Hagenberg Business Process Modelling Method

Felix Kossak · Christa Illibauer
Verena Geist · Christine Natschläger
Thomas Ziebermayr · Bernhard Freudenthaler
Theodorich Kopetzky · Klaus-Dieter Schewe

Hagenberg Business Process Modelling Method

 Springer

Felix Kossak
Christa Illibauer
Verena Geist
Christine Natschläger
Thomas Ziebermayr
Bernhard Freudenthaler
Theodorich Kopetzky
Klaus-Dieter Schewe

Software Competence Center Hagenberg GmbH
Hagenberg im Mühlkreis
Austria

ISBN 978-3-319-80825-3   ISBN 978-3-319-30496-0   (eBook)
DOI 10.1007/978-3-319-30496-0

Printed on acid-free paper

This Springer imprint is published by Springer Nature
The registered company is Springer International Publishing AG Switzerland

Preface

The Hagenberg Business Process Modelling (H-BPM) method constitutes a proposal for the design of Business Process Management (BPM) systems, which in addition to process modelling comprises several other important aspects like actor modelling, user interaction modelling, and an enhanced communication concept. On top of these aspects, we propose the enhanced Process Platform (eP^2) architecture to integrate the different models in a single tool.

The presented book gives insight into major results of a fundamental research project on business process modelling, called Vertical Model Integration (VMI), and its successor project, VMI 4.0, performed at the Software Competence Center Hagenberg (SCCH), Austria. It builds on a previous book, *A Rigorous Semantics for BPMN 2.0 Process Diagrams*[1], and like the latter, draws from our experience in large-scale business software development projects where we have experienced the need to go beyond BPM languages like BPMN.

This book mainly addresses researchers in the area of business process modelling, although we hope that it may also provide useful input to developers of modelling tools.

The introduced method is named after Hagenberg, a village in the district of Freistadt in the state of Upper Austria, situated on one of the green hills on the southern edge of the Bohemian Massif. Hagenberg is well known for the *Softwarepark Hagenberg*, a technology centre comprising 12 research institutes, 23 academic study programmes, and about 70 companies in the IT domain.

---

[1]Kossak, F., Illibauer, C., Geist, V., Kubovy, J., Natschläger, C., Ziebermayr, T., Kopetzky, T., Freudenthaler, B., Schewe, K.D.: A Rigorous Semantics for BPMN 2.0 Process Diagrams. Springer (2015)

The SCCH, where the H-BPM method has been developed, is one of the largest research institutions in the Softwarepark Hagenberg.

The research reported in this monograph has been partly supported by the Austrian Ministry for Transport, Innovation and Technology, the Federal Ministry of Science, Research and Economy, and the Province of Upper Austria in the frame of the COMET center SCCH.

This publication has been written within the projects "Vertical Model Integration (VMI)" and "VMI 4.0". Both projects have been supported within the programme "Regionale Wettbewerbsfähigkeit OÖ 2007–2013" by the European Fund for Regional Development as well as the State of Upper Austria.

This work was also supported in part by the *Austrian Research Promotion Agency* (FFG) under grant no. 842437.

Software Competence Center Hagenberg GmbH,   Felix Kossak
Hagenberg im Mühlkreis, Austria   Christa Illibauer
                                                       Verena Geist
                                                 Christine Natschläger
                                                    Thomas Ziebermayr
                                                 Bernhard Freudenthaler
                                                   Theodorich Kopetzky
                                                  Klaus-Dieter Schewe

Contents

Acronyms

ADL	Architectural Description Language
ARIS	Architecture of Integrated Information Systems
ASM	Abstract State Machine
AST	Abstract Syntax Tree
AUVA	Austrian Social Insurance Company for Occupational Risks
BPEL	Business Process Execution Language
BPM	Business Process Management
BPML	Business Process Modelling Language
BPMN	Business Process Model and Notation
CCS	Calculus of Communicating Systems
CPN	Coloured Petri-Net
CPS	Cyber Physical Systems
CPPS	Cyber Physical Production Systems
CSP	Communicating Sequential Process
DL	Description Logic
DSL	Domain-Specific Language
EAI	Enterprise Application Integration
eP^2	Enhanced Process Platform
EPC	Event-Driven Process Chain
ER	Entity-Relationship
H-BPM	Hagenberg Business Process Modelling
HCI	Human–Computer Interaction
HDM	Hypertext Design Model
ISO	International Organization for Standardization
IT	Information Technology
JSF	JavaServer Faces
MB-UIDE	Model-Based User Interface Development Environment
MDA	Model-Driven Architecture
OCL	Object Constraint Language
OMG	Object Management Group
OOHDM	Object-Oriented Hypertext Design Model

R2ML	REWERSE Rule Markup Language
RMM	Relationship Management Methodology
S-BPM	Subject-Oriented Business Process Management
SBVR	Semantics of Business Vocabulary and Rules
SME	Small- and Medium-sized Enterprise
SQL	Structured Query Language
SysML	Systems Modelling Language
UIML	User Interface Markup Language
UML	Unified Modeling Language
WebML	Web Modeling Language
WS-BPEL	Web Services Business Process Execution Language
XML	Extensible Markup Language
YAWL	Yet Another Workflow Language

Chapter 1
Introduction

This book contains a proposal for designing Business Process Management (BPM) systems which comprise much more than just process modelling. We see process modelling as a possible first step in BPM (though one could start with user-centric modelling as well, see [12]); but when it comes to business process *execution*, much more is needed for full-scale software support. At this point, if not already before, users (workers) will have to be added to the model, with issues from access control to user interfaces, and business data as well as cross-platform communication concepts have to be integrated.

We forgo an introduction to BPM in this place, as we rely on readers already having experience and knowledge in this field. Comprehensive introductions focussing on a classical approach can be found, amongst others, in the book of Dumas et al. on *Fundamentals of Business Process Management* [11] and in the book of ter Hofstede et al. on *Modern Business Process Automation* [45]; the book of Fleischmann et al. on *Subject-Oriented Business Process Management* [12], for instance, presents an alternative approach.

This book builds on a previous book, *A Rigorous Semantics for BPMN 2.0 Process Diagrams* [20] (not necessarily required for comprehending the current book), in which a formal specification of a purified semantics for the Business Process Model and Notation (BPMN) 2.0 was used, amongst others, to discuss a range of shortcomings of the BPMN standard [29]. Still, we think that BPMN, as a well-received international standard with ample tool support, forms a good basis for further development to service all the needs of BPM in practice.

Based on such a purified BPMN variant, we now present proposals for several important issues in BPM which have not or hardly been regarded in the BPMN 2.0 standard. Due to significant changes in comparison with BPMN as it stands today and, most of all, the extensive supplements we now propose, we have chosen to give the result an own name, the *Hagenberg Business Process Modelling (H-BPM)* method, named after the Upper Austrian village where it has been designed. The main issues discussed here are actor and user interaction modelling, rounded off by an enhanced communication concept. On top of these, we propose an enhanced

© Springer International Publishing Switzerland 2016
F. Kossak et al., *Hagenberg Business Process Modelling Method*,
DOI 10.1007/978-3-319-30496-0_1

Process Platform (eP^2) architecture capable of integrating all these aspects (as well as data modelling) in a single tool. We also describe how the different aspects and models work together.

In order to render models executable, the semantics of the modelling language needs to be described rigorously enough to prevent deviating interpretations by different tools. The semantics of the necessary concepts introduced in this book are defined using the Abstract State Machine (ASM) method [7], which is a system engineering method for developing software and systems seamlessly from requirements capture to their implementation. Within a precise but simple conceptual framework, the ASM method allows a modelling technique which integrates dynamic (operational) and static (declarative) descriptions, and an analysis technique that combines verification and validation methods at any desired level of detail. ASMs are an extension of finite state machines. The method has a rigorous mathematical foundation, yet a practitioner needs no special training to use the method since ASMs can be correctly understood as virtual machines working over abstract data structures.

1.1   Motivation

Today the success of enterprises and organisations depends very much on the speed with which they can create new business processes and adapt existing ones to react to increasingly fast changes in the environment and to take advantage of new trends and events.

Today's Trends—Factors of Influence

Due to the fact that communication is still becoming increasingly faster, easier, and more intense, more and more participants arc joining the global business landscape to find and grab new opportunities [21]. Not only large, international organisations, but also Small and Medium-sized Enterprises (SMEs) now have to adapt their business to face up to global competition.

Factors in pushing the need for more flexibility of workflows but also for more comprehensive and better integrated workflows are trends like just-in-time delivery, outsourcing and offshoring, product or service customisation right down to individualised products, and requirements of traceability not only of products themselves but also of raw materials and up to disposal or recycling. Extreme customisation as well as high integration of workflows transcending single places and organisations is envisaged, for instance, by the European "Industrie 4.0" initiative.

The term "Industrie 4.0", initialised by the German government [8], is designed to signify a fourth industrial revolution. The first industrial revolution (at the end of the eighteenth century) was fostered by the introduction of mechanical production facilities with the aid of water and steam power. The second industrial revolution (at the beginning of the twentieth century) was triggered by mass production with the aid of electricity. In the 1970s, the third industrial revolution was caused by the emergence of electronics and Information Technology (IT) [15].

Industrie 4.0 applies new trends from the information and communication technology to production systems. The goal is to create intelligent machines, logistic systems, and equipment that independently communicate with each other, that are able to trigger suitable events, and that are even able to mutually control each other [13]. Such networked (mostly over the internet) and communicating systems are called Cyber Physical Systems (CPS) or, when they are used in production, Cyber Physical Production Systems (CPPS) [26]. When, in addition to the production system, also sourcing and delivery (i.e. the supply chain) are included, such factories are called "Smart Factories". Special, domain-specific applications include "Smart Grid", "Smart Buildings", "Smart Products", "Smart Logistics", and "Smart Mobility"; all of them entail the same issues regarding communication between IT and software technologies on the one hand and electronic parts on the other [13].

With regard to implementations of Industrie 4.0 projects, Kagerman [15] emphasise the importance of a methodical approach comprising every aspect from requirements to product architecture and manufacture of the product. Furthermore they mention modelling and integration (horizontal integration through value networks, integration of engineering across the value chain, as well as vertical integration and networked manufacturing systems) as an essential challenge of enterprises for being prepared for Industrie 4.0.

H-BPM—A Holistic Modelling Approach

We have designed H-BPM to cover a range of aspects which we think are necessary to model business processes at the level required for automation and fit for Industrie 4.0. To motivate the holistic approach, for a start, consider an analogy from grammar: a sentence must—at least—consist of the central parts as are subject, predicate, and often also object in order to be valid and understandable; similarly, a business process with all its different aspects can only be understood in a holistic and intelligible way if the applied modelling method covers precise definitions for the essence of all BPM constructs and, particularly, supports accurate integration. To draw an analogy between a sentence and an H-BPM diagram, (i) the predicate is represented by a basic control-flow view on the process, including activities with deontic classifications to describe modalities and an enhanced communication concept for serving more sophisticated communication patterns for business processes, (ii) the subject is addressed by an extended actor modelling approach that provides a task-based assignment for actors, and (iii) the object is given by process data which corresponds to typed nodes of dialogues for user tasks. Thus, H-BPM is able to support the equivalent of full sentences. For only if all aspects are considered in a formal and integrated way, business processes can be understood with their full contexts.

Traditional process modelling languages like BPMN provide good support for the control-flow perspective and medium support for the data perspective, but the resource perspective is not well supported [49]. In [28], the limited support for actor modelling provided by rigid swimlane concepts is discussed in detail. Missing integration mechanisms for user interaction and data modelling are furthermore likely to pose communication problems and inconsistencies when planning and developing process-oriented systems [3]. Also simple communication patterns like those provided in BPMN often do not suffice for modelling the interplay between different processes, especially between very heterogeneous systems [19]. In particular, more flexibility and customisation are needed when human actors and user interaction are considered.

The number of models required for those different aspects, such as functionality, actors, user interaction, and communication, makes modelling information systems a complex endeavour [41]. In addition, those models are generally related to different abstraction layers, leading to discrepancies when integrating them.

The motivation for the development of a comprehensive modelling method proposing a design for BPM systems which comprise much more than just process modelling stems from several of our industrial projects (see [10, 28]), where business analysts and software developers struggled with redundancies and inconsistencies in system documentation due to missing integration. While different views on business processes represented by different models have been described before, to our knowledge, these different models have never been brought together in the available literature. In fact, it is their interplay which makes them useful in practice, and this interplay is not trivial.

Therefore, we suggest the H-BPM method for seamless modelling of business processes. Thereby, we take a static view regarding software component integration as well as a dynamic, runtime-related view on model integration. As a result, this new modelling method is able to seamlessly integrate different aspects of business process modelling, including organisational (actor), user interaction, data, and communication models, on all levels of abstraction.

Motivation for Formal Specification

Meeting modern challenges and the requirements for Industrie 4.0 will require trans-organisational workflows and a high level of interconnection between different systems. Consequently, it must be possible to exchange business process models between different organisations without undesired loss of information. Exchange of models, in turn, requires a rigidly specified standard.

The BPMN standard, arguably the most important international standard for business process modelling, is formulated in natural language. It is not so surprising, then, that we have identified numerous ambiguities, gaps, and inconsistencies in this standard [20]. Consequently, model interchange between different tools, despite being supported by an XML-based exchange format defined in the standard, is limited, as experiments by us, one of our partners, and others have shown; typically, imported models can be displayed but not run. Also the semantics of certain elements, e.g. the inclusive gateway, are interpreted differently, or such elements are not supported at all.

Thus, it is particularly important to guarantee that the executable behaviour of a process model is exactly as intended by the process designer. Consequently, the semantics of the modelling language and method needs to be specified *formally* such that no room for interpretation is left. Furthermore, a formal model allows for checking for certain properties, including safety and liveness properties.

We chose the notation of ASM for its closeness to natural language and its consequent understandability (despite its rigour). We can thereby also seamlessly build on our work in [20], where we rigorously defined a semantics for process models, following the BPMN standard as closely as possible; see also our discussion of the topic there.

1.2 Related Work and Comparison with Related Methods

In this section, an overview of related BPM methods and languages and a comparison with respect to considered aspects and their overall integration is provided. The results are summarised in Table 1.1.

The Subject-Oriented Business Process Management (S-BPM) method puts the focus on the subject of a process and defines two views: (i) the communication view, which depicts the process in its entirety (how the subjects collude in the process and which messages they interchange) and (ii) the internal subject view, which depicts the internal behaviour of a subject (which actions are to be processed and how to react or trigger communication). The formal foundation of S-BPM [32] is based on the Calculus of Communicating Systems (CCS) introduced by Milner [25]. The integration is done during process design; first the communication structure is specified and subsequently each subject models its behaviour from his or her perspective [22, 23].

Architecture of Integrated Information Systems (ARIS) is a method for optimising business processes as well as for implementing application systems. ARIS defines five views, which are symbolically presented in the form of the so-called ARIS house: (i) the organisational view (describing the organisational structure), (ii) the data view (business data and information), (iii) the control- or process-view (behaviour processes and their relations to services, organisation, functions and data), (iv) the functional view (tasks and business objectives, function hierarchies, etc.), and (v) the product (and service) view (products and services, their structures, relations, and product/service trees) [40]. ARIS further provides integration of concepts from other views [42, 48]. Formerly, the main ARIS model for processes was based on Event-Driven Process Chains (EPCs) [9], but recently also support for BPMN [2] has been added.

ADONIS is a business process management tool for designing, documenting, and optimising business processes, which supports business process management systems and BPMN 2.0. The idea of ADONIS is to encompass the phases identified within the business process management framework with the theory of a permanent lifecycle as depicted in most process management systems. The four key elements considered within ADONIS are: (i) products/services, (ii) processes, (iii) organisational structures, and (iv) information theory (including their dependencies) [5, 6].

The BPM-D framework is an architecture and toolset for establishing the BPM discipline in an organisation. The four major components of the framework are: (i) BPM-D Process: The process model is a reference model for project-based and asset-based processes and is detailed through four layers of decomposition with descriptions, reference methods, and best-practice examples. (ii) BPM-D Data: The information model is a reference model that details all major data entities. (iii) BPM-D Organisation: The organisation model is a reference model that comprises internal and external roles, their responsibilities and key performance metrics. It further includes a reference organisation structure together with examples of how this has been implemented in other organisations. (iv) BPM-D Value: The value model details the potential areas where value can be found and outlines pragmatic approaches to focus all development efforts on delivering this value [17].

The Horus method covers the whole life cycle of business process engineering and suggests steps to extend a process model with additional elements and to link (integrate) these elements with each other. The holistic business process management considers the following aspects: (i) process modelling with Petri nets, (ii) object modelling with business objects (e.g., documents, data objects, etc.), and (iii) organisational modelling. Besides the process-view, the Horus method also takes the service- and business-view with aspects such as ratio and risk analyses into account [43].

BPMN is a graphical modelling language for business processes and an international standard issued by the Object Management Group (OMG), a well-established group with a strong foundation in the industry [29]. It was formally published by the International Organization for Standardization (ISO) as the 2013 edition standard ISO/IEC 19510 [14]. BPMN has been widely adopted and is supported by various tools. Nevertheless, BPMN has major drawbacks like the lack of integrated user interaction and data modelling, a restricted support on organisational modelling and communication as well as only implicit expression of modalities [20].

The Yet Another Workflow Language (YAWL) system [45] is a service-oriented architecture and consists of an extensible set of YAWL services, each offering one or more interfaces. YAWL supports three different perspectives: control-flow, data, and resources. The formal foundation of YAWL makes its specifications unambiguous and enables automated verification. Additionally, YAWL offers two verification approaches, one based on Reset nets (Petri nets with reset arcs) and another one based on transition invariants. Aldred defines "process integration patterns", which could be seen as a support for communication aspects in an extension [1].

EPC is a popular business process modelling language introduced by Keller et al. [16] and defines the sequence-related connection of functions which are triggered by events. The main node types of EPCs are activities (functions), events and gateways (connectors). Connector operations describe "how" elements are connected (e.g. conjunction, disjunction or adjunction (and/or)) whereas the connection type defines which elements of the models are connected. An extension of EPC with data and resources is called eEPC [24, 39, 47].

The Unified Modeling Language (UML) [31] is a general-purpose modelling language maintained by the OMG and mainly used in software engineering. UML 2.5 defines 14 types of diagrams divided into the categories of structure and behaviour diagrams. Classified as structure diagrams are class, component, object, composite structure, deployment, package, and profile diagrams. The category of behaviour diagrams includes activity diagrams, use case diagrams, state machine diagrams and the sub-class of interaction diagrams comprising sequence diagrams, interaction overview diagrams, communication diagrams, and timing diagrams [31]. However, integration between these types of diagrams is only partly given based on the corresponding UML metamodel. Furthermore, also the integration between UML and BPMN diagrams, both specified by the OMG, is limited (cf. [18]). Additionally, for the design of user interfaces, different UML profiles have been specified [4, 33, 37]. Silva et al. provide a case study comprising common modelling problems of UML for modelling user interfaces [36].

The Systems Modelling Language (SysML), first released in 2006 by OMG, is a general-purpose visual modelling language for systems engineering. The systems may include hardware, software, information, processes, personnel, and facilities. SysML reuses a subset of UML 2 and provides additional extensions. SysML is especially applied to specify requirements, structure, behaviour, allocations, and constraints on system properties to support engineering analysis. SysML may be used to create models of the system (the entire model) as well as for viewpoints or view models of different stakeholders [30].

Petri nets, introduced by Adam Petri [34, 35], are a graphical and mathematical modelling language for concurrent, asynchronous, and distributed systems. A Petri net is a directed, weighted, bipartite graph, consisting of two kinds of nodes: (i) "places" (depicted as circles) and (ii) "transitions" (bars or boxes). Connecting arcs (either from a transition to a place or vice versa) can be labelled with weights. A marking can assign a non-negative integer k to a place (i.e. the place is marked with k "tokens") [27]. In modelling, places represent conditions whereas transitions represent events. A change of a state is denoted by the movement of tokens from places to places, effected by the firing of a transition. Van der Aalst studies the inability of classical Petri nets to model data and time and refers to three important extensions of Petri nets (called high-level Petri nets): (i) extension with colour to attach data value to tokens, (ii) extension with time, and (iii) extension with hierarchy for structuring large models [44]. Amongst others, Petri nets are used to formally specify the semantics of process modelling languages, e.g. YAWL (see above).

Workflow nets (WF-nets), introduced by van der Aalst [44], constitute a sub-type of Petri nets to model workflow process definitions. In a WF-net, tasks are modelled by transitions, conditions are modelled by places, and cases are modelled by tokens. WF-nets further satisfy the following requirements: they have exactly one input and one output place and there are no dangling tasks and/or conditions, so every transition is located on a path from the input to the output place [44, 46].

Like the proposed H-BPM method, S-BPM considers the business process model, actors, and the communication aspect, and even provides displaying user interfaces by triggering services. Similarly, ADONIS takes processes and organisational structures into account. ARIS suggests five views including processes, actors, and data. BPM-D comprises a process, actor, and data model as well as a value model to define the potential areas where value can be found. In addition, the Horus method considers not only the process-view with the process, data and organisational model, but also the business- and service-view throughout the whole business process lifecycle. All

Table 1.1 Comparison of BPM methods and languages

Name	Process	Organsational	Modality	User interaction	Data	Communication	Formal basis	Integration
BPM methods								
H-BPM	Yes	Yes	Yes	Yes	Partly	Yes	Yes	Yes
S-BPM	Yes	Yes	No	Service[a]	No	Yes	Yes	Yes
ARIS	Yes	Yes	No	Partly	Yes	No	Semi	Yes
ADONIS	Yes	Yes	No	No	No	No	No	No
BPM-D	Yes	Yes	No	No	Yes	No	No	No
Horus	Yes	Yes	No	No	Yes	No	Yes	Partly
BPM languages								
BPMN	Yes	Partly	No	No	Partly	Partly	Semi	Partly
YAWL	Yes	Yes	No	Yes	Yes	Ext[b]	Yes	Yes
EPC	Yes	Ext[b]	No	No	Ext[b]	Ext[b]	Semi	Ext[b]
UML/	Yes	Partly	No	Profile[c]	Yes	Partly	Semi	Partly
SysML	Yes	Yes	No	No	Yes	Partly	Semi	Partly
Petri net/	Yes	No	No	No	No	No	Yes	No
WF-net	Yes	Ext[b]	No	No	Ext[b]	No	Yes	Ext[b]

[a]By calling services
[b]In an extension
[c]In specific profiles

investigated approaches except ADONIS and BPM-D are built on a formal (or at least semi-formal) foundation. However, none of the aforementioned methods considers modalities and only S-BPM and ARIS (rudimentarily) define Human–Computer Interaction (HCI) as we provide it in our approach to user interaction modelling. Model integration, a main focus of the H-BPM method, is provided by S-BPM, ARIS, and partly by the Horus method.

Considering related BPM languages, BPMN provides only restricted support for data and organisational modelling and lacks integration of these aspects. Furthermore, UML, SysML, and YAWL consider data modelling and YAWL as well as SysML additionally support organisational aspects. All other investigated modelling languages either do not support organisational and data aspects or facilitate them either partly or only in an extension to the language (see Table 1.1). Only YAWL and UML (in specific profiles) support user interactions. Model integration is provided by YAWL and in an extension by EPC and WF-nets, however, partial integration of UML-based models (and also SysML models) can be done based on the corresponding UML metamodel [38, p. 187].

1.3 Outline

This book is structured as follows. We start with the way in which a user who has to perform tasks should be confronted with a process model. First, such a user need not be confronted with the whole process diagram (though knowledge about the whole process may often be very helpful); what they need in the first place is to be presented with a list of tasks which they are supposed to perform at a given moment. Second, those tasks may have different status—some tasks *have* to be performed (are obligatory), while others are optional (may but need not be performed); yet other tasks can be alternatives with respect to a group of further tasks. All these *modalities* can depend on certain conditions, and some tasks may even be forbidden under certain circumstances.

In a classical process diagram, the modality of a task is implicitly given by the structure of the whole diagram (or a part of the diagram). But this is not a comfortable and reliable way of detecting whether one must or may or must not perform a certain task. Instead, such modalities—like obligation or optionality—can be described in different flavours of deontic logic, which is the subject of Chap. 2. Even beyond looking at single tasks, the introduction of deontic modalities can often simplify process diagrams and render them better understandable. We use colour highlighting in combination with abbreviations for deontic operators to differentiate between modalities within a process diagram, and show how deontically modified diagrams are related to classical BPMN-style process diagrams.

Actor modelling, introduced in Chap. 3, then builds upon this deontic business process diagrams and allocates different modalities to different actors, depending on role permissions. We present a layered actor modelling approach with different views on the involvement of actors and their roles in a particular process, including task-based assignment of users, a hierarchical role model, and rules to define dependencies between tasks. Those rules can also be checked for consistency and derived rules can be generated.

Chapter 4 focuses on user interaction modelling, and thus on the user interface for those people who actually have to perform the user tasks defined in a process diagram. Such users, in their daily work, have a totally different view on a process than a business process analyst or higher level manager (compare, for instance, [12]). The core of a worker's view is represented by a *worklist* of tasks from which they can select. Selecting an item in their worklist, users are led through dialogues consisting of reports and forms. They give access to the data needed for the task and allow to perform actions (like entering data). Workflow charts also come with an own workflow model which, amongst others, allows to further structure tasks. Thereby, a user can be led through a dynamically assembled succession of dialogues, depending, amongst others, on their own actions and decisions.

In Chap. 5, we discuss how the event concept of BPMN can be generalised. BPMN provides a set of specific event types, like "Message" or "Signal", but those types do not cover all possibilities for communication. Those types are distinguished by different properties, and together with different types of *event pools*, we exploit those properties to define a generic event concept. Amongst others, event pools allow users to select messages and to subscribe or unsubscribe to public event pools, i.e. notification sources.

Having proposed several extensions to the workflow-centric language of BPMN and its purified version according to [20], we deal with the question of model integration in Chap. 6. We show how the different part models fit together, using a simple example process. We introduce the enhanced Process Platform (eP^2) architecture which binds all the different components together at runtime, so that the various business process modelling aspects can be supported by a single tool (cf. Sect. 6.4).

A detailed specification of the (eP^2) architecture and the integration of the different components therein are then given in Chap. 7.

Still more can be done towards a unified, comprehensive approach to BPM, though. In the Outlook in Chap. 8, we briefly recap the components of the H-BPM model introduced in this book and point out need for future work.

1.4   Recommendations for Readers

We tried to make the specific chapters as independent from each other as possible. However, *Actor Modelling* (Chap. 3) builds heavily on deontic process diagrams (Chap. 2), thus we suggest to read those two chapters together. Chapter 2 can be understood independently, however.

Not at all independent are the chapters on *Horizontal Model Integration* (Chap. 6) and the specification of the eP^2 architecture (Chap. 7), because they show how the separate parts presented in the previous chapters all fit together. Chapter 6 gives an overview of the eP^2 architecture (in Sect. 6.4) and can thus be understood independently of Chap. 7, but Chap. 7 builds on Chap. 6.

With those exceptions, it should be possible to read the more specific chapters independently of each other.

As in [20], wherever we consider it necessary to define the semantics of a concept rigorously, we resort to the ASM method. For our purposes in this book, ASM can simply be seen as "a rather intuitive form of abstract pseudo-code" [7, p. 2]. The foundation of the ASM method is a rigorous mathematical theory based on automata whose states are defined by arbitrarily complex data structures.

Functions define the data structure of an ASM. Concrete values of the parameters of a function define a *location* (comparable to a "memory address" of a computer at runtime), and concrete values of the functions for all locations define a particular state of the automaton. *Rules* define state transitions by modifying the function values at a finite number of locations. *Derived functions*, which constitute an important auxiliary element in ASM models, compute values from a combination of "proper" functions (or data) at runtime.

We trust that the ASM functions and rules we define in this book are intuitive to understand without any background knowledge of ASMs. For an understanding of the semantic subtleties, we recommend to consult "the ASM Book" by Börger and Stärk [7]; for a shortish introduction, see also [20, Chap. 3], amongst many other sources.

References

1. Aldred, L.: Process integration. In: ter Hofstede, A.M., van der Aalst, W.M.P., Adams, M., Russell, N. (eds.) Modern Business Process Automation: YAWL and its Support Environment, pp. 489–511. Springer, Heidelberg (2010)
2. ARIS Community: BPMN process modeling & free modeling tool. http://www.ariscommunity. com/aris-express/bpmn-2-free-process-modeling-tool (2015). Accessed 18 Sept 2015
3. Auer, D., Geist, V., Draheim, D.: Extending BPMN with submit/response-style user interaction modeling. In: Proceedings of CEC'09, pp. 368–374. IEEE Computer Society (2009)
4. Blankenhorn, K., Jeckle, M.: A UML profile for GUI layout. Object-Oriented and Internet-Based Technologies, pp. 110–121 (2004)
5. BOC Group: BPMS (Business Process Management System). http://www.boc-group.com/ products/adonis/bpms-method-life-cycle/ (2015). Accessed 18 Sept 2015
6. BOC Group: Business Process Management with ADONIS and the ADONIS Process Portal. http://www.boc-group.com/products/adonis/ (2015). Accessed 18 Sept 2015
7. Börger, E., Stärk, R.: Abstract State Machines: A Method for High-Level System Design and Analysis. Springer, Berlin (2003)
8. Bundesministerium für Bildung und Forschung: Zukunftsprojekt Industrie 4.0. http://www. bmbf.de/de/9072.php (2015). Accessed 30 Sept 2015
9. Davis, R., Brabander, E.: ARIS Design Platform: Getting Started with BPM. Springer, Berlin (2007)
10. Draheim, D., Geist, V., Natschläger, C.: Integrated framework for seamless modeling of business and technical aspects in process-oriented enterprise applications. Int. J. Softw. Eng. Knowl. Eng. 22(05), 645–674 (2012)
11. Dumas, M., La Rosa, M., Mendling, J., Reijers, H.A.: Fundamentals of Business Process Management. Springer, Berlin (2013)
12. Fleischmann, A., Schmidt, W., Stary, C., Obermeier, S., Börger, E.: Subject-Oriented Business Process Management. Springer, Berlin (2012)

13. International Controller Association (ICV): Industrie 4.0 - Controlling in the Age of Intelligent Networks. http://www.icv-controlling.com/fileadmin/Assets/Content/AK/Ideenwerkstatt/ Files/Dream_Car_Industrie_4.0_EN.pdf (2015). Accessed 23 Dec 2015

14. International Organization for Standardization: Information technology – Object Management Group: Business Process Model and Notation. http://www.omg.org/spec/BPMN/ISO/19510/ PDF/ (2013). Accessed 28 Sept 2015. iSO/IEC 19510

15. Kagermann, P., Wahlster, P., Helbig, D.: Recommendations for implementing the strategic initiative INDUSTRIE 4.0 (2013). Accessed 23 Dec 2015

16. Keller, G., Nüttgens, M., Scheer, A.W.: Semantische Prozeßmodellierung auf der Grundlage Ereignisgesteuerter Prozeßketten (EPK). http://www.econbiz.de/archiv/sb/usb/iwi/ prozessmodellierung_grundlage_prozessketten.pdf (1992). Accessed 08 Oct 2015

17. Kirchmer, M., Franz, P.: BPM-discipline framework. http://bpm-d.com/framework (2015). Accessed 28 Sept 2015

18. Kleinschmidt, T.: Integration von BPMN und UML: Wie Mars und Venus oder doch zwei Seiten einer Medaille? OBJEKTspektrum **04**, 60–65 (2015)

19. Kossak, F., Geist, V.: An enhanced communication concept for business processes. In: Kolb, J., Leopold, H., Mendling, J. (eds.) Enterprise Modelling and Information Systems Architectures – Proceedings of EMISA 2015. Lecture Notes in Informatics, vol. 248, pp. 77–91. Gesellschaft für Informatik (2015)

20. Kossak, F., Illibauer, C., Geist, V., Kubovy, J., Natschläger, C., Ziebermayr, T., Kopetzky, T., Freudenthaler, B., Schewe, K.D.: A Rigorous Semantics for BPMN 2.0 Process Diagrams. Springer, Berlin (2015)

21. Lawlor, B.: The Age of Globalization: Impact of Information Technology on Global Business Strategies. Honors Projects in Computer Information Systems. Paper 1. http://digitalcommons. bryant.edu/honors_cis/1 (2007). Accessed 08 Oct 2015

22. Metasonic: Modeling with S-BPM. https://www.metasonic.de/en/modeling-with-s-bpm (2015). Accessed 08 Oct 2015

23. Metasonic: What's S-BPM. https://www.metasonic.de/en/s-bpm (2015). Accessed 08 Oct 2015

24. Meyer, A., Smirnov, S., Weske, M.: Data in business processes. EMISA Forum **31**(3), 5–31 (2011)

25. Milner, R.: A Calculus of Communicating Systems. Springer, Secaucus (1982)

26. Monostori, L.: Cyber-physical production systems: roots, expectations and R&D challenges. Procedia CIRP **17**, 9–13 (2014)

27. Murata, T.: Petri nets: properties, analysis and applications. Proc. IEEE **77**(4), 541–580 (1989)

28. Natschläger, C., Geist, V.: A layered approach for actor modelling in business processes. Bus. Process Manag. J. **19**, 917–932 (2013)

29. Object Management Group: Business Process Model and Notation (BPMN) 2.0. http://www. omg.org/spec/BPMN/2.0 (2011). Accessed 06 Oct 2015

30. Object Management Group: OMG Systems Modelling Language (OMG SysML). http://www. omg.org/spec/SysML (2015). Accessed 23 Sept 2015

31. Object Management Group: OMG Unified Modeling Language (OMG UML), version 2.5. http://www.omg.org/spec/UML/2.5 (2015). Accessed 06 Oct 2015

32. Oppl, S., Fleischmann, A.: S-BPM ONE - education and industrial developments. In: 4th International Conference, S-BPM ONE 2012, Vienna, Austria, 4–5 April 2012. Proceedings. Communications in Computer and Information Science. Springer, Berlin Heidelberg (2012)

33. Perisic, B., Milosavljevic, G., Dejanovic, I., Milosavljevic, B.: UML profile for specifying user interfaces of business applications. Comput. Sci. Inf. Syst. **8**(2), 405–426 (2011)

34. Petri, C.A.: Kommunikation mit Automaten. Ph.D. thesis, Universität Hamburg (1962)

35. Petri, C.A.: Communication with automata. Rome Air Development Center (New York). TR-65-377 / DTIC Research Report AD0630125 (1966)

36. Pinheiro da Silva, P., Paton, N.: User interface modelling with UML. In: Proceedings of the 10th European-Japanese Conference on Information Modelling and Knowledge Bases (2000)

37. Rauf, A., Rahim, M., Ramzan, M., Shahid, A.: Extending UML to model GUI: a new profile. In: 2010 The 2nd International Conference on Computer and Automation Engineering (ICCAE), vol. 1, pp. 349–353 (2010)
38. Rittgen, P.: Enterprise Modeling and Computing with UML. ITPro collection, Idea Group Pub (2006)
39. Scheer, A.W.: ARIS - Business Process Modeling. Springer, Berlin (2000)
40. Scheer, A., Abolhassan, F., Jost, W., Kirchmer, M.: Business Process Excellence: ARIS in Practice. Springer, Berlin (2012)
41. Schewe, K.D.: Horizontal and vertical business process model integration. In: Decker, H., Lenka, L., Link, S., Basl, J., Tjoa, A. (eds.) Database and Expert Systems Applications. Lecture Notes in Computer Science, vol. 8055, pp. 1–3. Springer, Berlin (2013)
42. Schuster, T.: Modellierung. Integration und Analyse von Ressourcen in Geschäftsprozessen, Karlsruher Institut für Technologie (2014)
43. Schönthaler, F., Vossen, G., Oberweis, A., Karle, T.: Geschäftsprozesse für Business Communities. Oldenbourg Verlag München (2011)
44. van der Aalst, W.M.P.: The application of petri nets to workflow management. J. Circuits Syst. Comput. **8**(1), 21–66 (1998)
45. ter Hofstede, A.M., van der Aalst, W.M.P., Adams, M., Russell, N. (eds.): Modern Business Process Automation: YAWL and its Support Environment. Springer, Heidelberg (2010)
46. van der Aalst, W.M.P., van Hee, K.M., ter Hofstede, A.H.M., Sidorova, N., Verbeek, H.M.W., Voorhoeve, M., Wynn, M.T.: Soundness of workflow nets: classification, decidability, and analysis. Form. Asp. Comput. **23**(3), 333–363 (2011)
47. van Hee, K.M., Oanea, O., Sidorova, N.: Colored petri nets to verify extended event-driven process chains. In: Meersman, R., Tari, Z., Hacid, M.S., Mylopoulos, J., Pernici, B., Babaoglu, Z., Jacobsen, H.A., Loyall, J.P., Kifer, M., Spaccapietra, S. (eds.) OTM Conferences (1). Lecture Notes in Computer Science, vol. 3760, pp. 183–201. Springer, Berlin (2005)
48. Wakayama, T., Kannapan, S., Khoong, C., Navathe, S., Yates, J.: Information and Process Integration in Enterprises: Rethinking Documents. The Springer International Series in Engineering and Computer Science, Springer (2012)
49. Wohed, P., van der Aalst, W., Dumas, M., ter Hofstede, A., Russell, N.: On the suitability of BPMN for business process modelling. In: Dustdar, S., Fiadeiro, J., Sheth, A. (eds.) Business Process Management. Lecture Notes in Computer Science, vol. 4102, pp. 161–176. Springer, Berlin (2006)

Chapter 2
Deontic Process Diagrams

In this chapter, we present a deontic classification of tasks, that is, we classify tasks as *obligatory*, *permissible*, *forbidden*, or *alternative* with respect to others. Such a classification can also be made conditional, and we will resort to such conditional deontic modality in our concept of actor modelling (a particular weakness of many Business Process Modelling Languages (BPML)) in Chap. 3.

For such a classification, we employ (modal) deontic logic, a family of modal logics which were originally developed for reasoning on ethical theories (and laws). The name is derived from classical Greek, "deon", which means "obligation"; and obligation has been cho sen in most deontic logics as the most basic modal operator.

In the following, we present a notation for deontically classified tasks, combining symbols and colour encoding, demonstrate their usage based on the *Control-Flow Patterns* (part of the *Workflow Patterns* introduced by van der Aalst et al. [32]), provide a semantics for such tasks, and a model transformation from classical process diagrams to deontic process diagrams. We also show that such a transformation is reliable, or "trusted". An approach to extend the Business Process Model and Notation (BPMN) with deontic logic was suggested by Natschläger [21], which was extended in [23, 24] and subsequently adapted to the Hagenberg Business Process Modelling (H-BPM) method. We consider deontic classification to be optional.

In most BPMLs, deontic modality is only implicitly expressed through the structure of the process flow, but it cannot be seen when just looking at the task in question. In such languages, all activities are (tacitly) obligatory, and whenever something should be optional, a gateway is used to split the process flow, which offers the possibility to execute the activity or to do nothing (expressed by an empty, alternative path). This requires additional modelling elements to split and merge the process flow and a comprehensive understanding of the whole process to identify obligatory, permissible, and alternative activities.

Deontic process diagrams improve readability by highlighting obligatory, permissible, and alternative activities. This further allows reducing the number of gateways and sequence flows and consequently, the structural complexity of the diagram. An algebraic graph transformation from BPMN to Deontic BPMN was suggested by Natschläger [21] and shown to be trusted (reliable) in [23]. According to

© Springer International Publishing Switzerland 2016

F. Kossak et al., *Hagenberg Business Process Modelling Method*,

DOI 10.1007/978-3-319-30496-0_2

Varró et al. [34], the most important correctness properties of a trusted model trans-formation are termination, uniqueness (confluence), and behaviour preservation. We adapt the graph transformation to H-BPM and show that the transformation from classical process diagrams to deontic process diagrams is also terminating and con-fluent, which implies global determinism, and that the original diagram and the deontic diagram are semantically equivalent.

This chapter is structured as follows: Sect. 2.1 provides the motivation for extend-ing process diagrams with deontic logic and Sect. 2.2 on related work will focus on deontic logic in process modelling. Afterwards, Sect. 2.3 introduces possible deontic classifications of an activity and provides a discussion of user decisions and condi-tional decisions and an overview to which extent deontic concepts can be used in process flows. Then the *Workflow Patterns* are presented, which describe the main constructs of BPMLs. Extended with deontic logic are the *Control-Flow Patterns*, which specify the process flow (see Sect. 2.4). The benefits of deontic process dia-grams are further demonstrated by an application scenario study (see Sect. 2.5) and Sect. 2.6 provides a semantic model for deontic activities. Finally, we introduce in Sect. 2.7 a graph transformation from classical process diagrams to deontic process diagrams and show that this transformation is trusted, i.e. confluent, terminating, and preserving semantics. We sum up the results in Sect. 2.8.

2.1   Motivation

In standard process diagrams, all activities are implicitly obligatory, and whenever an activity should be optional, the process flow is split so one can choose to do nothing by means of an alternative, empty path (i.e. a path without an activity). This implies that the decision whether to execute one or more activities is described within another element, that is, the splitting element (e.g. a gateway). The separation between decision and execution leads to the following problems:

- Limited readability: It is difficult to identify obligatory, permissible, and alternative activities at first sight.
- Complex structure: Additional elements are necessary to express modality, which complicates the structure of the diagram.
- Duplication: Various agents with different normative concepts for the same activity require a duplication of the activity.

Regarding the last issue, in most BPMLs, activities have to be duplicated if modal-ity depends on a particular role. For example, a task *Attend Conference* might be obligatory for the main author of a paper but permissible for reviewers and co-authors.

Problems with implicit modality were also observed by the authors in an industrial project where an order execution process and a business travel process contained several permissible activities (see Sect. 2.5). The resulting process diagrams were complex and a distinction between obligatory and permissible activities would have been advantageous.

Thus we extend process diagrams with deontic logic, which allows to highlight the modality and to reduce the structural complexity of the process flow. Decisions are specified within the corresponding activities, which permits a fine-granular capture of rights and obligations.

2.2 Related Work

An overview of the main applications of deontic logic in computer science is given by Wieringa and Meyer [37]. Broersen et al. identified ten problems of deontic logic and normative reasoning in computer science [6]. Amongst these problems is how to combine legal ontologies, normative systems, business process notations, and compliance checking tools. For this purpose, the authors recommend the Semantics of Business Vocabulary and Rules (SBVR) for interaction between norms and business processes. SBVR employs alethic and deontic modal logics (see [25]), but it considers neither the influence on the process flow (such as readability or reduction of structural complexity) nor the model transformation.

According to Goedertier and Vanthienen [12], most process modelling languages, such as UML Activity Diagrams (UML ADs), BPMN and the Business Process Execution Language (BPEL), are procedural and only implicitly keep track of why design choices have been made. In contrast, these authors present a vocabulary for declarative process modelling that supports business concerns, execution scenarios, execution mechanisms, modality, rule enforcement, and communication. Considering modality, procedural modelling only specifies what *must* be the case while declarative process modelling supports the modalities *must*, *ought*, and *can* based on deontic logic. In [11], the same authors introduce a language to express temporal rules about obligations and permissions in business interaction, called *Penelope*. Those publications provide a good foundation for the suggested deontic extension of process diagrams. However, the focus of the normative concepts is more on agents and temporal constraints, whereas neither optimisation capabilities nor model transformation are studied.

Other publications focus on formal models of normative reasoning and deontic logic in combination with business rules and process modelling. Padmanabhan et al. [26] consider process modelling and deontic logic. They develop a logical framework based on multi-modal logic to capture the normative positions among agents in an organisational setting. Governatori and Milosevic present a language for expressing contract conditions in terms of deontic concepts, called *Business Contract Language (BCL)* [13]. However, these publications focus on agents and their contractual relationships and do not provide a detailed study of modality.

Further approaches ensure business process compliance based on deontic logic. According to Sadiq et al., process and control modelling are two distinct specifications, but convergence is necessary to achieve business practices that are compliant with control objectives [30]. The authors propose a *Formal Contract Language (FCL)* as a formalism to express normative specifications. This language is a combination of defeasible logic and a deontic logic of violations. Ghose and Koliadis [10] present an approach to enhance business process modelling notations with the capability to detect and resolve compliance-related issues. They define a framework for auditing BPMN process models and suggest that activity, event, and decision inclusion may be defined with deontic modalities.

Deontic logic is also used by Asirelli et al. for modelling the behavioural variability in product family descriptions [2]. According to this publication, deontic logic became very popular for formalising descriptional and behavioural aspects of systems, since it provides a natural way to formalise concepts such as violation, obligation, permission, and prohibition.

Furthermore, an approach by Weigand et al. [35] provides a bridge between interoperable transactions and business process models based on deontic logic.

Although several approaches use deontic logic in combination with process modelling, none of them studies the influence on the process flow (such as readability and optimisation capabilities) or considers model transformation. Thus, an own approach which extends BPMN with deontic logic has been developed by Natschläger [21]. This approach has been adopted in H-BPM and is employed in this chapter.

2.3 Deontic Classification

In this section, all deontic constructs used for the extension of process diagrams are presented. In particular, we use the deontic modalities of obligation, permission, prohibition, and commitment in the form of conditional obligation (cf. [1]). Alternatives (i.e. choice of one out of a set) can be expressed as conditional obligations. These modal operators are added to classical propositional logic. We will use, in particular, the propositional connectives of negation ($\neg$), conjunction ($\wedge$), disjunction ($\vee$), and contravalence ($\dot{\vee}$).

While monadic deontic logic models unconditional normative concepts, conditional obligations and permissions can be expressed by an additional argument to the respective modal operator, i.e. the respective condition; this family of deontic logics is called dyadic deontic logic (because of the two arguments to the modal operators; compare [16]). In case of unstructured diagrams, multiple deontic classifications might be necessary and are described in the third subsection. The fourth subsection then comprises a concept of agency, allowing to consider users and roles. Moreover, for the deontic classification of choices (exclusive or multi-choice), user decisions and conditional decisions must be distinguished. Finally, different levels concerning the extent to which deontic logic affects the process flow are presented.

2.3.1 Monadic Deontic Logic

Monadic deontic logic comprises unconditional or absolute normative concepts [1, p. 148]. The core concepts are *obligation* (O), *permission* (P), and *prohibition* (F for "forbidden") extended with a further operator for *alternative* (X). In addition, for the deontic classification of business processes, we specify an empty path (or *Phi*-Path). A path is called a *Phi*-Path (Φ), if it consists of a sequence flow that directly connects a split with the corresponding merge and thereby offers the possibility to do nothing.

The deontic concept for obligation (O) is expressed in natural language by the word "must" [1, p. 148]. In the deontic extension, an obligatory (or mandatory) activity is highlighted with a red background colour and by surrounding the text with O() for obligatory as shown in Fig. 2.1a. All obligatory activities must be executed within every process instance.

Activities are obligatory if they are, for example, defined in the main flow (*Start*; *A*; *B*; *C*; *End* $\equiv$ *Start*; $O(A)$; $O(B)$; $O(C)$; *End*) or after a parallel split in the main flow (*Start*; $A \wedge B$; *End* $\equiv$ *Start*; $O(A) \wedge O(B)$; *End*).

The deontic concept for permission (P) is expressed in natural language by the word "may" ($P(Task) \equiv \neg O(\neg Task)$) [1, p. 148ff]. In the deontic extension, a permissible activity is highlighted with a green background colour and by surrounding the text with P() for permissible (see Fig. 2.1b). The semantics of a permissible task is that if a token reaches the task, it can either be executed or not; if the task is not executed, the token is immediately passed on.

Activities are permissible if they are, for example, specified after an exclusive or multi-choice and if there is at least one alternative *Phi*-Path (*Start*; $A \mathbin{\dot\vee} B \mathbin{\dot\vee} Phi$; *End* $\equiv$ *Start*; $P(A) \mathbin{\dot\vee} P(B)$; *End*). Examples for exclusive or multi-choices in H-BPM are unconditional gateways (modelled as exclusive, inclusive, or complex gateways with conditions where the user is free to decide (see description of *User Choice* in Sect. 2.3.5)). In the deontic extension, the *Phi*-Paths can be removed, since the optionality is directly expressed within the corresponding activity.

Note that in deontic logic, the concepts of permission (P) and optionality (K) (also called deontic contingency) are similar, but slightly different. Optionality is defined as $K(Task) \equiv \neg O(Task) \wedge \neg O(\neg Task)$ and, thus, extends the definition of permission with an additional $\neg O(\neg Task)$ [27]. Hence, whenever a split offers the possibility to execute an activity or to do nothing, the activity is in fact optional. However, every optional activity is also permissible (since the definition of permission is more general), and we will, therefore, resort to the more familiar concept of permission in the proposed extension of H-BPM.

The deontic concept for prohibition (F) is expressed in natural language by the term "must not" [1, p. 148] and can alternatively be expressed with the concepts for obligation or permission ($F(Task) \equiv O(\neg Task) \equiv \neg P(Task)$). In the deontic extension of process diagrams, a forbidden (or prohibited) activity is highlighted with a blue background colour and by surrounding the text with F() for forbidden as shown in Fig. 2.1c. The semantics of a forbidden activity is that if a token reaches the activity, the activity is neither executed nor is the token passed on. Thus, the question remains how to deal with this situation. In a first step, the condition can be

regularly re-evaluated until a given deadline is reached (an additional attribute would
be required for that). However, if the prohibition remains, then possible solutions are,
e.g. to throw an exception, to wait indefinitely, or to consume the token silently. The
concrete reaction depends on the underlying BPML, since the deontic extension
must not change the behaviour of the process flow. Thus, different situations may
also require different reactions, e.g. in BPMN, an exception is thrown if no condition
of a splitting exclusive or inclusive gateway evaluates to true, but the behaviour of a
catch event that never catches an event is undefined (the token waits for an indefinite
time).

Activities that are only forbidden (monadic concept) are rare, since the intention
of process flows is to comprise activities that might be executed. However, more
common is the use of activities that are forbidden under some circumstances (dyadic
deontic logic), especially in case of multiple deontic classifications.

The deontic concept for alternative (X) is expressed in natural language by the
phrase "either …or …". This concept will be used to simplify the otherwise complex
definition of contravalence. The concept of alternatives is also defined in [3]:

$$X(A, B) \equiv (O(A) \vee O(B)) \wedge \neg(P(A) \wedge P(B))$$

In the deontic extension of process diagrams, an alternative activity is highlighted
with a yellow background colour and by surrounding the text with X() for alternative
as shown in Fig. 2.1d. The semantics of an alternative task is that it is obligatory
to execute the task if no alternative task will be executed and forbidden otherwise.
Alternative tasks are currently identified through the structure of the process flow
(i.e. located on alternative paths originating from the same split). For more complex
examples (e.g. higher gradings of deontic classification as described in Sect. 2.3.6),
an explicit definition of alternative tasks is required.

Activities are alternative if they are, for example, defined after an exclusive choice
and if there is no alternative *Phi*-Path (*Start*; $A \dot\vee B$; *End* $\equiv$ *Start*; $X(A) \dot\vee X(B)$; *End*).

Fig. 2.1 Unconditional
normative concepts. **a**
Obligation, **b** Permission, **c**
Prohibition, **d** Alternative

(a)   **(b)**   **(c)**   **(d)**

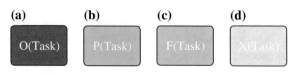

So, in addition to the deontic prefix, we suggested to highlight deontic activities with a background colour. Highlighting through colours is also discussed in
[20]. Moody describes colour as "one of the most cognitively effective of all visual
variables". He adds, however, that colour "should only be used for redundant cod-
ing" to provide for colour-blind people and print-outs in black-and-white. Consequently, we use colour in combination with the respective modal operators, "O",
"P", "F", and "X". However, we do not want to restrict other modellers to this formal
representation, so we suggested alternatives in [22], e.g. optional activities can also
be presented with a marker or with a dashed line style.

2.3.2 Dyadic Deontic Logic

Dyadic deontic logic supports conditional or relative normative concepts and, thus, the concept of commitment [1, p. 148]. Every monadic deontic operator can be extended with a precondition, for example, a conditional obligation is expressed in natural language by the sentence "if..., then it must be the case that" [1, p. 148].

Different notations have been proposed to specify conditions, e.g. a task A with a precondition B can be defined as AfB (A "fordert" (requires) B) [18], $A \Rightarrow O(B)$ (A implies that B is obligatory) [3], $O_B A$ (A is obligatory given B) [1, p. 151], or $O(A|B)$ (it is obligatory that A given B) [16]. Several conditions can then be concatenated with $\wedge$ or $\vee$. In our deontic extension of process diagrams, the last notation type ($O(A|B)$) is used due to its understandability (see Fig. 2.2). Furthermore, the extension of process diagrams with dyadic deontic logic allows for additional definitions that have not been possible in the original language. For example, it is criticised in [38] that BPMN does not directly support pre- and postconditions, which can be defined with the deontic extension.

Fig. 2.2 Conditional normative concepts

The semantics of a conditional activity is that the deontic expression must only be fulfilled in process instances where the condition evaluates to true. If an obligatory activity specifies as precondition the completion of the previous activity, then this activity must only be executed if the previous activity was executed before. However, if the previous activity was not executed, then the behaviour is undefined. A complete formal definition would specify the behaviour in case the condition is not fulfilled, e.g. define that the activity is forbidden. However, it can also be assumed that whenever the behaviour is undefined, the execution is forbidden and the token is passed on. This approach provides a shorter and better understandable definition and will, thus, be used for the deontic extension of process diagrams. Note that the evaluation of a condition may also have a third state "undecided", e.g. in case of a deferred choice (see Sect. 2.4). If the evaluation of a condition is in this state, then the token is blocked until a decision is reached.

2.3.3 Multiple Deontic Classifications

The concept of multiple deontic classification is necessary, as in case of unstructured diagrams. According to Liu and Kumar [17], a structured workflow is the one in which each split element is matched with a properly nested join element of the same type. The authors identified four basic types of structured workflows (based on the definition of structured workflows by Kiepuszewski et al. [15]): sequence, decision structure, parallel structure, and structured loop. Diagrams that are restricted to these types are well structured.

On the contrary, unstructured constructs allow arbitrary connections between activities, so a construct may have multiple entry or exit points [7]. Hence, an activity may be addressed by different splitting gateways. For example, Fig. 2.3a shows an unstructured diagram, in which task *A* is on the one hand an alternative to task *B* if the splitting gateway after the start event is taken into account and on the other hand permissible according to the splitting gateway after task *B*. Unstructured workflows are presented in more detail in [17], and the weaknesses of unstructured business process modelling languages are studied in particular in [7].

Multiple deontic classifications are, however, not restricted to unstructured diagrams. Examples of structured diagrams that require multiple deontic classifications are multi-choices without *Phi*-Path, or more complex constructs as described by the patterns *Deferred Choice, Milestone, Transient Trigger*, and *Persistent Trigger* in Sect. 2.4.2.

Multiple deontic classification then means that several deontic expressions are concatenated, for example, with ∧ or ∨. The unstructured diagram in Fig. 2.3a can be extended with deontic concepts as shown in Fig. 2.3b. Task *A* is classified as alternative and as permissible and the background colour is a mixture of yellow and green (if supported by the modelling tool, an alternative is to colour the upper part of the task yellow and the lower part green). Furthermore, preconditions can be used to define which classification is applicable under which circumstances and to remove the *Phi*-Path as well as the surrounding gateways as shown in Fig. 2.3c.

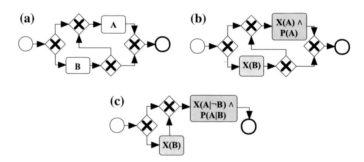

Fig. 2.3 Multiple deontic classification in an unstructured diagram. **a** Unstructured diagram. **b** Multiple deontic classification. **c** With preconditions

The semantics of an activity with multiple deontic classifications depends on the number of applicable expressions as follows:

- If no expression evaluates to true, then the activity is forbidden as described in Sect. 2.3.1.

- If one expression is applicable, for example task *A* in Fig. 2.3 is either alternative or permissible depending on the previous task, then only this expression must be considered.
- If several expressions are applicable at the same time, then all expressions must be fulfilled. For example, every activity after a multi-choice (inclusive gateway) without *Phi*-Path is permissible, and it is obligatory if no alternative activity is executed ($P(A) \land O(A|\neg AlterActivity)$). When the precondition evaluates to true, the activity is simultaneously permissible and obligatory, so it must be executed. However, the applicable expressions can also be contradictory, e.g. an activity is obligatory and forbidden at the same time. Due to the contradiction, the activity is neither executed nor is the token passed on, resulting in a runtime exception.

2.3.4 Deontic Logic with Agency

A further concept of deontic logic is the definition of actors. For example, an action description can have the form $Do(r, p)$, where *Do* is a modal operator for action or agency, *r* stands for an agent (or role), and *p* describes a propositional expression (e.g. an action *A*) [14]. Every deontic operator can then be extended with an action description, e.g. $O\ do(r, A)$, $P\ do(r, A)$, or $F\ do(r, A)$ (a user with role *r* is obliged/permitted/forbidden to perform action *A*). Since the deontic logic used in this book is based on actions, the modal operator *Do* (expressed e.g. as "ought to do" or "permitted to do") can either be used implicitly or explicitly. In the following, the modal operator is only used explicitly if agents are defined.

2.3.5 User Versus Conditional Choice

According to the Workflow Patterns and the most concrete BPMLs like BPMN and UML ADs, all exclusive and multi-choices must define conditions on the outgoing paths. The conditions depend on the outcome of a preceding task, on the evaluation of data or an expression, or on another programmatic selection mechanism. The only exception is represented by default arcs, which have their own semantics and do not specify an explicit condition (cf. for this paragraph [33]).

However, an important aspect for the deontic classification is the differentiation of human (or user) and state-based (or conditional) decisions. The result of both decisions can be determined, e.g. within a preceding task, but in the first case the user can freely decide whereas in the second case the outgoing path is selected based on a state, data, or rule. For example, an exclusive choice with the decision "Choose Colour" could describe a user choice, whereas the answer to the question "Credit Card Valid?" would be based on the verification of the credit card.

The reason for the differentiation of user choices and conditional choices is that the deontic extension is intended for a different level of abstraction than most BPMLs.

For example, in classical process diagrams, the level of abstraction is such that the resulting models can be executed by a business process engine and every model is supposed to be deterministic. The deontic extension, however, takes the viewpoint of the user, who is not seen as a deterministically operating machine, but as an agent who is capable of autonomously taking decisions and also authorised to do so. Thus, the tasks following such a user choice are classified as permissible or alternative.

To be able to compare standard models and their deontic extensions, the deontically classified models must be transformed to the same level of abstraction. In a standard model, every task must be seen as obligatory as soon as the firing conditions are met, e.g. by a token on the incoming path. In order to establish a relation between a permissible and a standard task, a permissible task can be considered to be a conditionally obligatory task, where the precondition is determined by user input ("UserChoice"). The precondition "UserChoice" then has to be matched with the firing condition of the respective outgoing path of the choice (gateway) which leads to the task in question. It should also be noted that due to the different layers addressed, the deontically extended models may show a certain redundancy where user-centric and process-engine-centric concepts overlap. This redundancy is assumed to be very helpful from the user's point of view.

2.3.6 Levels of Deontic Classification

Regarding the deontic classification of process flows, different levels are possible concerning the extent to which deontic concepts affect the process flow, and they range from highlighting modalities to a detailed work list in which the process flow can be omitted. The following levels of deontic classification can be distinguished:

1. Deontic logic is used to highlight the modality of activities by classifying them as obligatory, alternative, or permissible. However, the classification does not affect the representation of process flow and, thus, the number of gateways and sequence flows remains the same.
2. The deontic classification affects the representation of process flow and reduces the structural complexity as follows:

   a. The number of gateways and sequence flows can be reduced by removing the *Phi*-Paths and possible surrounding gateways in case only one further path is addressed.
   b. The exclusive and inclusive choices are replaced by parallel splits, resulting in only one gateway type without conditions and irrelevant order of the outgoing paths.

3. The entire process flow is expressed with deontic logic, for example, by using preconditions or deontic rules to define the dependencies. The activities can then be provided in a work list starting with those activities that have no defined

precondition or where the precondition is already fulfilled. The representation of process flow is no more required (see also workflow charts in Chap. 4).

In general, it can be said that the lower levels (1 and 2a) increase human understandability. Modalities are highlighted and the structural complexity might be reduced, but the applied deontic constructs are easy to understand. However, the higher levels (2b and 3) may comprise complex deontic expressions. The resulting expressions are hard to understand for humans, but simplify the execution by a process engine.

The goal of the current work is to increase the human understandability. Thus, the necessary deontic extensions for reaching level 2a are presented. For a definition of the required extension for reaching level 2b, see [24].

2.4 Workflow Patterns

This section considers the *Workflow Patterns* (WP) developed by research groups around Wil van der Aalst and Arthur ter Hofstede [33] and describes how the patterns of the control-flow perspective, the *Control-Flow Patterns*, can be extended with deontic concepts to highlight modalities.

2.4.1 Overview

The *Workflow Patterns* define requirements for workflow and BPMLs by a collection of patterns divided into four perspectives (control-flow, resource, data, and exception handling) with the goal to provide a conceptual basis for process technology [32, 33]. The Workflow Patterns have been developed by research groups around Wil van der Aalst and Arthur ter Hofstede since 1999 and are presented on the Workflow Patterns Homepage (see [33]) and in corresponding publications (e.g. [29, 32] for Control-Flow Patterns). A major advantage of the Workflow Patterns is that they are independent of concrete BPMLs and, thus, an extension defined for the Workflow Patterns can be easily adapted for most concrete BPMLs including H-BPM, BPMN, UML ADs, and (EPCs).

The first perspective comprises the *Control-Flow Patterns*, which specify the requirements for the process flow and include patterns for branching, synchronising, multiple instances, cancellation, iteration, termination, and triggering [33]. The original 20 patterns described in [32] have been extended in 2006 to 43 patterns presented in [29]. For each pattern, a formal description is provided in the form of a Coloured Petri-Net (CPN). The Control-Flow Patterns are extended with deontic logic in Sect. 2.4.2.

The 43 *Workflow Resource Patterns* are used to capture the various ways in which resources are represented and utilised in workflows and business processes [28]. These patterns are described in more detail in Sect. 3.6. Similarly, the 40 *Workflow*

Data Patterns describe how data is represented in workflows and business processes [33]. For the last perspective, the *Exception Handling Patterns*, a classification framework for exception handling based on patterns, has been developed [33]. Neither the Workflow Data Patterns nor the Exception Handling Patterns are extended with deontic logic.

The research groups further analysed whether and how patterns are implemented in 14 commercial products (Staffware, IBM WebSphere MQ, FLOWer, COSA, iPlanet, SAP Workflow, FileNet, BPEL, WebSphere Integration Developer, Oracle BPEL, BPMN 1.0, XPDL, UML ADs, and EPCs) [29]. Three additional commercial products (jBPM, OpenWFE, and Enhydra Shark) are considered in a more current analysis provided in [33]. An analysis of EPCs based on the Workflow Patterns is provided in [19]. White, one of the specification editors of BPMN, studied how BPMN and UML ADs can represent the Control-Flow Patterns [36]. A more comprehensive comparison of BPMN and the WPs also considering the resource and data perspective is presented in [38]. According to this analysis, BPMN provides a good support for the Control-Flow Patterns, a medium support for the Data Patterns, but only a low support for the Resource Patterns. Thus, considering actor modelling in process diagrams is important and addressed in Chap. 3.

Interesting is also the formal specification of the 43 Control-Flow Patterns in terms of Abstract State Machine (ASMs) by Börger (see [4]). Eight basic workflow patterns were identified, four for sequential (sequence, iteration, begin/termination, and selection) and four for parallel control-flows (splitting, merging, interleaving, and trigger). Although this definition helps to structure the WPs, the refined patterns must be considered for the deontic analysis, since the deontic classification depends, e.g. on how many outgoing paths of a selection (or choice) may be taken. Börger further criticised the WPs for their ambiguous and incomplete description and the unsuitable comparison with other approaches (no consideration of *workarounds*) in [5].

However, although the Workflow Patterns are widely used and often referenced as shown by the *Impact* section on the homepage (see [33]), no approach is available that extends the Workflow Patterns with deontic logic. Nevertheless, some publications focus on the organisational part of process modelling and either reference the Workflow Patterns or deontic logic as related work (e.g. [26]).

2.4.2 Control-Flow Patterns with Deontic Logic

In this section, the *Control-Flow Patterns* are studied and extended with deontic concepts. An overview of the 43 Control-Flow Patterns is given in Table 2.1. The first column provides the pattern number, the second column the pattern name, and the third column specifies whether the pattern requires a deontic classification. For example, some tasks in the *Sequence* and *Parallel Split* patterns can be classified as obligatory whereas in the *Synchronisation* pattern, several parallel paths converge into a single path without affecting the deontic classification.

Table 2.1 Overview of Control-Flow Patterns based on [33]

No.	Pattern name	Deontic extension
Basic Control-Flow Patterns		
1	Sequence	Yes
2	Parallel split	Yes
3	Synchronisation	No
4	Exclusive choice	Yes
5	Simple Merge	No
Advanced branching and synchronisation patterns		
6	Multi-choice	Yes
7	Structured synchronising merge	No
8	Multi-merge	No
9	Structured discriminator	No
28	Blocking discriminator	No
29	Cancelling discriminator	No
30	Structured partial join	No
31	Blocking partial join	No
32	Cancelling partial join	No
33	Generalised AND-join	No
37	Local synchronising merge	No
38	General synchronising merge	No
41	Thread merge	No
42	Thread split	No
Multiple instance patterns		
12	Multiple instances without synchronisation	No
13	Multiple instances with a priori design-time knowledge	No
14	Multiple instances with a priori runtime knowledge	No
15	Multiple instances without a priori runtime knowledge	No
34	Static partial join for multiple instances	No
35	Cancelling partial join for multiple instances	No
36	Dynamic partial join for multiple instances	No
State-based patterns		
16	Deferred choice	Yes
17	Interleaved parallel routing	No
18	Milestone	Yes
39	Critical section	No
40	Interleaved routing	No
Cancellation and force completion patterns		
19	Cancel task	No
20	Cancel case	No

(continued)

Table 2.1 (continued)

No.	Pattern name	Deontic extension
25	Cancel region	No
26	Cancel multiple instance activity	No
27	Complete multiple instance activity	No
Iteration patterns		
10	Arbitrary cycles	Yes
21	Structured loop	Yes
22	Recursion	No
Termination patterns		
11	Implicit termination	No
43	Explicit termination	No
Trigger patterns		
23	Transient trigger	Yes
24	Persistent trigger	Yes

2.4.2.1 Pattern 1: Sequence

The first pattern describes a sequence of tasks, where each task is enabled after the completion of the preceding task and no condition is associated with the control-flow edge [33]. The CPN of the *Sequence* pattern is shown in Fig. 2.4.

Fig. 2.4 Pattern 1: Sequence (*Source* [33], © 2010–2011 workflow patterns initiative, reprinted with permission (This © will also apply to all forthcoming reprints from [33]))

The circles contain the places (input labels (*i1..in*), internal labels (*p1..pn*), and output labels (*o1..on*)), whereas the rectangles describe the transitions (*A..Z*) [29]. Places represent conditions, which can either be seen as precondition if placed before the transition or as postcondition if placed afterwards [31, p. 167]. The places and transitions are connected by edges that represent the control-flow (*c*). Since Petri nets are directed bipartite graphs, every edge has as source either a place or a transition and as target the respective other element [31, p. 165].

Considering the deontic classification, three cases are distinguished as shown in Fig. 2.5. The second and every further task of a sequence are obligatory and enabled after the completion of the preceding task. Thus, in all three cases, these tasks are classified as obligatory under the precondition that the previous task was executed, e.g. $O(B|A)$. A forbidden statement is only necessary in cases where the previous task may be forbidden. The difference between the three cases shown in Fig. 2.5, however, is the classification of the first task.

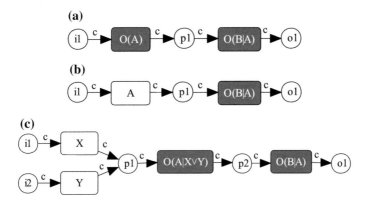

Fig. 2.5 Deontic classification of *Sequence* pattern. **a** Starting process. **b** Preceding splitting node. **c** Preceding tasks

In the first case shown in Fig. 2.5a, it is assumed that task *A* starts the process and there is no other preceding task or start event. In this case, task *A* is marked as obligatory ($O(A)$).

In the second case shown in Fig. 2.5b, task *A* is addressed by a splitting node, for example, a parallel split or a choice. In this case, task *A* is deontically classified by the corresponding split or the choice pattern and remains unclassified in the sequence pattern.

The third case is shown in Fig. 2.5c and comprises all scenarios where the first task of the sequence has one or more preceding tasks or events. In this case, task *A* is obligatory, but all preceding tasks or events must be summarised in the precondition, e.g. $O(A|X \vee Y)$ in case of a preceding multi-merge, $O(A|X \wedge Y)$ in case of parallel incoming paths, or $O(A|StartEvent)$ in case of a preceding start event.

However, preconditions decrease the understandability. Thus, a pragmatic approach is suggested, which allows to omit the preconditions (see Fig. 2.6) if the sequence is part of the main flow and the execution order is also expressed by sequence flows.

Fig. 2.6 Pragmatic approach to the *Sequence* pattern

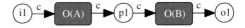

Nevertheless, the preconditions must remain if the sequence follows an exclusive or multi-choice as shown by the process diagram in Fig. 2.7a with the deontic classification provided in Fig. 2.7b. The preconditions are necessary to define that if the first task is not executed, then also the further tasks must not be executed, thereby representing the *Phi*-Path. Removing the preconditions (see Fig. 2.7d) would require to execute the further tasks and lead to the assumption that the former process model only comprised task *A* within the choice and defined the other tasks after the merge as shown in Fig. 2.7c.

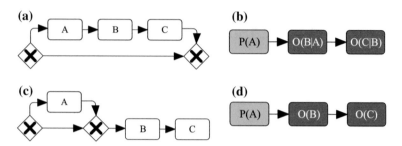

Fig. 2.7 Examples of *Sequence* pattern. **a** Example 1: classical process diagram. **b** Example 1: deontic process diagram. **c** Example 2: classical process diagram. **d** Example 2: Deontic process diagram

2.4.2.2 Pattern 2: Parallel Split

The *Parallel Split* pattern describes the split of a branch into two or more parallel branches, which are executed concurrently as shown in Fig. 2.8 [33]. The parallel split does not define any conditions on the outgoing control-flow edges.

Fig. 2.8 Pattern 2: Parallel split (*Source* [33])

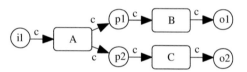

The deontic classification of the *Parallel Split* pattern is shown in Fig. 2.9. Tasks B and C are always executed and, thus, classified as obligatory under the precondition that the previous task has been completed ($O(B|A)$, $O(C|A)$). The preconditions can be omitted if the split is defined in the main flow, since in this case, all parallel paths must be executed within every process instance ($B \wedge C \Rightarrow O(B) \wedge O(C)$).

Fig. 2.9 Deontic classification of *Parallel Split* pattern

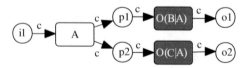

Since parallel splits do not specify conditions, a possible *Phi*-Path has no additional semantics and can be removed.

$$B \wedge \Phi \Rightarrow O(B) \qquad B \wedge C \wedge \Phi \Rightarrow O(B) \wedge O(C)$$

If there is only one other path besides the *Phi*-Path, then removing the *Phi*-Path also allows removing the parallel split.

2.4.2.3   Pattern 4: Exclusive Choice

The *Exclusive Choice* pattern describes the divergence of one branch into two or more branches, but the thread of control is only passed to exactly one outgoing branch as shown in Fig. 2.10. The selection of the outgoing branch is based on an evaluation of the conditions defined for the outgoing paths [33]. Not specified is the behaviour if several conditions evaluate to true; e.g. BPMN refers to an undefined ordering of the outgoing paths.

Fig. 2.10 Pattern 4: Exclusive choice (*Source* [33])

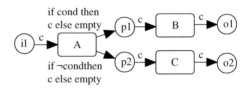

The deontic classification depends on the type of choice (user vs. conditional) and on a possible *Phi*-Path (see Fig. 2.11). If the exclusive choice provides a user decision without *Phi*-Path, then all tasks are alternatives as shown in Fig. 2.11a.

$$B \stackrel{.}{\vee} C \Rightarrow X(B) \stackrel{.}{\vee} X(C)$$

Fig. 2.11 Deontic classification of *Exclusive Choice* pattern. **a** User choice without *Phi*-Path. **b** User choice with *Phi*-Path. **c** Conditional choice

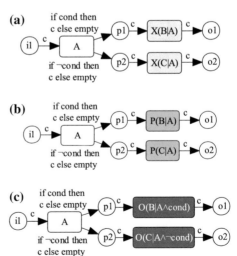

However, if one or more *Phi*-Paths exist, then these paths can be removed and all other tasks are classified as permissible as shown in Fig. 2.11b. If there is only one other path apart from the *Phi*-Path, then also the exclusive choice can be removed.

$$B \ \dot\vee \ \Phi \ \Rightarrow \ P(B) \qquad B \ \dot\vee \ C \ \dot\vee \ \Phi \ \Rightarrow \ P(B) \ \dot\vee \ P(C)$$

However, if the exclusive choice provides a conditional decision, then the tasks are obligatory under the precondition that the condition is fulfilled as shown in Fig. 2.11c, and possible *Phi*-Paths must remain.

$$(B|cond) \ \dot\vee \ (C|\neg cond) \ \Rightarrow \ O(B|cond) \ \dot\vee \ O(C|\neg cond)$$

All tasks specify as precondition the completion of the previous task. This precondition can be omitted if the choice is defined in the main flow.

Preconditions are, however, necessary for nested choices as shown by the process diagram in Fig. 2.12a with the deontic classification in Fig. 2.12b. The precondition is necessary to define that task *B* is permissible but can only be executed if task *A* was executed before. Removing the precondition (see Fig. 2.12d) would allow to execute task *B* in any case and lead to the assumption that the process diagram defined task *A* and task *B* within two different choices on the same level as shown in Fig. 2.12c.

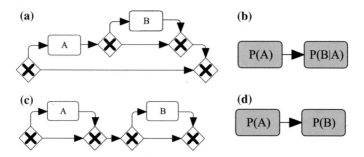

Fig. 2.12 Examples of *Exclusive Choice* pattern. **a** Example 1: classical process diagram. **b** Example 1: Deontic process diagram. **c** Example 2: classical process diagram. **d** Example 2: deontic process diagram

2.4.2.4   Pattern 6: Multi-choice

The *Multi-choice* pattern describes the splitting of one branch into two or more branches, where the thread of control is immediately passed to one or more branches as shown in Fig. 2.13 [33]. The selection of the outgoing branches is based on an evaluation of the conditions defined for the outgoing paths [33].

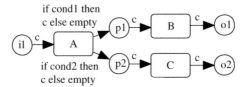

Fig. 2.13 Pattern 6: Multi-choice (*Source* [33])

Similar to the exclusive choice pattern, the deontic classification of the multi-choice pattern depends on the type of choice (user vs. conditional) and on a possible *Phi*-Path (see Fig. 2.14). If the multi-choice provides a user decision without *Phi*-Path, then all tasks are permissible, and obligatory if no alternative task will be executed, as shown in Fig. 2.14a.

$$B \ \lor \ C \Rightarrow (P(B) \ \land \ O(B|\neg C)) \ \lor \ (P(C) \ \land \ O(C|\neg B))$$

However, if one or more *Phi*-Paths exist, then these paths can be removed and all other tasks are classified as permissible as shown in Fig. 2.14b. If there is only one other path apart from the *Phi*-Path, then also the multi-choice can be removed.

$$B \ \lor \ \Phi \Rightarrow P(B) \quad B \ \lor \ C \ \lor \ \Phi \Rightarrow P(B) \ \lor \ P(C)$$

The deontic classification of tasks in a multi-choice with *Phi*-Path can be justified by considering all possible combinations of paths, e.g. the structure $(A \lor B \lor \Phi)$ can be transformed as follows:

$$\phi \ \dot\lor \ A \ \dot\lor \ B \ \dot\lor \ (A \land B) \ \dot\lor \ (A \land \phi) \ \dot\lor \ (B \land \phi) \ \dot\lor \ (A \land B \land \phi)$$
$$\phi \ \dot\lor \ A \ \dot\lor \ B \ \dot\lor \ (A \land B)$$
$$P(A \ \dot\lor \ B \ \dot\lor \ (A \land B))$$
$$P(A \lor B)$$

If $A \lor B$ is permitted, then certainly *at least* either A or B must be permitted. But the performance of $A \lor B$ does not rule out that both A *and* B are performed, so from $P(A \lor B)$ follows $P(A) \lor P(B)$. Thus, all tasks following a multi-choice with *Phi*-Path are permissible.

However, if the multi-choice provides a conditional decision, then every task is obligatory under the precondition that the condition is fulfilled and possible *Phi*-Paths must remain (see Fig. 2.14c).

$$(B|cond1) \ \lor \ (C|cond2) \Rightarrow O(B|cond1) \ \lor \ O(C|cond2)$$

Fig. 2.14 Deontic
classification of *Multi-choice*
pattern. **a** User choice
without *Phi*-Path. **b** User
choice with *Phi*-Path. **c**
Conditional choice

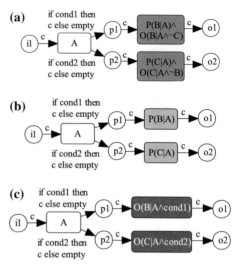

Furthermore, all tasks in Fig. 2.14 specify as precondition the completion of the previous task. This precondition can be omitted if the choice is defined in the main flow.

2.4.2.5   Pattern 16: Deferred Choice

The *Deferred Choice* pattern offers the possibility to choose one of several outgoing branches based on an interaction with the operating system as shown in Fig. 2.15. In a first step, all branches are possible and the decision is made by initiating the first task, thereby withdrawing all other tasks [33].

Fig. 2.15 Pattern 16:
Deferred choice
(*Source* [33])

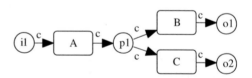

This pattern is similar to the exclusive choice pattern with conditions, but it must be specified that only the branch of the first initiated task is taken. Thus, every task is obligatory if the previous task completed and the condition evaluates to true, but forbidden if already an alternative task is executed (see Fig. 2.16). All tasks specify as precondition the completion of the previous task. This precondition can be omitted if the choice is defined in the main flow.

$$(B|cond1) \dot{\vee} (C|cond2) \Rightarrow (O(B|cond1) \wedge F(B|C)) \vee (O(C|cond2) \wedge F(C|B))$$

Fig. 2.16 Deontic classification of *Deferred Choice* pattern

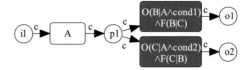

2.4.2.6 Pattern 18: Milestone

The *Milestone* pattern defines that a task is only enabled if the process instance has reached a specific state (milestone) and not progressed beyond this state (deadline) (see Fig. 2.17; B is milestone and C is deadline) [33].

Fig. 2.17 Pattern 18: Milestone (*Source* [33])

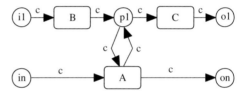

For the deontic classification, the task must already be classified as obligatory, alternative, or permissible based on the other patterns. This classification is then extended with the precondition that the milestone must have been reached and a forbidden statement that prohibits the execution of the task if the deadline already has expired. The forbidden statement assures that neither the task is executed nor the token is passed on. The further behaviour then depends on the underlying BPML. Since most BPMLs like H-BPM and BPMN only support this pattern in their deontic extension, we can specify the behaviour and suggest to throw an exception that can be caught and handled by an alternative task.

$$(A|Milestone \wedge \neg Deadline) \Rightarrow O(A|Milestone) \wedge F(A|Deadline)$$

The deontic classification of three different tasks and the milestone pattern with an obligatory task is presented in Fig. 2.18. All tasks specify as precondition the completion of the previous task. This precondition can be omitted if the task is defined in the main flow.

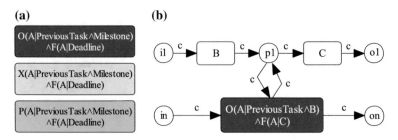

Fig. 2.18 Deontic classification of *Milestone* pattern. **a** All tasks. **b** *Milestone* pattern (Obligatory task)

The milestone pattern is only supported by the product COSA and partly by FLOWer [33]. However, an extension with deontic logic permits that also standards (or notations) such as H-BPM, BPMN, UML ADs, and EPCs can support this pattern.

2.4.2.7 Patterns 10 and 21: Arbitrary Cycles and Structured Loop

The two patterns, *Arbitrary Cycles* and *Structured Loop*, are both defined in this section, since the deontic classification is the same. The arbitrary cycles pattern is shown in Fig. 2.19 and represents cycles with more than one entry or exit point. In contrast, the structured loop pattern provides the possibility to execute a task or sub-process repeatedly within a loop that has a single entry and exit point. The structured loop pattern distinguishes between the pre-test or while loop (see Fig. 2.20a) and the post-test or repeat loop (see Fig. 2.20b) (cf. for this paragraph [33]).

A cycle or loop has a limited deontic influence, since the elements in between are just repeated and the only question is how often a task is executed. In case of a repeat loop the elements in between are executed at least once (1..*n*), whereas a while loop might not be executed at all (0..*n*). Nevertheless, the elements in the loop are classified based on other patterns and the loop or cycle only affects the precondition of the tasks following the entry points as well as the classification of the task following the exit point in case the loop only defines one exit point.

Considering the deontic classification of the arbitrary cycles pattern (see Fig. 2.21), task *D* is the second task of a sequence and, thus, obligatory under the precondition

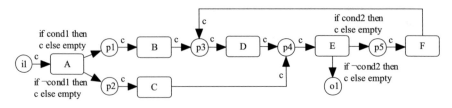

Fig. 2.19 Pattern 10: Arbitrary cycles (*Source* [33])

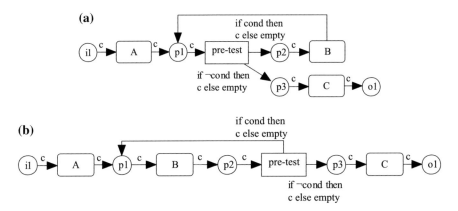

Fig. 2.20 Pattern 21: Structured loop (*Source* [33]). **a** While variant. **b** Repeat variant

that the previous task B was executed. This precondition is extended with task F based on the cycle. Furthermore, task D is consisted in a type of repeat loop and at least executed once, which corresponds to the obligatory classification. Task E follows the simple merge and is considered as a single task, whose deontic classification is explained in a subsequent section. Task E is classified as obligatory under the precondition that the previous tasks were executed and is not affected by the cycle. Also not affected by the cycle is task F, which is classified based on the preceding exclusive choice (e.g. as alternative in case of a user choice). This task is consisted in a type of while loop and might not be executed at all, which corresponds to the deontic classification. Interesting, however, is the classification of a task following the exit point $o1$. Normally, the task would also be classified as alternative due to the preceding exclusive choice. However, since there is no other exit point within the cycle and this task must be executed sooner or later, the task can be classified as obligatory. In this case the classification of the exclusive choice pattern is overruled by the arbitrary cycle pattern.

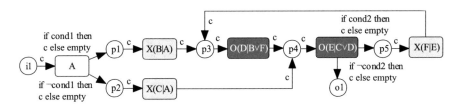

Fig. 2.21 Deontic classification of the *Arbitrary Cycles* pattern

The classification of tasks in a structured loop is shown in Fig. 2.22 with the while loop being presented in Fig. 2.22a. Task B is classified as alternative due to the preceding exclusive choice (assumed to be a user choice) and the precondition refers to task *A* or *B*. The alternative classification corresponds to the fact that a while loop might not be executed at all. The task can also be classified as permissible if the exclusive choice with user decision has a preceding empty path (see explanation below). The loop further affects the classification of the task following the exit point, since this task will be executed sooner or later. Thus, task *C* is classified as obligatory under the precondition that either task *A* or *B* was completed before.

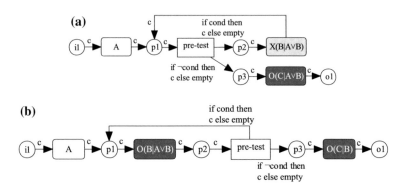

Fig. 2.22 Deontic classification of *Structured Loop* pattern. **a** While variant. **b** Repeat variant

The classification of a structured repeat loop is presented in Fig. 2.22b. In this case, task *B* is the second task of a sequence and classified as obligatory. This classification corresponds to the fact that a repeat loop must be executed at least once. The precondition further specifies that either task *A* or *B* must have been executed before. In addition, task *C* follows the loop and is classified as obligatory. The precondition only refers to task *B*, which is executed at least once and, thus, the only possible preceding task.

As mentioned earlier, a task in a structured while loop with an exclusive choice that provides a user decision and has a preceding empty (*Phi*) path may also be classified as permissible. For example, in Fig. 2.22a, task *B* can be classified as permissible since no task is defined between place *p1* and transition *pre-test*. Nevertheless, the gateways and sequence flows must remain to express the loop. Thus, the definition of a task in a while loop without deontic classification ([*A*]) is different from that of a task with permissible classification ([[*A*]]) (syntax based on *Extended Backus–Naur Form* (EBNF)), but the semantics is the same and the task can be executed as often as desired. The permissible classification corresponds to the classification of a task following an exclusive choice with user decision and *Phi*-Path in the main flow. However, if the path before the exclusive choice is not empty, then the task must not be classified as permissible. For example, the standard process diagram shown in Fig. 2.23a (*A*, [*B*, *A*]) is semantically different from the deontic process diagram shown in Fig. 2.23b (*A*, [[*B*], *A*]).

Fig. 2.23 Example: invalid classification of a *Structured Loop*. **a** Standard process diagram. **b** Deontic process diagram

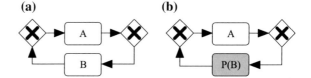

2.4.2.8 Patterns 23 and 24: Transient Trigger and Persistent Trigger

The two patterns *Transient Trigger* and *Persistent Trigger* are defined in one section, since the patterns are similar and the deontic classification is the same. The transient trigger pattern provides the possibility that a task is triggered by a signal from another part of the process or from the external environment. However, the triggers are transient and lost if the receiving task does not immediately act upon the trigger (see Fig. 2.24a for the unsafe variant of the transient trigger pattern). The persistent trigger pattern is very similar and also describes the triggering of a task by a signal. In contrast to transient triggers, persistent triggers are, however, retained by the process until the receiving task can act on the trigger (see Fig. 2.24b) [33].

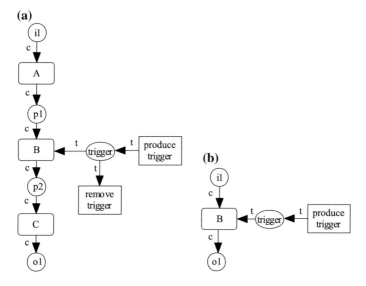

Fig. 2.24 Patterns 23 and 24: Transient and persistent trigger (*Source* [33]). **a** Transient trigger. **b** Persistent trigger

The deontic classification of different tasks that require a trigger is shown in Fig. 2.25a. The tasks are already classified as obligatory, alternative, or permissible based on other patterns. This classification is extended with the precondition that the trigger occurred and a forbidden statement that prohibits the execution of the task if no trigger is available. The behaviour of a forbidden task must correspond with the original BPML. In H-BPM, and also BPMN, a catch event waits for the trigger for an indefinite time (i.e. the expression is regularly re-evaluated). Thus, the same behaviour is suggested for the deontic extension.

$$(B|Trigger) \Rightarrow O(B|Trigger) \land F(B|\neg Trigger)$$

The deontic classification does not differ between the transient and persistent trigger patterns, since it makes no difference whether the task receives a trigger signal directly or from a buffer. The deontic classification of the two patterns with an obligatory task is shown in Fig. 2.25b, c.

The transient trigger pattern is not supported by all BPMLs, e.g. BPMN 1.0 only supports the persistent trigger pattern through the use of message events [33]. However, in BPMN 2.0 and H-BPM, a signal event is provided, which is used for broadcasting and may support the transient trigger pattern.

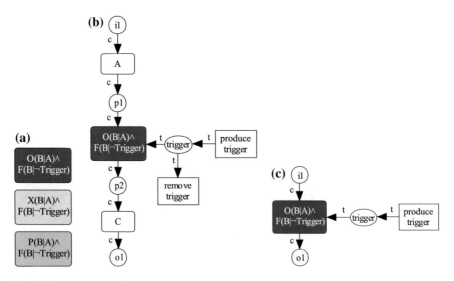

Fig. 2.25 Deontic classification of the *Transient* and *Persistent Trigger* patterns. **a** All tasks. **b** Transient trigger. **c** Persistent trigger

2.4.2.9 Single Task

The extension of the Control-Flow Patterns with deontic concepts highlights the modality of most tasks. However, not classified are some tasks that may occur after an event or merge and are not part of a sequence. These tasks are called *Single Tasks* and are studied in this section. For example, in Fig. 2.26, tasks *A*, *E*, and *F* are single tasks and not classified by one of the WPs.

Not a single task is, however, the first task after a splitting node, even if a merge is defined in between, since this task is classified by the corresponding split pattern. For example, in Fig. 2.26, task *B* is the first task after a splitting node with a merge in between and, thus, not a single task. Instead, task *B* requires multiple deontic classifications as explained in Sect. 2.3.3.

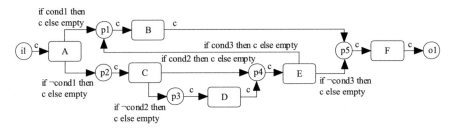

Fig. 2.26 Single task

The deontic classification of a single task is the same as for the first task of a sequence. The task is classified as obligatory under the precondition that all possible previous tasks and events have been completed as shown in Fig. 2.27. Furthermore, the precondition can be omitted if the task starts the process or if the task is part of the main flow (pragmatic approach).

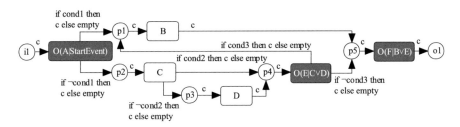

Fig. 2.27 Deontic classification of *Single Task*

2.5 Application Scenario

We now present two examples which are taken from a real-life industrial project in which we were involved. The first example describes a typical order execution process as it can be found in many companies (with certain variations). The standard process diagram of the order execution process is shown in Fig. 2.28. The process comprises the following tasks: *Create Request* (CR), *ModifyRequest* (MR), *Delete Request* (DR), *Reject Request* (RJR), *Approve Order* (AO), *Create/Modify Appointment* (CMA), *Remove Appointment* (RA), *Approve Appointment* (AA), *Reject Appointment* (RJA), *Order in Progress* (OP), *Execute Order* (EO), *Create Report* (RC), *Modify Report* (RM), *Formally Correct Report* (RFC), *Formally Incorrect Report* (RFI) and *Close Order* (CO). These tasks are specified within three lanes that describe the roles *Assistant*, *Consultant*, and *Approver*.

The order execution process essentially defines that a request can be created by any of the three roles. If an assistant or a consultant creates the request, then this request can be modified by the consultant and is afterwards either deleted or sent to the approver, who can approve or reject the order. If the order is created by the approver, then it will always be approved. The approved order is then sent to the consultant who may define an appointment or specify that the order is in progress. Subsequently, every order must be executed by the consultant. The consultant can then create and modify a report which might be sent to the approver for approval. Finally, the consultant closes the order.

Considering the order execution process, all splitting gateways provide user choices and do not depend on any state or data. The entire diagram contains 26 gateways and 64 sequence flows and is quite complex. Thus, it is difficult to identify the permissible and obligatory tasks.

The corresponding deontic process diagram is shown in Fig. 2.29. The deontic process diagram highlights that it is obligatory to create a request (CR) (only the roles are alternative) and obligatory to approve (AO), execute (EO), and close the order (CO). Additionally, it defines that the two tasks *Delete Request* (DR) and *Reject Request* (RJR) are alternatives to the main flow. All other tasks are permissible. It is further necessary to deontically classify two sequence flows, since a report may only be modified or sent for approval if it has been created before. This classification, however, highlights that the two tasks *Formally Correct Report* (RFC) and *Formally Incorrect Report* (RFI) are alternatives within a permissible structure.

The deontic process diagram provides two advantages with respect to intelligibility. First, this diagram contains only 18 gateways and 49 sequence flows. So it was possible to remove eight gateways and 15 sequence flows and thereby reduce the structural complexity of the process flow. Second, obligatory and permissible tasks can be distinguished at first sight based on the coloured highlighting. It is still necessary to decide whether a permissible task is executed or not but instead of describing this decision through separate gateways and alternative paths, the decision is described within the corresponding task. The advantages are accompanied by additional deontic constructs requiring a basic understanding by the user.

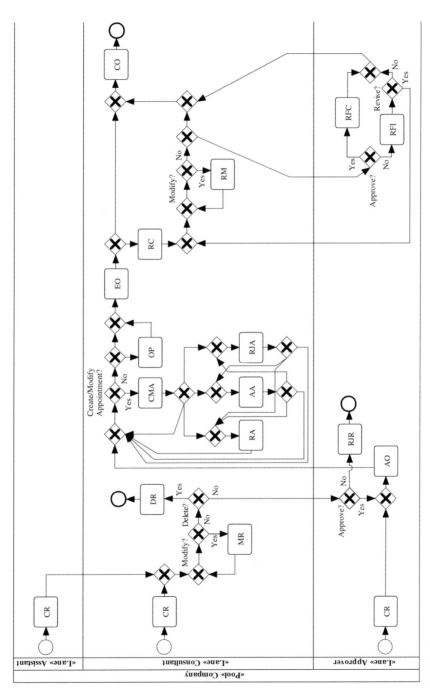

Fig. 2.28 Order execution: standard process diagram

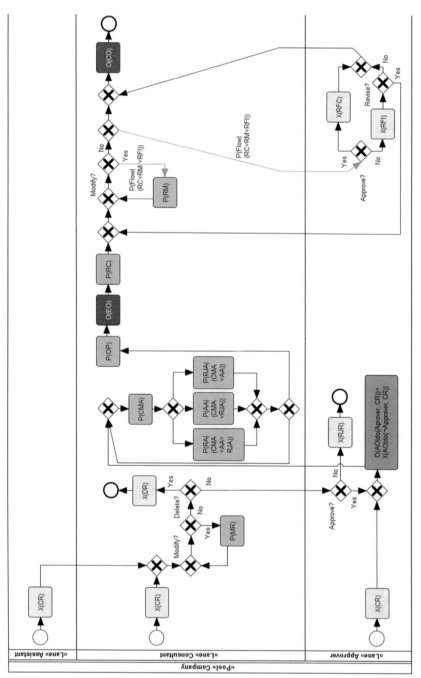

Fig. 2.29 Order execution: deontic process diagram

However, the more complex constructs (such as preconditions) are only relevant for a more detailed understanding of the process.

The second example describes a business travel process and the standard process diagram is shown in Fig. 2.30. The process comprises the tasks: *Create BT*, *Modify BT*, *Send for Approval*, *Review BT*, *Reject Review*, *Approve BT*, *Reject BT*, and *Execute and Close BT*. The abbreviation *BT* stands for *Business Travel*. These tasks are specified within three lanes that describe the roles *Owner*, *Reviewer*, and *Approver*.

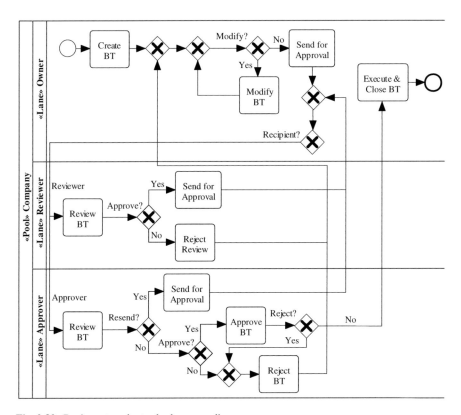

Fig. 2.30 Business travel: standard process diagram

This process essentially defines that a business travel is created by its owner and can then be modified. Afterwards, the business travel is sent for approval to either a reviewer or an approver. If the business travel is sent to a reviewer, then the reviewer reviews it and either resends it for approval or rejects the review in which case the owner is supposed to modify the business travel. If, however, the recipient of the business travel is an approver, then the approver has to review the business travel and can either resend it (e.g. to another approver) or approve/reject it. If the approver rejects the business travel, then the owner is again supposed to modify it, but if the

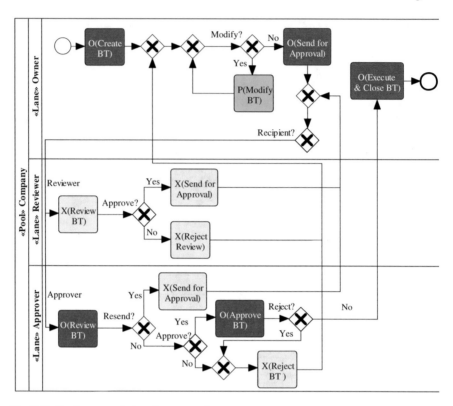

Fig. 2.31 Business travel: deontic process diagram

approver approves the business travel, then the owner must execute and close the business travel.

Considering the business travel process, again all splitting gateways provide user choices and the entire model consists of 10 gateways and 28 sequence flows. So although this model is less complex than that of the order execution process, it is still difficult to identify the obligatory and permissible tasks at first sight.

The corresponding deontic process diagram is shown in Fig. 2.31. The tasks *Create BT*, *Send for Approval* (by the owner), *Review BT* (by an approver), *Approve BT*, and *Execute and Close BT* are obligatory. All tasks executed by a reviewer as well as the tasks *Send for Approval* and *Reject BT* specified within the approver lane are alternatives. The only permissible task is *Modify BT*, which is defined within a loop and may be executed as often as desired.

In this case, the deontic classification does not affect the structure of the process flow and the number of gateways and sequence flows remains the same. However, the deontic classification increases the understandability, since obligatory and permissible tasks can be distinguished at first sight. Furthermore, the business travel process provides an example that does not require complex deontic constructs like preconditions, classified paths, or multiple deontic classifications.

Note that the complexity of the two examples (standard and deontic process diagrams) is also caused by a duplication of tasks for different roles (e.g. task *Create Order* in the order execution process and task *Send for Approval* in the business travel process are defined three times). We address this issue by a task-based assignment of actors in Chap. 3.

In summary, this section demonstrated the transformation from standard to deontic process diagrams within an application scenario consisting of an order execution and a business travel process. In the first case, some complex deontic operators were necessary, but the modalities were highlighted and the structural complexity was reduced. In the second case, the structural complexity remained the same, but only simple deontic operators were necessary to highlight the modalities. The reduction in structural complexity and highlighting of the modalities comes at the cost of an increased complexity of the process modelling language: one further attribute with four different values (i.e. O, P, X, and F) and possible conditions have been added. We expect that the average possible reduction in structural complexity will outweigh this increased complexity of the language, but only an investigation of a wide range of different, real-life examples (e.g. with respect to Halstaed complexity) will tell, which can only be done once the method has been put into widespread use. Moreover, the benefits also depend on the particular use of a diagram, that is, how much the deontic aspects are relevant for a particular user.

Nevertheless, it seems that the understandability of the business process is increased by the deontic extension. To confirm this statement, the understandability of deontic classification in business processes was further studied within a preliminary survey (see [21, 24] for more details). All in all, the results of the preliminary survey are satisfying and indicate that the deontic classification increases the understandability of a process model.

2.6 The Semantics of Deontic Activities

The deontic extension is intended to aid the user in designing and understanding business processes while preserving the design capacities of standard diagrams. That this is possible will become clear when we introduce a graph transformation system from (a subset of) standard process diagrams to (a subset of) deontic process diagrams (both defined with H-BPM) further below.

In this section, we introduce a formal semantics for deontic process diagrams and compare it with the relevant subset of standard process diagrams (both defined with H-BPM). For better understanding, we need to stress that standard and deontic process diagrams serve different levels of abstraction.

2.6.1 Different Levels of Abstraction

In standard process diagrams, the level of abstraction is such that the resulting models can be executed by a business process engine. This entails that models are supposed to be deterministic in every detail. The deontic extension, however, takes the viewpoint of the (human) user who is capable of autonomously taking decisions. Consequently, deontic process diagrams leave choices open to the user (see description of "UserChoice" in Sect. 2.3.5). Such choices are modelled as permitted tasks (or "P(task)").

To be able to compare standard and deontic process diagrams, we have to transform deontic process models to the level of abstraction suitable for a process engine. In particular, in order to establish a relation between a permitted task and a standard task, we translate a permitted task to a conditionally obligatory task, where the condition (subsequently called "precondition") is determined by user input—or, in terms of the ASM formalism, through a monitored function. Note that this does not mean that "permission" and "conditional obligation" would be equivalent in our deontic logic (they are not). "Permission" is a concept of the level of abstraction of deontic process diagrams, while "conditional obligation" here is the translation to the level of abstraction of standard process diagrams, where user choice *as such* cannot be modelled (except in ad hoc sub-processes, which we do not consider here).

As also a conditionally obligatory task is a deontic task (and not an element of standard process diagrams), this translation is performed within the deontic process framework. However, by means of this translation, we can make the step down to the abstraction layer of standard process diagrams. The precondition "UserChoice" will then have to be matched with the firing condition of the respective outgoing sequence flow of a splitting gateway which leads to the task in question, as we will show in more detail further below.

It should also be noted that due to the different layers addressed, deontic process models may show a certain redundancy where user-centric and process engine-centric concepts overlap. For instance, the information that a particular task is obligatory may be derived from the context of the task alone in certain (but not all) cases. We assert that this redundancy is actually very helpful from the user's point of view.

2.6.2 Criteria for Comparing Standard and Deontic Process Diagrams Semantically

In order to show that a deontic process diagram generated by transformation of a standard process diagram has the same semantics as the latter, we assert that there is a bijective mapping between (standard or deontic) tasks before and after the transformation. This is fulfilled by the transformation rules suggested in Sect. 2.7. Then we have to show that

1. whenever a particular task would have been performed in the original diagram, also the corresponding deontic task is performed after transformation; and
2. a partial order with respect to the performance of tasks in time is preserved (i.e. where relevant, tasks are performed in the same order one after the other).

When we look at the graph transformation rules, it will suffice to consider only the subdiagrams affected by particular graph transformation steps.

A final note may be due on a certain issue of performance time. We will suggest graph transformation rules which dispose of gateways. One might assume that with two flow nodes (i.e. a pair of gateways) less, the switching time of those gateways would now be missing and thus the overall time consumption of the subdiagram in question would be sped up. One can construct examples where different speeds in different branches may lead to different decisions later on and thus change the overall behaviour of the diagram at runtime.

However, relevant for this is only the time consumption of the whole subdiagram that is being transformed. First of all, the necessary transition is not eliminated—it is just transferred from the splitting gateway to the deontic task; second, in our considerations presented here, we only deal with user choices, waiting for which will not change in either way; and third, any potentially remaining variation in time due to this will be extremely small compared with the performance of tasks, and with variations in the performances of tasks. Hence we think that this potential problem can be safely ignored.

To put it in ASM language: Such a (sub)graph transformation constitutes an $n:m$-refinement which affects only intermediate steps of "threads" of the machine in between two points of interest for synchronisation.

2.6.3 General Semantic Differences Between Standard and Deontic Process Diagrams

For comparison, we re-state the general semantics of a flow node defined in H-BPM as follows:

```
rule NodeTransition(flowNode) =
  if eventCondition(flowNode) and controlCondition(flowNode) and
     dataCondition(flowNode) and resourceCondition(flowNode)
        then
  parblock
    EventOperation(flowNode)
    ControlOperation (flowNode)
    DataOperation(flowNode)
    ResourceOperation(flowNode)
  endparblock
```

For the purpose of this chapter, we can simplify this by summarising all the operations in a single `PerformanceOperation`. Furthermore, we only need to distinguish between two kinds of conditions, namely `controlCondition` and `performanceCondition` (consisting of a conjunction of the other conditions). This leads to the following simplified rule:

```
rule NodeTransition(flowNode) =
  if controlCondition(flowNode)
      and performanceCondition(flowNode) then
    PerformanceOperation(flowNode)
```

In the case of certain deontic tasks, however, we have to provide for the possibility that they are not supposed to perform the `PerformanceOperation` under certain conditions, but still pass tokens on along their outgoing sequence flows. This is the case with "conditional" tasks—e.g. permissible tasks (which we translate to conditionally obligatory tasks): if such a task gets a token (i.e. `controlCondition` is fulfilled), and the other conditions are not relevant, the user may still decide whether the task shall be performed or not; yet if it is not performed, it still has to pass on a token towards other activities or towards a gateway waiting for it.

Consequently we have to introduce a new "`choiceCondition`" representing the user's choice to model this behaviour as follows:

```
rule NodeTransitionDeontic(flowNode) =
  if choiceCondition(flowNode) then
    if controlCondition(flowNode)
        and performanceCondition(flowNode) then
      PerformanceOperation(flowNode)
  else
    if controlCondition(flowNode) then
      ControlFlowOperation(flowNode)
```

where `ControlFlowOperation` simply passes a token on to outgoing sequence flows without doing anything else, while `ControlOperation` (hidden in `PerformanceOperation`) first performs the actual task before it passes tokens on.

In the above formulation, it can be easily seen that `NodeTransitionDeontic` is a conservative extension of `NodeTransition`: the original code is retained and just nested into a more complex rule. We can reformulate this to the following, logically equivalent rule, where the actual behaviour can be identified and compared even easier:

```
rule NodeTransitionDeontic(flowNode) =
  if controlCondition(flowNode) then
    if choiceCondition(flowNode) then
      if performanceCondition(flowNode) then
        PerformanceOperation(flowNode)
      else
        skip
    else
      ControlFlowOperation(flowNode)
```

For instance, we can now easily see that the user's choice is only relevant and asked for once the `controlCondition` is fulfilled. Note that it is still obvious that we can model standard flow nodes with `NodeTransitionDeontic` by setting `choiceCondition := true` for all standard flow nodes. We will use this last formulation of `NodeTransitionDeontic` in our following considerations.

If `choiceCondition` is true for all standard tasks but not for all deontic tasks, we will not be able to achieve the same semantics unless we can match `choiceCondition` with some other feature in standard process diagrams. To this end, we cannot simply compare a standard task with its corresponding deontic task, but we have to look at whole *subdiagrams*.

We assert that a deontic task where `choiceCondition` is relevant, in particular a permissible task, will always be in a place where the corresponding standard task is downstream of an exclusive or inclusive gateway. The graph transformation rules suggested below fulfil this assertion. Each outgoing sequence flow of such a gateway (except for a default sequence flow) is associated with a `conditionExpression` which determines whether, upon firing, this sequence flow will get a token or not. We will show that we can match this `conditionExpression` with the `choiceCondition` of the respective deontic task.

We do not alter the semantics of gateways for deontic process diagrams. However, we assume that for splitting gateways with user choice, `conditionExpression` is derived from a monitored function which corresponds to the `choiceCondition` in `NodeTransitionDeontic`, so that we can define some mathematical function f with

```
conditionExpression(sequenceFlow) =
       f(choiceCondition(deonticTask)),
```

where `sequenceFlow` marks the start of a path leading to `deonticTask`.

For proving semantic equivalence of standard and deontic process diagrams, we further have to assume a bracketing condition for gateways, that is, that every splitting gateway has a matching merging gateway such that every path outgoing from the splitting gateway eventually leads to the merging gateway. The graph transformation rules suggested in Sect. 2.7 only work for such matches. And finally, we assume that, conforming to best practice, condition expressions of outgoing sequence flows of splitting exclusive gateways are mutually exclusive and, if no default sequence flow is defined, also complete, such that always exactly one outgoing sequence flow is deterministically selected.

2.6.4 The Semantics of Tasks

For the semantics of standard tasks, we can use `NodeTransitionDeontic` with the constraints that

1. `choiceCondition` is always `true` and
2. there is exactly one incoming and one outgoing sequence flow.

For deontic process diagrams (the subset introduced here), we distinguish five different types of tasks as follows:

- obligatory tasks,
- permissible tasks,
- alternative tasks,
- conditionally obligatory tasks with the possible preconditions

  - "PreviousTask",
  - "NOT(AlternativeTask(s))", and
  - "UserChoice", as well as

- permissible and conditionally obligatory tasks with precondition "NOT(AlternativeTask(s))".

Obligatory tasks have exactly the same semantics as standard tasks: they only pass a token on after the actual task has been performed.

Permissible tasks can be seen as conditionally obligatory tasks with precondition "UserChoice".

Alternative tasks can also be seen as conditionally obligatory tasks but with precondition "NOT(AlternativeTask(s))". It should be noted that the precondition "NOT(AlternativeTask(s))" is actually an insufficient condition, for user choice must be considered as well. The point is that users are only allowed to choose, if they have not already chosen another task. For brevity of the respective markings, we omit the reference to user choice and regard it as implied.

Thus all that remains to do is to look at *conditionally obligatory tasks*, which we have to do separately for the three different, possible preconditions, and *permissible and conditionally obligatory tasks*. We now treat all those in more detail.

Conditionally Obligatory Tasks with Precondition "PreviousTask"

We assert that the source of the incoming sequence flow of a conditionally obligatory task with precondition "PreviousTask" is also some kind of task, which is guaranteed by the graph transformation rules which we use. Then, if the previous task was indeed performed, also the task in question will perform once it receives a token. In that case the behaviour is the same as that of a standard or obligatory task.

If the task in question receives a token, but the previous task (which passed this token on) was *not* performed, then that previous task must also be a conditionally obligatory task (as neither a standard task nor an (unconditionally) obligatory task can behave in this way). Now we can assume that a chain of conditionally obligatory tasks with precondition "PreviousTask" has a beginning, that is, there exists a conditionally obligatory task with another precondition in front of such a chain (which we will call the "starting task"). So the task in question will behave like the starting task: once it gets a token, it will perform if the starting task did and not perform if the starting task did not. (We define that whenever a task is not explicitly permitted or obligatory, it is forbidden.)

We can assert that both possible candidates for such a "starting" task (with preconditions "UserChoice" or "NOT(AlternativeTask(s))") are only used if the corresponding standard task came after a splitting gateway (which is also guaranteed by our graph transformation rules). Thus the task in question will lie on a (not further branched) path in between two gateways and will perform or not perform like all other tasks on that path—which is exactly the behaviour we expect and which is achieved in standard process diagrams by means of tokens alone.

We conclude that the semantics of a conditionally obligatory task with precondition "PreviousTask" is always the same as that of some other conditionally obligatory task with some other precondition; we investigate both of these other task types now.

Conditionally Obligatory Tasks with Precondition "NOT(AlternativeTask(s))"

We assert that conditionally obligatory tasks with precondition "NOT(Alternative Task(s))" are only used in between exclusive gateways, and that those gateways are retained during graph transformation, for otherwise, there would not exist any alternative tasks. This assertion holds for our graph transformation rules.

Then `choiceCondition` will be `true` if the task gets a token, i.e. if the `conditionExpression` of the respective sequence flow outgoing from the splitting gateway evaluates to `true`, and `choiceCondition` will be `false` if the `conditionExpression` evaluates to `false`. So the value of `choiceCondition` turns out to be redundant (for the user's comfort only), and such a task behaves exactly like a standard task.

Conditionally Obligatory Tasks with Precondition "UserChoice"

We assert that a conditionally obligatory task with precondition "UserChoice" is only used in the place of a standard task which is located after a splitting exclusive or inclusive gateway, because these are the only places where a choice is possible in a standard process diagram. Then we can match the `conditionExpression` of the respective sequence flow outgoing from the splitting gateway with the `choiceCondition` of this task. Such a task corresponds to a *permissible task*.

A permissible task may make the enclosing gateways redundant (in particular, when an empty path (Φ) would have been the only alternative). In this case, `choiceCondition(task)` will replace `conditionExpression( sequenceFlow)`. The eliminated empty path will be simulated by setting `choiceCondition` to `false` (in case Φ would have been chosen at the gateway), whereby the task will not be performed but a token will be passed on.

If the enclosing gateways are retained (because there are other alternatives), then `choiceCondition` will be formally redundant, because the task will get a token if and only if `choiceCondition` = `true` (by way of the coupling of

`conditionExpression(sequenceFlow)`   and   `choiceCondition`
(`task`)). Thus the task will behave like an obligatory or standard task.

Permissible and Conditionally Obligatory Tasks with Precondition "NOT (AlternativeTask(s))"

Depending on the runtime evaluation of the precondition, a permissible and conditionally obligatory task with precondition "NOT(AlternativeTask(s))" behaves either like a conditionally obligatory task with precondition "NOT(AlternativeTask(s))", if the precondition evaluates to true, or else like a permissible task, that is, like a conditionally obligatory task with precondition "UserChoice". Both of these task types have been treated above; it remains to show, for each situation where such a task can be employed, that in both cases the initial behaviour is retained. We have done this for each graph transformation rule individually in [23] (for (Deontic) BPMN, which is equivalent to (Deontic) H-BPM in this respect).

2.7 Graph Transformation

This section describes an algebraic graph transformation from a subset of standard process diagrams to deontic process diagrams (both defined within H-BPM) called DeonticBpmGTS. The main idea of graph transformation is rule-based modification of a graph, where each application of a rule leads to a transformation step. The transformation of a graph LHS (left-hand side) to a graph RHS (right-hand side) is based on a rule r (also called production). Applying the rule $r = $ (LHS, RHS) entails finding a match of LHS in the source graph and replacing LHS by RHS, leading to the target graph of the transformation. Different approaches for graph transformation have been proposed, such as node label replacement, hyperedge replacement, or the algebraic approach. DeonticBpmGTS uses the algebraic approach, which was developed by Ehrig, Pfender and Schneider in 1973 (see [8]). We use a tool for attributed graph grammar systems (AGG) to define graph transformations from classical process diagrams to diagrams with deontic activities (compare [9, p. 3ff]).

In DeonticBpmGTS, specific standard process models are taken as input and transformed to deontic process models, thereby highlighting the deontic concepts. The GTS comprises the basic transformations described in Sect. 2.4, but is limited to the following:

- Structured Diagrams: All gateways are defined in a bracket structure (see description of structured diagrams in Sect. 2.3.3).
- Basic Set of Elements: DeonticBpmGTS supports sequence flows, parallel, exclusive and inclusive gateways with user choice, start/end events and tasks. All supported node and edge types are shown in the type graph (see Fig. 2.32).
- One Task per Path: DeonticBpmGTS is limited to one task per path following a splitting gateway and is also prohibiting most types of nested gateways.

An attributed type graph with inheritance is then defined for DeonticBpmGTS and shown in Fig. 2.32. The basic element of the type graph is *Node* with the derived types *Gateway*, *DeonticTask*, *BpmTask*, and *Event*. These elements are abstract node types as highlighted by the curly brackets. Further concrete node types are the three gateways (*ParallelGateway*, *InclusiveGateway* and *ExclusiveGateway*), the concrete task (*Task*), the deontic tasks (*O(Task)*, *X(Task)*, *P(Task)*, *O(Task|Precondition)*, *X(Task|Precondition)*, *P(Task|Precondition)* and *P(Task)&O(Task|Precondition)*), and two events (*StartEvent* and *EndEvent*). One further node type is called *MeasuredValues* and used to store meta-information like the number of gateways and sequence flows in order to study the reduction of structural complexity. In addition, DeonticBpmGTS provides one edge label called *SF* for sequence flows representing several edge types.

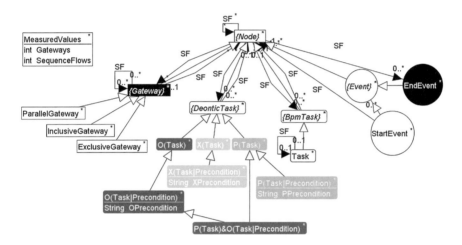

Fig. 2.32 Type graph of *DeonticBpmGTS*

The overall graph transformation system consists of 18 rules with application conditions distributed across four layers as shown in Table 2.2. The table comprises the layers, all rule names, the number of negative (NAC) and positive (PAC) application conditions, and a description of the transformation rule. Due to space limitation, all gateways are abbreviated: parallel gateway (PG), exclusive gateway (EG), and inclusive gateway (IG). In the following, we only present the rule *ExclusiveWithPhi-DualRule* in more detail and prove the semantic equivalence. A detailed description of all other rules with proven semantic equivalence is provided in [23, 24].

The rule *ExclusiveWithPhiDualRule* takes an exclusive gateway with a task and a *Phi*-Path (LHS) and transforms it to a permissible task (RHS) (see Fig. 2.33). The negative application condition (NAC) forbids further alternative nodes and thereby avoids dangling edges. The transformation leads to a reduction of two gateways and three sequence flows.

In order to check that the semantics are preserved by this rule, as explained before, we have to transform the new permissible task into a conditionally obligatory task

Table 2.2 Graph transformation rules of DeonticBpmGTS

Name	NAC	PAC	Description
Layer 0			
SeveralPhiReductionRule			Removes duplicate *Phi*-Paths
IterationRepeatUntilRule	2	1	class. task in repeat-until loop as O(Task)
SequenceRuleBase			class. second task of sequence as O(Task|PreviousTask)
SequenceRuleExtended			class. further tasks of sequence as O(Task|PreviousTask)
Layer 1			
SequenceRuleFinish	1		class. first task of sequence in main flow as O(Task)
Layer 2			
ParallelWithPhiDualRule	1		Replaces PGs with one task and *Phi*-Path with O(Task)
ParallelRule		1	class. task between PGs as O(Task)
ParallelRuleFinish	1		Removes *Phi*-Path between PGs
ExclusiveWithPhiDualRule	1		Replaces EGs with one task and *Phi*-Path with P(Task)
ExclusiveWithPhiRule		1	class. task between EGs with *Phi*-Path as P(Task)
ExclusiveWithPhiRuleFinish	1		Removes *Phi*-Path between EGs with classified P(Task)s
ExclusiveWithoutPhiRule	3	1	class. task between EGs without *Phi*-Path as X(Task)
InclusiveWithPhiDualRule	1		Replaces IGs with one task and *Phi*-Path with P(Task)
InclusiveWithPhiRule		1	class. task between IGs with *Phi*-Path as P(Task)
InclusiveWithPhiRuleFinish	1		Removes *Phi*-Path between IGs with classified P(Task)s
InclusiveWithoutPhiRule	3	1	class. task betw. IGs without *Phi*-Path as P(Task)&O(Task|NOT(AlternativeTask(s)))
Layer 3			
SequenceBpmRulePragmatic	3		transf. O(Task|PreviousTask) to O(Task) if one incoming flow from *BpmTask*
SequenceDeonticRulePragmatic	3		transf. O(Task|PreviousTask) to O(Task) if one incoming flow from *DeonticTask*

with precondition "UserChoice" before we can compare the diagrams before and after the transformation. The precondition "UserChoice" is reflected in the boolean function `choiceCondition(task)` in our ASM model. Let *sf7* and *sf9* be the sequence flows marked in Fig. 2.33 with "7: SF" and "9: SF", and let *task3* be the

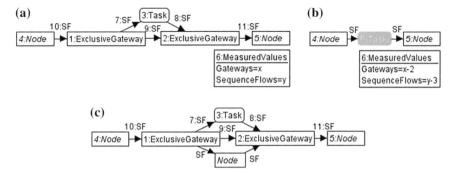

Fig. 2.33 ExclusiveWithPhiDualRule

task marked with "3: Task" and *pTask* the resulting conditionally obligatory task. We distinguish two cases.

Case 1: In the standard model (LHS of the transformation rule), `select-OutgoingSequenceFlows(splitGateway)` yields {*sf7*} at runtime (i.e. *sf7* was chosen by the user, i.e. `firingCondition(sf7) = true`). Then *task3* received a token, thus it is performed (as `choiceCondition(flowNode)` is `true` for all non-deontic tasks) and passes a token on. After the graph transformation, `choiceCondition(pTask)` will be `true`, thus *pTask* will behave like *task3*, i.e. it will be performed and pass a token on.

Case 2: In the standard model, `selectOutgoingSequenceFlows (splitGateway)` yields {*sf9*}. In this case *task3* is not performed, and the merging gateway receives a token via *sf9*. After the graph transformation, `choiceCondition(pTask)` will be `false`, therefore *pTask* will not be performed (like *task3*), yet will pass on a token towards the merging gateway. Thus the behaviour of the subdiagram is again the same.

After defining all rules, a typed graph can be created for a specific standard process model and is then transformed to a deontic process model. This is demonstrated by an example whose standard process model is shown in Fig. 2.34a. The gateways are displayed in their image view. According to the *MeasuredValues* element, the standard process model consists of eight gateways and 29 sequence flows.

The resulting deontic process model is shown in Fig. 2.34b. The transformation leads to a reduction of two gateways and five sequence flows. In addition, the obligatory, alternative, and permissible tasks can be distinguished on first sight based on their prefix and background colour.

Finally, we want to show that DeonticBpmGTS is a trusted model transformation. According to Varró et al. (see [34]), the most important correctness properties of a trusted model transformation are termination, uniqueness (confluence), and behaviour preservation. In DeonticBpmGTS, the source and target graph of every transformation rule are semantically equivalent. Moreover, it can be shown that DeonticBpmGTS is strictly AC-confluent and terminating, which implies that the

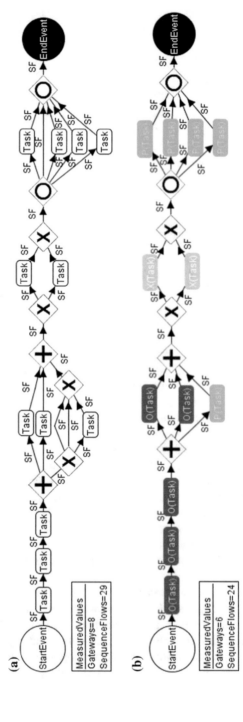

Fig. 2.34 Example: standard and deontic process model. **a** Standard. **b** Deontic

transformation is globally deterministic (the proof is provided for (Deontic) BPMN in [23, 24], which is equivalent to (Deontic) H-BPM in this respect). Thus, DeonticBpmGTS can be called a trusted model transformation.

2.8 Summary

In this chapter, we presented an extension of BPMLs with deontic concepts to highlight modalities. The motivation for the extension comprised difficulties with the identification of modalities and the increased structural complexity of the process flow that results from expressing optional activities. Related work regarding deontic logic and process modelling was studied, and although several approaches use deontic logic in combination with process modelling, none of them studies the influence on the process flow such as understandability and optimisation capabilities. Thus, we introduced a deontic classification of activities and presented monadic and dyadic deontic logic, multiple deontic classifications, as well as deontic logic with agency. In addition, user choices and conditional choices were distinguished and different levels of deontic classifications specified. Afterwards, we extended the *Control-Flow Patterns* with deontic concepts, since this extension can be applied to several BPMLs including H-BPM, BPMN, UML ADs, and EPCs. The application of deontic concepts and their benefits are then demonstrated by an application scenario comprising two processes taken from an industrial project. Furthermore, we introduced a formal semantics for deontic process diagrams and showed that (a subset of) standard process diagrams and deontic process diagrams are semantically equivalent. Finally, we presented an algebraic graph transformation from standard to deontic process diagrams called DeonticBpmGTS and proved that it is a trusted model transformation.

Summing up, extending process diagrams with deontic logic provides the possibility to highlight modalities, reduce the structural complexity of the process flow, and increase expressiveness (i.e. further patterns are supported). However, the advantages are accompanied by additional deontic constructs that can be quite complex. The complexity of the deontic constructs largely depends on the reduction of structural complexity, i.e. if the process structure remains the same, then less complex deontic constructs suffice. Thus, our next goal is to find a balance between the reduction of structural complexity and the complexity of the modelling language and to suggest corresponding modelling guidelines.

A further open issue is the explicit definition of alternatives. Currently, alternative activities are marked with an X, but the concrete alternatives are only implicitly given by the structure of the process flow. This keeps the deontic expression simple, but requires an analysis of the process flow to identify all alternatives. Thus, our goal is to identify process structures in which an explicit definition of alternatives is helpful (e.g. if an activity is multiply classified as alternative) or possibly also necessary (e.g. for higher gradings of deontic classification in which the process flow is omitted).

Another open issue is the deontic classification of nested structures. Up to now, we only considered multiple gateways addressing an activity alternatively (i.e. we defined multiple alternative deontic classifications). Thus, our next step is to also consider activities that are addressed by several hierarchically nested gateways. For example, an exclusive choice without *Phi*-Path that is addressed by an exclusive choice with *Phi*-Path requires to also nest the deontic classifications (e.g. $P(X(A))$). We assume that the definition of nested deontic constructs is straightforward, but it will be more challenging to determine the semantics and to simplify the deontic expressions, for example, by merging fitting deontic operators and overlapping preconditions.

Furthermore, in this work we have only considered the lower gradings of deontic classification that increase human understandability. An extension that replaces exclusive and inclusive choices with parallel splits was presented by Natschläger [24]. Left for future work is the complete definition of the process flow with deontic concepts allowing to omit the process flow and to provide the activities in a work list (see also workflow charts in Chap. 4).

Finally, deontic logic can also be used for a task-based definition of actors and roles. Compared to the rigid swimlane concepts suggested, e.g. in BPMN, this would further reduce the structural complexity of the process flow and increase the expressiveness. Thus, in the following chapter, we will present a layered approach for actor modelling that provides a task-based assignment of actors and roles based on deontic logic.

References

1. Åqvist, L.: Deontic logic. Handbook of Philosophical Logic, vol. 8, 2nd edn, pp. 147–264. Kluwer Academic, Dordrecht (2002)
2. Asirelli, P., ter Beek, M.H., Gnesi, S., Fantechi, A.: Deontic logics for modeling behavioural variability. In: Benavides, D., Metzger, A., Eisenecker, U.W. (eds.) VaMoS'09. ICB Research Report, vol. 29, pp. 71–76. Universität Duisburg-Essen (2009)
3. Asirelli, P., ter Beek, M.H., Gnesi, S., Fantechi, A.: A deontic logical framework for modelling product families. In: Benavides, D., Batory, D.S., Grünbacher, P. (eds.) 4th International Workshop on Variability Modelling of Software-intensive Systems (VaMoS'10). ICB-Research Report, vol. 37, pp. 37–44. Universität Duisburg-Essen (2010)
4. Börger, E.: Modeling workflow patterns from first principles. In: Parent, C., Schewe, K.D., Storey, V., Thalheim, B. (eds.) Conceptual Modeling - ER 2007. Lecture Notes in Computer Science, vol. 4801, pp. 1–20. Springer, Berlin (2007)
5. Börger, E.: Approaches to modeling business processes: a critical analysis of BPMN, workflow patterns and YAWL. Softw. Syst. Model. **11**(3), 305–318 (2012)
6. Broersen, J., Van der Torre, L.: Ten problems of deontic logic and normative reasoning in computer science. In: European Summer School of Logic, Language and Information (ESSLLI) (2010)
7. Combi, C., Gambini, M.: Flaws in the flow: The weakness of unstructured business process modeling languages dealing with data. In: Meersman, R., Dillon, T., Herrero, P. (eds.) On the Move to Meaningful Internet Systems: OTM 2009. Lecture Notes in Computer Science, vol. 5870, pp. 42–59. Springer, Berlin (2009)

8. Ehrig, H., Pfender, M., Schneider, H.J.: Graph-grammars: an algebraic approach. In: Proceedings of FOCS 1973, pp. 167–180. IEEE (1973)
9. Ehrig, H., Ehrig, K., Prange, U., Taentzer, G.: Fundamentals of Algebraic Graph Transformation. Springer, Heidelberg (2006)
10. Ghose, A., Koliadis, G.: Auditing business process compliance. Service-Oriented Computing (ICSOC). Lecture Notes in Computer Science, vol. 4749, pp. 169–180. Springer, Berlin (2007)
11. Goedertier, S., Vanthienen, J.: Designing compliant business processes with obligations and permissions. In: Eder, J., Dustdar, S. (eds.) Business Process Management Workshops. Lecture Notes in Computer Science, vol. 4103, pp. 5–14. Springer, Vienna (2006)
12. Goedertier, S., Vanthienen, J.: Declarative process modeling with business vocabulary and business rules. In: Meersman, R., Tari, Z., Herrero, P. (eds.) On the Move to Meaningful Internet Systems 2007: OTM 2007 Workshops. Lecture Notes in Computer Science, vol. 4805, pp. 603–612. Springer, Berlin (2007)
13. Governatori, G., Milosevic, Z.: A formal analysis of a business contract language. Int. J. Coop. Inf. Syst. **15**(4), 659–685 (2006)
14. Hilpinen, R.: Deontic logic. In: Goble, L. (ed.) The Blackwell Guide to Philosophical Logic, chap. 8, pp. 159–182. Blackwell Publishers, Hoboken (2001)
15. Kiepuszewski, B., ter Hofstede, A., Bussler, C.: On structured workflow modelling. In: Wangler, B., Bergman, L. (eds.) Advanced Information Systems Engineering. Lecture Notes in Computer Science, vol. 1789, pp. 431–445. Springer, Berlin (2000)
16. Lewis, D.: Semantic analyses for dyadic deontic logic. In: Stenlund, S. (ed.) Logical Theory and Semantic Analysis: Essays Dedicated to Stig Kanger on His Fiftieth Birthday, pp. 1–14. Reidel Publishing Co., Boston (1974)
17. Liu, R., Kumar, A.: An analysis and taxonomy of unstructured workflows. In: van der Aalst, W., Benatallah, B., Casati, F., Curbera, F. (eds.) Business Process Management. Lecture Notes in Computer Science, vol. 3649, pp. 268–284. Springer, Berlin (2005)
18. Lokhorst, G.J.C., Goble, L.: Mally's deontic logic. Grazer philosophische Studien **67**, 37–57 (2004)
19. Mendling, J., Neumann, G., Nüttgens, M.: Towards workflow pattern support of event-driven process chains (EPC). In: Second GI-Workshop of XML for Business Process Management (XML4BPM 2005). CEUR Workshop Proceedings, vol. 145, pp. 23–28. Karlsruhe, Germany (2005)
20. Moody, D.L.: The "physics" of notations: Toward a scientific basis for constructing visual notations in software engineering. IEEE Trans. Softw. Eng. **35**(6), 756–779 (2009)
21. Natschläger, C.: Deontic BPMN. In: Hameurlain, A., Liddle, S., Schewe, K., Zhou, X. (eds.) Database and Expert Systems Applications. Lecture Notes in Computer Science, vol. 6861, pp. 264–278. Springer, Berlin (2011)
22. Natschläger, C., Geist, V., Kossak, F., Freudenthaler, B.: Optional activities in process flows. In: Rinderle-Ma, S., Weske, M. (eds.) EMISA 2012 – Der Mensch im Zentrum der Modellierung, pp. 67–80 (2012)
23. Natschläger, C., Kossak, F., Schewe, K.D.: Deontic BPMN: a powerful extension of BPMN with a trusted model transformation. Softw. Syst. Model. pp. 1–29 (2013)
24. Natschläger-Carpella, C.: Extending BPMN with Deontic Logic. Logos Verlag, Berlin (2012)
25. Object Management Group: Semantics of business vocabulary and business rules (SBVR), v1.0. http://www.omg.org/spec/SBVR/1.0 (2008). Accessed 25 Sept 2015
26. Padmanabhan, V., Governatori, G., Sadiq, S., Colomb, R., Rotolo, A.: Process modelling: The deontic way. Proceedings of the 3rd Asia-Pacific Conference on Conceptual Modelling, vol. 53, pp. 75–84. Australian Computer Society Inc., Darlinghurst, Australia (2006)
27. Rönnedal, D.: An Introduction to Deontic Logic (2009). ISBN:978-1-4499-1694-7
28. Russell, N., ter Hofstede, A., Edmond, D., van der Aalst, W.: Workflow Resource Patterns. BETA Working Paper Series WP 127, Eindhoven University of Technology, Eindhoven (2004)
29. Russell, N., ter Hofstede, A., van der Aalst, W., Mulyar, N.: Workflow Control-Flow Patterns: A Revised View. Technical report, BPMcenter.org (2006)

30. Sadiq, S., Governatori, G., Namiri, K.: Modeling control objectives for business process compliance. In: Alonso, G., Dadam, P., Rosemann, M. (eds.) Business Process Management. Lecture Notes in Computer Science, vol. 4714, pp. 149–164. Springer, Berlin (2007)
31. van der Aalst, W.M.: Workflow verification: finding control-flow errors using Petri-net-based techniques. In: van der Aalst, W., Desel, J., Oberweis, A. (eds.) Business Process Management. Lecture Notes in Computer Science, vol. 1806, pp. 19–128. Springer, Berlin (2000)
32. van der Aalst, W.M., ter Hofstede, A.H., Kiepuszewski, B., Barros, A.P.: Workflow patterns. Distrib. Parallel Databases **14**, 5–51 (2003)
33. van der Aalst, W.M., ter Hofstede, A.H.: Workflow patterns homepage. http://www.workflowpatterns.com. Accessed 25 Sept 2015
34. Varró, D., Varró-Gyapay, S., Ehrig, H., Prange, U., Taentzer, G.: Termination analysis of model transformations by petri nets. In: Corradini, A., Ehrig, H., Montanari, U., Ribeiro, L., Rozenberg, G. (eds.) Graph Transformations. Lecture Notes in Computer Science, vol. 4178, pp. 260–274. Springer, Berlin (2006)
35. Weigand, H., Verharen, E., Dignum, F.: Interoperable transactions in business models - a structured approach. In: Constantopoulos, P., Mylopoulos, J., Vassiliou, Y. (eds.) Advanced Information Systems Engineering. Lecture Notes in Computer Science, vol. 1080, pp. 193–209. Springer, Berlin (1996)
36. White, S.A.: Process Modeling Notations and Workflow Patterns. http://www.bptrends.com/process-modeling-notations-and-workflow-patterns (2004). Accessed 25 Sept 2015
37. Wieringa, R., Meyer, J.J.: Applications of deontic logic in computer science: A concise overview. Deontic Logic in Computer Science: Normative System Specification, pp. 17–40. Wiley, Chichester (1993)
38. Wohed, P., van der Aalst, W., Dumas, M., ter Hofstede, A., Russell, N.: On the suitability of BPMN for business process modelling. In: Dustdar, S., Fiadeiro, J., Sheth, A. (eds.) Business Process Management. Lecture Notes in Computer Science, vol. 4102, pp. 161–176. Springer, New York (2006)

Chapter 3
A Layered Approach for Actor Modelling

Several Business Process Modelling Languages (BPMLs) that primarily express the flow of activities provide only limited support for actor modelling. For example, the Business Process Model and Notation (BPMN) and UML activity diagrams suggest rigid swimlane concepts to model roles and actors. Thus, in this chapter, we present a task-based approach for actor modelling, extended with deontic logic and speech act theory. An extension of process diagrams with deontic logic to highlight modalities and to reduce the structural complexity of the process flow was already suggested in the previous chapter. In addition, another issue that can be addressed with deontic logic is the limited support for actor modelling. The new approach for actor modelling is more expressive and provides the possibility to reduce the structural complexity of the process flow as shown by an application scenario and an evaluation based on the *Workflow Resource Patterns*. The actor modelling approach was previously applied to BPMN by Natschläger in [19] and by Natschläger and Geist in [18], and is now adopted to the Hagenberg Business Process Modelling (H-BPM) method.

The remainder of this chapter is structured as follows: Sect. 3.1 provides the motivation for a task-based approach for actor modelling and Sect. 3.2 on related work will focus on current actor definitions in process modelling. In Sect. 3.3, we describe the underlying research base of our work and present the hypothesis for the actor modelling approach. We then discuss the different aspects of the layered actor modelling approach in Sect. 3.4. Afterwards, we evaluate the suitability of the approach by means of an application scenario (see Sect. 3.5) and by a comparison with a modelling approach using swimlanes based on the *Workflow Resource Patterns* (see Sect. 3.6). Finally, we conclude our work with a summary of the results and a description of future goals in Sect. 3.7.

© Springer International Publishing Switzerland 2016   63
F. Kossak et al., *Hagenberg Business Process Modelling Method*,
DOI 10.1007/978-3-319-30496-0_3

3.1   Motivation

Many BPMLs that primarily express the flow of activities provide only limited support for organisational modelling. For example, BPMN, a popular and successful standard for business process modelling, leaves the definition of organisational models and resources out of its scope [21, p. 22]. Nevertheless, one of the five basic categories of BPMN elements is called *swimlanes* and provides two concepts, *pools* and *lanes*, which can be used to model participants. These two concepts reveal the need for organisational modelling and are frequently used by BPMN modellers as shown by an analysis of 1210 BPMN models in which more than 60 % of the models comprised pools and lanes [14].

However, pools and lanes are also repeatedly criticised for their restricted support for organisational modelling [23, 24, 32]. For example, Recker presents a global survey with 590 BPMN users [23], in which five major issues are identified, one of them being organisational modelling with the ambiguity of the pool and lane concepts. The ambiguity that comes with the flexible semantics stands in contrast to the ease with which the two concepts can be used for process modelling. Furthermore, Wohed et al. study the suitability of BPMN for business process modelling and use the Workflow Patterns as an evaluation framework [32]. According to this publication, BPMN provides good support for the control-flow perspective, medium support for the data perspective, but only low support for the resource perspective. Considering the resource perspective, BPMN supports only 8 out of the 43 Workflow Resource Patterns, since swimlanes are specified in a restrictive manner.

Summing up, modelling participants, i.e. entities and roles [21, p. 502], are limited by the fact that an activity can only be located in at most one lane. This leads to the following issues:

- Expressiveness: There is no possibility to express that an activity (e.g. a sub-process) can be executed by two or more roles in collaboration.
- Inaccuracy: Lanes may comprise all types of elements including those that are automatically executed, like business rules and scripts.
- Redundancy: An activity that is executed by two or more roles on parallel or alternative paths must be duplicated for every additional lane.

We also identified the demand for actor modelling in some of our industrial projects. For example, considering the application scenario presented in the previous chapter (see Sect. 2.5), it was not possible to specify in the order execution process that the creation of an appointment as well as the execution and closure of the order must be done by the same consultant (*Retain Familiar* pattern) or in the business travel process that the owner and approver of a business travel must be different (*Separation of Duties* pattern). Thus, there is a need for a clear and expressive actor modelling approach that provides more than just rigid modelling constructs, e.g. pools and lanes, and overcomes currently prevailing restrictions. In this chapter, we want to emphasise the gap regarding *subjects* in control-flow-based business process modelling languages and present a novel approach based on deontic logic and speech act theory to model actors and constraints. In doing so, we aim at putting forward the important role of actors in business process modelling languages that primarily express the flow of activities, following more resource-centric approaches as, e.g. Subject-Oriented Business Process Management (S-BPM) [7].

3.2 Related Work

To address problems with actor modelling, several extensions for BPMN have been suggested. For example, Awad et al. propose a task-based human resource allocation and extend the BPMN metamodel with the Object Constraint Language (OCL) to express resource allocation constraints [2]. Task-based authorisation constraints for BPMN supporting different patterns like *Separation of Duties*, role-based allocation, or case handling are further presented by Wolter and Schaad [33]. In addition, a BPMN extension considering security requirements like access control, nonrepudiation, privacy, or integrity is proposed by Rodríguez et al. [25]. Furthermore, Korherr and List extend BPMN with goals and performance measures [12] and Milanović et al. provide a rule-based extension of the BPMN metamodel based on the REWERSE Rule Markup Language (R2ML) [15]. However, although several extensions suggest a task-based approach for actor modelling, pool and lane concepts are still used to express the role hierarchy resulting in a mixture of different resource definitions. It is further not possible to specify generic restrictions (e.g. every business travel must be approved by the corresponding manager) or dependencies between tasks concerning the executing roles.

Considering other BPMLs, some of them provide a task-based definition of resources. For example, the recommended way to express roles and actors in UML activity diagrams is to use activity partitions (swimlane concept). However, the specification also permits to define participants above the activity name in parentheses, thereby representing a task-based approach. Several partition names can be specified within a comma-delimited list, expressing that the node is contained in more than one partition [22, p. 406f]. Although this alternative approach is only mentioned briefly in the UML specification, it reveals the need for a task-based assignment of actors. Other BPMLs that provide a task-based approach for specifying participants are Event-Driven Process Chains (EPCs), which define an own element for organisational units that is referenced by a function [29], and Yet Another Workflow Language (YAWL), in which any manual atomic task may provide a distribution set of resources to which the task should be offered at runtime. YAWL further supports three different perspectives: control-flow, data, and resources. The resource perspective provides an organisational model that comprises the participants of an organisation, their roles and capabilities, as well as managerial hierarchies [1].

Enterprise architecture frameworks such as ARIS or the Zachman Framework comprise several views also including process and organisational models. ARIS, for example, consists of five views that are symbolically presented in the form of a house, the so-called ARIS house, with the *organization view* as the roof, the *data view*, *control view*, and *function view* as the three pillars, and the *output view* as the basis of the house [27, 28]. According to Scheer [27], the designations "function", "process", and "activity" are used synonymously, thus, the *function view* is similar to our *process view*. Furthermore, the *organization view* of ARIS comprises a hierarchical organisational model with organisational units and concrete instances [28, p.52ff.], and resembles the *organisational view* of our actor modelling approach. In addition, the Zachman Framework consists of six rows for the viewpoints (*Scope, Enterprise* (or *Business*) *Model, System Model, Technology Model, Detailed Representations*, and *Functioning Enterprise*) and six columns for the aspects (*Data, Function, Network, People, Time*, and *Motivation*). The aspect *Function* contains the business process model and is similar to our *process view*. Furthermore, the aspect *People* contains the workflow or organisational model with organisational units and hierarchical dependencies defined between them [16, 35].

Considering related work regarding deontic rules and constraints, the use of deontic rule sets to connect the organisational model to the activities in the process flow is recommended by Hohwiller et al. [11]. In addition, Grossi et al. propose a semantic framework based on dynamic logic with deontic expressions in which responsibilities between groups and agents are divided into three dimensions (power (delegation), coordination (information), and control (monitoring)) and formally characterised [9]. Furthermore, also the Semantics of Business Vocabulary and Rules (SBVR), which is, like BPMN, a standard of the Object Management Group (OMG), recommends deontic logic for specifying business rules [20].

The consistency of task-based authorisation constraints was studied by Tan et al. [30]. The authors define a formal model with a set of consistency rules for constraints that guarantee a sound constrained workflow authorisation schema. Similar to our approach are the role-based access control and the task-based definition of constraints. However, an open issue of the proposed approach for actor modelling is the case of actors that violate obligations. If actors do not execute the activities they are obliged to perform, the process must be adapted and, for example, the activity assigned to another actor. The specification of error-tolerant software agents based on deontic logic has, for example, been studied by Eiter et al. [6]. In addition, Governatori and Milosevic present a formal system based on deontic concepts for reasoning about violations of obligations in contracts [8].

Finally, considering related work regarding speech acts, Dignum and Weigand combine illocutionary logic and dynamic deontic logic to model communication processes [5]. The authors distinguish four basic speech acts (*request, commit, assert*, and *declare*), which are executed by agents based on power, authorisation, or charity. The work of Dignum and Weigand inspired our approach to extend control-flow based business process modelling languages with actor modelling. Furthermore, Colombetti introduced an agent communication language based on speech acts that supports conversations of agents [4].

3.3 Foundations of the Theory

We base our approach for actor modelling on several pieces of previous scientific work. In particular, we described an actor modelling approach for BPMN in the Ph.D. thesis by Natschläger (cf. [19]) and in an article by Natschläger and Geist (cf. [18]). In the following, we adopt this approach to H-BPM.

In order to identify the shortcomings and gaps of flow-based BPMLs, we formally defined the syntactical restrictions of BPMN within an ontology, called the *BPMN 2.0 Ontology* [17]. The ontology can be used as a knowledge base to investigate BPMN elements, to infer additional knowledge, and for syntax checking of concrete models.

We further defined the semantics of a modified version of BPMN 2.0 (on which H-BPM is based) as an Abstract State Machine (ASM) ground model in [13]. We build on this work when we specify the execution semantics of the actor modelling approach in Sect. 6.

Also important for the actor modelling approach is the extension of process diagrams with deontic logic presented in the previous chapter. Deontic logic was used to highlight modalities and we provided a precise specification of deontic concepts such as obligations (O), permissions (P), alternatives (X), and prohibitions (F). The explicit definition of modalities is deemed to be more intuitive and also positively affects the structural complexity as well as the understandability of the process flow. The deontic classification (also for actor modelling) is defined in detail in Sect. 2.3.

Furthermore, we investigated the *Workflow Patterns* and deontically classified the *Control-Flow Patterns* in Sect. 2.4. In this chapter, we will extend the classification and also consider the *Workflow Resource Patterns*.

So the suggested actor modelling approach is based on the elaborated deontic concepts and comprises further extensions that increase expressiveness and avoid inaccuracy and redundancy as stated by the following hypothesis:

> The suggested actor modelling approach for process diagrams is more expressive than the swimlane concept provided by modelling notations such as BPMN or UML Activity Diagrams.

3.4 Approach for Actor Modelling

This section starts with a description of the three different views of the actor modelling approach, i.e. the *process view*, *organisational view*, and *rule view*. Afterwards, different layers to which extent the suggested concepts can be used for actor modelling are distinguished and comprise task-based assignment of individual roles and actors, extension with further additional or alternative roles and actors, specification of deontic rules and corresponding inference techniques, and speech acts.

3.4.1 Views of Actor Modelling Approach

The approach consists of three different views (see Fig. 3.1). The first view is called the *process view* and comprises the process flow. All activities in the process flow are deontically classified according to the description in Chap. 2. In addition, the deontic classification of manual or human activities (or abstract activities with a human executor) is extended with an action description of the form $Do(r, p)$, where Do is a modal operator for action or agency, r stands for the executing agent or role (several roles can be concatenated with "and" or "or") and p describes a propositional expression (e.g. an action A) [10]. Instead of the modal operator for agency, speech acts may also be defined. Speech act theory treats communication as action and distinguishes between five different types of speech acts: representatives (e.g. inform), directives (e.g. request), commissives (e.g. commit), declarations (e.g. declare), and expressives (e.g. thank) [34, p. 132ff]. The last type (expressives) is not relevant for process modelling, but all other types may be used to support collaboration of actors. In summary, the supplemented process diagrams provide a task-based definition of possible actors based on deontic logic and speech act theory. Thus, pool and lane concepts are no more required.

The second view is called the *organisational view* and provides an organisation chart with a simple specification of possible roles and groups, the definition of the role hierarchy, and individuals that can be assigned to roles and groups. Thus, this view comprises the dependencies and relationships between roles, groups, and individuals.

Finally, the third view is called the *rule view* and includes additional rules that specify restrictions which cannot be defined within the process flow. For example, the first rule shown in Fig. 3.1 specifies that the individual c of role C (written as *hasRole(c, C)*) who is executing the order (*ExecuteOrder*) must also close the order (*CloseOrder*) (*Retain Familiar* pattern). The second rule specifies that the individual y who is deleting the request (*DeleteRequest*) or approving the order (*ApproveOrder*) must have a higher role than the individual x who created the request (*CreateRequest*). In addition, the third rule defines that if a group leader g approves an order, g must inform a department head about the approved order. The defined rules are then evaluated and with the help of inference techniques new rules are derived and contradictions are identified. For example, considering the second rule, if a group leader creates a request, then a department head must delete the request or approve the order; however, if a department head creates a request, then no higher role can execute the following activities, resulting in a contradiction.

3.4.2 Layers of the Actor Modelling Approach

Considering the suggested concepts for actor modelling, not all of them are required for every process model. For example, to achieve the same expressiveness as swim-lanes, only the *process view* with deontic classifications and the definition of at most

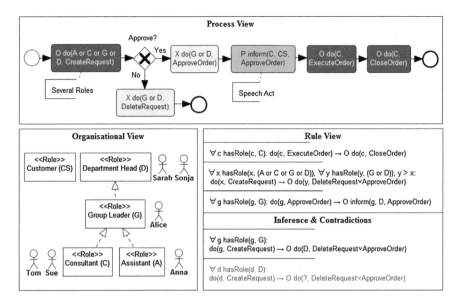

Fig. 3.1 Approach for actor modelling

one role or actor for an activity as well as the *organisational view* (including roles, a role hierarchy, and individuals where applicable) are necessary. However, the usage of further concepts increases the expressiveness. Thus, the following layers to which extent the suggested concepts can be used for actor modelling are distinguished.

Deontic Classification and Task-Based Assignment

First, all activities in the process flow are deontically classified according to the definition of deontic process diagrams described in Chap. 2. In addition, if an activity is executed by a human actor, then deontic logic with agency is used to define the executing role, e.g. $O\ do(role, Activity)$. The advantage of the task-based definition is that every activity has its own specification of allowed roles and actors. The organisational model further comprises groups, roles, hierarchical relationships between roles, and individuals that can be assigned to roles and groups. The hierarchical relationships are necessary, since also swimlanes can be nested, thereby expressing hierarchical dependencies. Summing up, this layer has the same expressiveness as swimlanes, but is more flexible and also solves the problem of inaccuracy mentioned in Sect. 3.1, i.e. that all types of elements can be defined in a lane (also those that are automatically executed).

Extended Actor Modelling

The next step is to extend the actor modelling approach by supporting several roles that can execute an activity either together (concatenated with "and") or alternatively (concatenated with "or"). Note that "and" can only be used in case of non-atomic activities (e.g. sub-processes). This extension then solves the other two problems described in Sect. 3.1, i.e. redundancy and expressiveness. So activities that can be executed by two or more roles on parallel or alternative paths must not be duplicated any more, thereby reducing the structural complexity of the process flow. It is further possible to specify that activities can be executed by two or more roles in collaboration.

Deontic Rules, Inference, and Contradictions

Further deontic rules that cannot be expressed within the process flow are defined in the *rule view*. In addition, predicate logic may be used to define quantifiers and higher or lower roles may be expressed with the operators $\prec$ and $\succ$. Although such rules increase the complexity of the diagram, they also allow to define constraints that could not have been specified within the process flow. For example, the restriction that the first task can be executed by an arbitrary individual of a given role but the subsequent task must be executed by another individual (*Separation of Duties* pattern) is often required but can neither be expressed with swimlane concepts nor with a task-based assignment of roles.

In a next step, inference techniques are used to analyse the deontic rules and to derive new rules, thereby making implicit knowledge explicit. Furthermore, with the help of inference, contradictions in the rule definitions are identified and highlighted for the modeller. All derived rules and potential contradictions are shown in the lower part of the *rule view*. This extension does not increase the expressiveness of the diagram but it reduces the complexity from the perspective of the modeller, since derived rules explicitly express already existing knowledge and the identification of contradictions supports the modeller by highlighting mistakes in the original rule definitions.

Speech Acts

In the last step, the approach for actor modelling is extended with speech act theory to support communication, coordination, and cooperation between actors. Speech acts are, according to Wooldridge, the "conceptual foundation for agent communication" [34]. Speech act theory was introduced by Austin in 1962 and extended by Searle in 1969. It treats communication as action with the assumption that speech actions are performed by agents like any other action. Speech act theory distinguishes three different aspects of speech acts: locutionary act (act of making an utterance), illocutionary act (action performed in saying something), and perlocution (effect of the act). In the following, only illocutionary acts are considered, which are further classified as representatives (e.g. *inform*), directives (e.g. *request*), commissives (e.g. *commit*), declarations (e.g. *declare*), and expressives (e.g. *thank*) [34, p.132ff.]. For process modelling, the last type (*expressives*) is not relevant. Thus, the following speech acts may be defined within the process flow or as additional rules (speaker s, hearer h, proposition ϕ, action α—based on [34, p.132ff.]):

- inform(s, h, ϕ)
- request(s, h, α)
- commit(s, h, α)

- declare(s, h, ϕ)

Speech acts are easy to understand and only slightly increase the complexity of the diagram but allow to express collaboration of actors. For example, in the process flow shown in Fig. 3.1, the consultant informs the customer about the proposition that the order was approved. Hence, the speech act *inform* supports *communication* between actors. Furthermore, all speech acts together support *coordination* and *cooperation*. Every speech act can then be extended with deontic concepts to define that the speech act is obligatory, permissible, or forbidden.

In addition, the inference techniques described before must be extended to support rules with speech acts. Also speech acts can be expressed with roles in Description Logics (DLs), however, speech acts require ternary relations. Some DLs support *n*-ary relations and, thus, also provide inference concepts for such roles. However, if a DL does not support *n*-ary relations, then the concept of reified relationships can be used and a new concept with *n* properties (functional roles) can be created for the relationship [3].

3.5 Application Scenario

In order to study the suitability of the actor modelling approach for practical scenarios, this section provides an application scenario based on the order execution and business travel process presented in Sect. 2.5. The deontic process diagrams of both processes are considered and extended with the actor modelling approach.

The deontic process diagram of the order execution process is shown in Fig. 2.29 and comprises 3 start events, 18 tasks, 18 gateways, and 49 sequence flows. The actor modelling approach replaces the pools and lanes with an organisational model and a task-based authorization as shown in Fig. 3.2. This, on the one hand, allows a flexible positioning of the elements that is no more restricted by lanes and, on the other hand, the three *Create Request* (CR) tasks can be unified in one task that is executed by either one of the three roles. The resulting task is classified as obligatory (which is more appropriate than three alternative tasks) and two start events, two tasks, two gateways, and six sequence flows can be removed, thereby reducing the structural complexity of the process flow.

Furthermore, it was not possible to specify in the standard or deontic process diagram that the creation of an appointment as well as the execution and closure of the order must be done by the same consultant (*Retain Familiar* pattern). With the actor modelling approach, this restriction can be defined by additional rules in the *rule view*.

We admit that the deontic classification of the tasks in the order execution process is complex and difficult to understand. On the one hand, we had to abbreviate task and roles names due to space limitation. On the other hand, we use an extensive formal definition that comprises deontic operators, roles, task names, and preconditions. Thus, for practical usage, we recommend an alternative graphical representation,

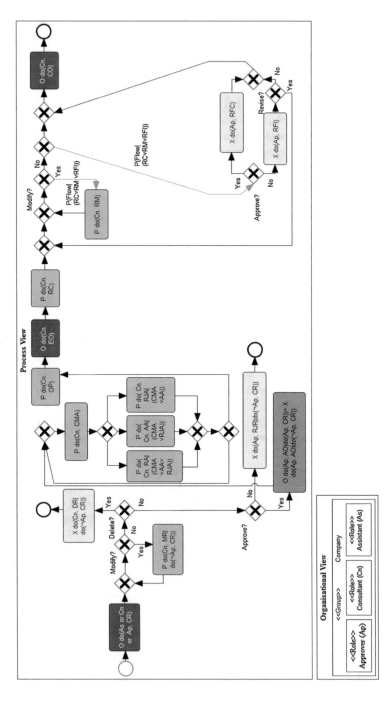

Fig. 3.2 Order execution process: deontic process diagram with actor modelling

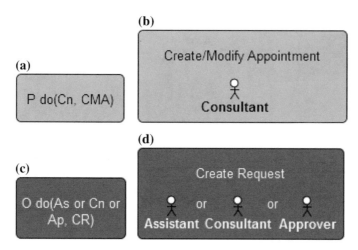

Fig. 3.3 Alternative graphical representations. **a** Original. **b** Alternative representation. **c** Original. **b** Alternative representation

e.g. the tasks *Create Request* (CR) and *Create/Modify Appointment* (CMA) shown in Fig. 3.3a, c can also be represented as shown in Fig. 3.3b, d. In this case, the executing roles are explicitly shown as possible actors and the deontic classification is implicitly given by the colour of the task (alternatively a new symbol can be used to express optionality).

The deontic process diagram of the business travel process is shown in Fig. 2.31 and consists of 11 tasks, 10 gateways, and 28 sequence flows. The resulting deontic process diagram with actor modelling comprises 8 tasks, 10 gateways, and 24 sequence flows and is shown in Fig. 3.4. In the course of the transformation, the two tasks *Review Business Travel (BT)* are unified in one task, which allows a reduction of one task and two sequence flows. The exclusive gateway with the question "Recipient?" is placed after the unified task. Subsequently, the three *Send for Approval* tasks are unified in one task, resulting in a reduction of two tasks and two sequence flows. If, however, only the two *Send for Approval* tasks that are executed by the *Reviewer* and the *Approver* are unified in one task, then an additional merging gateway and a further sequence flow would have been necessary. Thus, the modeller can freely decide whether to unify tasks or not (and whether the reduction of a task outbalances an additional gateway and a sequence flow).

In addition, if a hierarchical dependency is defined between the roles *Approver* and *Reviewer* in the *organisational view*, then it would be possible to specify only *Reviewer* instead of *Reviewer or Approver* as the executing role of a task. However, this abbreviation is only recommended, if *Reviewer* is the standard role, which is sometimes substituted by an *Approver*. Considering the task *Review BT*, both roles should be specified to highlight that an *Approver* is not only a substitute, but is required to execute the task at least once in every process instance.

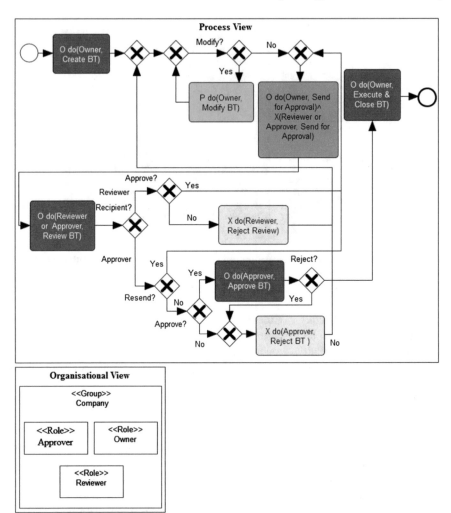

Fig. 3.4 Business travel process: deontic process diagram with actor modelling

In summary, this section showed the application of the actor modelling approach within an application scenario consisting of an order execution and a business travel process. In both cases, it was possible to reduce the number of tasks by unifying duplicated tasks which, in most cases, also reduced the number of gateways and sequence flows. However, in one case, the unification of tasks would require an additional merging gateway. Thus, the modeller can freely decide whether to unify tasks or not. So without unification of tasks, the structure of the process flow remains the same, resulting in the same structural complexity. In addition, the unification of some tasks provides the possibility to reduce the structural complexity of the process flow. Thus, there is at least one transformation from deontic process diagrams with swimlanes to deontic process diagrams with the suggested actor modelling concept with an equal or reduced structural complexity.

However, the main objective of the actor modelling approach is to increase expressiveness. In the application scenario, the resulting deontic process diagrams with actor modelling had the same expressiveness due to the transformation. It has only been mentioned for the order execution process that additional rules are possible to define that some tasks must be executed by the same individual. Since it was not possible to study the increased expressiveness within the application scenario, the expressiveness of the actor modelling approach is evaluated based on the *Workflow Resource Patterns* in the next section.

3.6 Workflow Resource Patterns

It has been claimed by the hypothesis in Sect. 3.3 that the entire approach for actor modelling increases expressiveness. This hypothesis will now be validated by a comparison of a standard process modelling approach with swimlanes (e.g. BPMN) and the actor modelling approach, based on the 43 *Resource Patterns*, which are used to capture the various ways in which resources are represented and utilized in workflows and business processes [26]. An overview of the 43 Resource Patterns is given in Table 3.1. The first column provides the pattern number, the second column the pattern name and the third and fourth columns specify whether the pattern is supported by swimlane concepts (abbreviated with *Swim*) and the actor modelling approach (abbreviated with *Actors*). For example, the pattern *Case Handling* is only supported by the actor modelling approach. Furthermore, the pattern *Role-Based Distribution* is supported by swimlane concepts, but the support in deontic process diagrams with actor modelling is more comprehensive.

So a process modelling approach with swimlanes (we consider BPMN) only supports 8 out of 43 Resource Patterns. A major reason for the limited support is the restrictive manner in which the pool and lane concepts are specified. In addition, several patterns requiring a work list or queue are not supported, since the focus of BPMN (and also H-BPM) is primarily on business process modelling and not on workflows and resources. If a more resource-centric approach for business process modelling is desired, then subject-oriented business process management (S-BPM) (see [7]) is recommended. Nevertheless, the actor modelling approach provides full support for 15 patterns and partial or enhanced support for 4 further patterns and is, thus, more expressive than swimlane concepts. In the following, the patterns supported by the suggested actor modelling approach are described in detail.

Pattern 1: Direct Distribution

The *Direct Distribution* pattern describes the ability to specify, at design-time, the individual (or resource) to which instances of the task will be distributed at runtime. This pattern is supported by the pool and lane concept of BPMN, since pools and lanes may also denote individuals (cf. for this paragraph [31]).

Table 3.1 Overview workflow resource patterns based on [31]

No.	Pattern name	Swim	Actors
Creation patterns			
1	Direct distribution	Yes	Yes
2	Role-based distribution	Yes	Yes(+)
3	Deferred distribution	No	No
4	Authorization	No	No
5	Separation of duties	No	Yes
6	Case handling	No	Yes
7	Retain familiar	No	Yes
8	Capability-based distribution	No	No(+)
9	History-based distribution	No	No
10	Organisational distribution	No	Yes
11	Automatic execution	Yes	Yes
Push patterns			
12	Distribution by offer—single resource	No	No(+)
13	Distribution by offer—multiple resources	No	No(+)
14	Distribution by allocation—single resource	Yes	Yes
15	Random allocation	No	No
16	Round Robin allocation	No	No
17	Shortest queue	No	No
18	Early distribution	No	Yes
19	Distribution on enablement	Yes	Yes
20	Late distribution	No	No
Pull patterns			
21	Resource-initiated allocation	No	Yes
22	Resource-initiated execution—allocated work item	No	Yes
23	Resource-initiated execution—offered work item	No	No
24	System-determined work queue content	No	No
25	Resource-determined work queue content	No	No
26	Selection autonomy	No	No
Detour patterns			
27	Delegation	No	No
28	Escalation	No	No
29	Deallocation	No	No
30	Stateful reallocation	No	No
31	Stateless reallocation	No	No
32	Suspension-resumption	No	No
33	Skip	No	No
34	Redo	No	No
35	Pre-Do	No	No

(continued)

Table 3.1 (continued)

No.	Pattern name	Swim	Actors
Auto-start patterns			
36	Commencement on creation	Yes	Yes
37	Commencement on allocation	No	No
38	Piled execution	No	No
39	Chained execution	Yes	Yes
Visibility patterns			
40	Configurable unallocated work item visibility	No	No
41	Configurable allocated work item visibility	No	No
Multiple resource patterns			
42	Simultaneous execution	Yes	Yes
43	Additional resources	No	No

This pattern is also supported by the actor modelling approach by the definition of individuals in the *Organisational View* and the assignment of these individuals to activities.

Pattern 2: Role-Based Distribution

The *Role-Based Distribution* pattern defines the ability to specify, at design-time, one or more roles to which instances of the task will be distributed at runtime. This pattern is supported by the pool and lane concept of BPMN, since pools and lanes may also denote general roles (cf. for this paragraph [31]).

However, the BPMN support for this pattern is limited, since tasks can only be located in at most one lane. Thus, the assignment to several roles is only supported if the roles have a hierarchical relationship and the lanes are nested. In all other cases, several roles require a duplication of the task. Furthermore, it is not possible to specify that an activity (e.g. a sub-process) is executed by several roles in collaboration. Note that also the support of many BPMLs with a task-based assignment of roles is limited for this pattern, since more formal definitions are required.

In the suggested actor modelling approach, one or more roles can be assigned to a task without the necessity to duplicate the task. Several roles can be concatenated with "and" or "or". Thus, it can also be specified that an activity is executed by several roles in collaboration. So deontic process diagrams with actor modelling provide a more comprehensive support for the *Role-Based Distribution* pattern.

Pattern 5: Separation of Duties

The fifth pattern describes the ability to specify that two tasks must be executed by different individuals in a given process instance. This pattern is not supported by BPMN (cf. for this paragraph [31]).

However, the *Separation of Duties* pattern is supported by deontic process diagrams with actor modelling by the definition of additional rules. For example, it can be specified in the process flow that two tasks are executed by the same role (X), but an additional rule defines that the individuals must be different (e.g. $\forall x\ hasRole(x, X) : do(x, A1) \rightarrow F\ do(x, A2)$).

Pattern 6: Case Handling

The sixth pattern describes the ability to allocate all work items within a process instance to the same individual. This pattern is not supported by BPMN (cf. for this paragraph [31]).

However, the *Case Handling* pattern is supported by the actor modelling approach by the definition of additional rules. For example, it can be specified in the process flow that every task is executed by the same role (X) and additional rules define for every task that also the individuals must be the same (e.g. $\forall x\ hasRole(x, X) : do(x, A1) \rightarrow O\ do(x, A2), \forall x\ hasRole(x, X) : do(x, A1) \rightarrow O\ do(x, A3), ...$).

Pattern 7: Retain Familiar

The *Retain Familiar* pattern describes the ability to allocate a work item within a process instance to the same individual that undertook a preceding work item. In contrast to the *Case Handling* pattern, this pattern applies to single work items and not to all work items within a process instance. This pattern is not supported by BPMN (cf. for this paragraph [31]).

However, the *Retain Familiar* pattern is supported by the actor modelling approach by the definition of additional rules. For example, it can be specified in the process flow that two tasks are executed by the same role (X) and an additional rule defines that also the individuals must be the same (e.g. $\forall x\ hasRole(x, X) : do(x, A1) \rightarrow O\ do(x, A2)$).

Pattern 8: Capability-Based Distribution

The eighth pattern describes the ability to distribute work items to individuals based on specific capabilities they possess. The capabilities are defined for individuals as part of the organisational model. This pattern is not supported by BPMN (cf. for this paragraph [31]).

The *Capability-Based Distribution* is currently also not supported by the actor modelling approach. However, the organisational model can be easily extended to also comprise the capabilities of actors. Furthermore, additional rules can be defined to restrict the assignment of a task to those actors who provide the required capabilities. Thus, a minor extension of the actor modelling approach would allow to support this pattern.

Pattern 10: Organisational Distribution

The *Organisational Distribution* pattern describes the ability to distribute work items to resources based on their position within the organisation and their relationship with other resources. This pattern is not supported by BPMN (cf. for this paragraph [31]).

The *Organisational Distribution* pattern is, however, supported by the actor modelling approach. Roles and groups are defined in the *organisational view* and then assigned to activities in the process flow. In addition, the actor modelling approach supports the distribution of work items based on the relationship with other resources by additional rules in the *rule view*. For example, an additional rule may define that an order created by any employee must be approved by a higher role (e.g. $\forall x \, hasRole(x, (A \text{ or } B \text{ or } C)), \forall y \, hasRole(y, (A \text{ or } B \text{ or } C)), y \succ x : do(x, CO) \rightarrow O \, do(y, AO))$.

Pattern 11: Automatic Execution

The *Automatic Execution* pattern describes the ability of a task instance to execute without needing to utilize the services of a resource. The automatic execution of tasks that do not involve human interaction is not effected by actor modelling and, thus, supported by BPMN and the actor modelling approach (cf. for this paragraph [31]).

Pattern 12: Distribution by Offer—Single Resource

The *Distribution by Offer—Single Resource* pattern describes the ability to distribute a work item to an individual on a non-binding basis. The actor is informed of the work item being offered but is not committed to execute it. This pattern is not supported by BPMN (cf. for this paragraph [31]).

However, this pattern is partly supported by the actor modelling approach by additional tasks with speech acts. For example, a task in the process flow can specify that an actor x $(hasRole(x, R))$ requests an actor y $(hasRole(y, R))$ to perform task A (e.g. $O \, request(x, y, A)$). Two further tasks addressed by an exclusive gateway then define that actor y can either commit or decline to execute the task (e.g. $X \, commit(y, x, A)$ and $X \, commit(y, x, \neg A)$). If actor y commits to execute the task, then actor y is obliged to perform task A (e.g. $O \, do(y, A)$). If actor y declines, then another actor z $(hasRole(z, R))$ can be asked to execute the task (e.g. $O \, request(x, z, A)$). Note that actor y can decide at runtime whether to commit or decline the execution of the task. However, the actors and the order in which they are asked must be defined at design-time within the tasks in the process flow. Thus, this pattern is only partly supported by the actor modelling approach.

Pattern 13: Distribution by Offer—Multiple Resources

The *Distribution by Offer—Multiple Resources* pattern describes the ability to distribute a work item to a group of selected resources on a non-binding basis. This pattern is not supported by BPMN (cf. for this paragraph [31]).

However, the *Distribution by Offer—Multiple Resources* pattern is partly supported by the actor modelling approach by additional tasks with speech acts. For example, a task in the process flow can specify that all actors of a given group are requested to perform task A (e.g. $O \, request(system, G1, A)$). Every actor of the group can then either commit or decline to execute the task (e.g. $X \, commit(x, system, A)$ and $X \, commit(x, system, \neg A)$ and $X \, commit(y, system, A)$ and $X \, commit(y, system, \neg A)$). As soon as the first actor commits to execute the task, all other actors are interrupted and, in addition, forbidden to execute the task (e.g. $commit(x, system, A) \rightarrow F \, do(y, A)$ and $commit(y, system, A) \rightarrow F \, do(x, A)$). If all actors decline to execute the task, then the task can be assigned to another group (e.g. $O \, request(system, G2, A)$). However, similar to the previous pattern, the communication must be defined at design-time. Thus, also this pattern is only partly supported by the actor modelling approach.

Pattern 14: Distribution by Allocation—Single Resource

The *Distribution by Allocation—Single Resource* pattern describes the ability to distribute a work item to a specific resource for execution on a binding basis. This pattern is supported in BPMN by the pool and lane concept (cf. for this paragraph [31]).

The *Distribution by Allocation—Single Resource* pattern is also supported by the task-based assignment of the actor modelling approach. If an obligatory task is assigned to an actor or role (e.g. $O\ do(x, A)$), then the actor or role is obliged to execute the task.

Pattern 18: Early Distribution

The *Early Distribution* pattern describes the ability to advertise and potentially distribute a work item to resources ahead of the moment at which it is actually enabled, but the notification does not imply that the work item is ready for execution. This pattern is not supported by BPMN (cf. for this paragraph [31]).

However, the pattern is supported by the actor modelling approach by the speech act *inform*. For example, an additional rule can define that consultant c must inform approver a after the creation of a business travel about its upcoming approval (e.g. $do(c,\ Create\ BT) \rightarrow O\ inform(c, a, Approve\ BT)$), although the consultant can still modify the business travel before sending it to the approver.

Pattern 19: Distribution on Enablement

The *Distribution on Enablement* pattern describes the ability to distribute a work item to resources at the moment that the task to which it corresponds is enabled for execution. This pattern is supported by the pool and lane concept of BPMN (cf. for this paragraph [31]).

The *Distribution on Enablement* pattern is also supported by the task-based assignment of the actor modelling approach. If an obligatory task is enabled for execution, then this task is immediately distributed to the assigned actor or role.

Pattern 21: Resource-Initiated Allocation

This pattern describes the ability of an actor to commit to undertake a work item without needing to commence working on it immediately. This pattern is not supported by BPMN (cf. for this paragraph [31]).

However, the pattern is supported by the actor modelling approach by the speech act *commit*. An actor that is requested to execute a task (e.g. $O\ request(x, y, A)$) can commit to execute the task (e.g. $X\ commit(y, x, A)$). After the commitment, a further task in the process flow defines that the actor is obligated to perform task A (e.g. $O\ do(y, A)$). However, the actor can start task A later and, e.g. execute tasks on parallel paths before.

Pattern 22: Resource-Initiated Execution—Allocated Work Item

This pattern describes the ability of an actor to commence work on a work item that is allocated to him/her and that the actor has committed to execute. Moreover, the actor should have the possibility to inform others about the commencement. This pattern is not supported by BPMN (cf. for this paragraph [31]).

However, this pattern is supported by the actor modelling approach by speech acts. After an actor has committed to execute a task (e.g. $X\ commit(y, x, A)$), the actor can start the task at an arbitrary point in time. Furthermore, the actor can inform others about the commencement (e.g. $do(y, start(A)) \rightarrow P\ inform(y, x, start(A))$).

Pattern 36: Commencement on Creation

The *Commencement on Creation* pattern describes the ability of a resource to commence execution on a work item as soon as it is created. This pattern is supported by BPMN, since an activity is enabled as soon as it receives the required token(s) (cf. for this paragraph [31]).

This pattern is also supported by the task-based assignment of the actor modelling approach. If an obligatory task is assigned to an actor or role (e.g. $O\ do(x, A)$), then the actor or role can commence execution as soon as the task is enabled.

Pattern 39: Chained Execution

The *Chained Execution* pattern describes the ability to automatically start the next work item in a process instance once the previous one has completed. This pattern is supported by BPMN, since once an activity is completed, subsequent activities receive a token and are triggered immediately (cf. for this paragraph [31]).

This pattern is also supported by the task-based assignment of the actor modelling approach. If an activity has completed, subsequent activities are triggered immediately.

Pattern 42: Simultaneous Execution

The *Simultaneous Execution* pattern describes the ability of an actor to execute more than one work item simultaneously. This pattern is supported by BPMN, since there are no constraints on how many instances of a task specified within a pool or lane can be active (cf. for this paragraph [31]).

This pattern is also supported by the task-based assignment of the actor modelling approach. Several instances of a task can be active simultaneously (e.g. multi-instance activity) and are executed by the same actor.

So the proposed actor modelling approach supports almost twice as many patterns as an ordinary modelling approach with swimlanes, including essential ones like *Separation of Duties* and *Retain Familiar*. However, in order to support the remaining patterns, a more resource-centric approach with work lists and dynamic reallocation is necessary. Nevertheless, it has been shown that our actor modelling approach is, concerning the resource perspective, more expressive than an ordinary approach, thereby validating the hypothesis in Sect. 3.3.

3.7 Summary

A major problem of business process modelling languages that primarily express the flow of activities, e.g. BPMN, is the limited support for actor modelling. Several research groups criticised that the swimlane concept is specified in a very restrictive manner, resulting in a gap of defining the "subject" in business process models. In this chapter, we put forward the important role of actors in control-flow based business process modelling languages and suggested a new approach based on deontic logic and speech act theory to model actors and constraints. A major excellence of the actor modelling approach is that it supports different layers of abstraction, thereby increasing the expressiveness and avoiding inaccuracy and redundancy. Since it has been claimed that the expressiveness in every layer is increased or remains the same, the entire approach for actor modelling should increase the expressiveness as stated by the hypothesis. This hypothesis is validated on the basis of the *Workflow Resource Patterns*, i.e., using the proposed actor modelling approach, almost twice as many patterns are supported compared to using an ordinary modelling approach with swimlanes, including important patterns such as *Separation of Duties* and *Retain Familiar*. Furthermore, we studied the suitability of the actor modelling approach within an application scenario, which showed a possible reduction of structural complexity in business process models.

In addition, practical applications are also considered since different layers concerning the extent to which actor modelling is supported are distinguished. For example, a simple task-based assignment of actors without additional rules can give a good visual presentation for a high-level process description. To model more specific situations, the diagrams can be extended with further concepts without loss of information but with additional possibilities for expression. The new diagrams can then be refined accordingly, being clear without ambiguity, not leaving relevant information open, and providing high expressiveness. Thus, higher layers are, for example, more complex but also more expressive. Further important elements of process modelling, such as legibility and maintainability, are also considered (e.g. by using inference techniques to identify contradictions). This way, it is possible to bridge the gap between theory and practice.

In future work, we plan to extend the approach for actor modelling to also consider additional elements like events and gateways. So far, only activities were assigned to actors within the proposed approach. However, pools and lanes may also comprise further elements like events and gateways. Although such elements may be executed automatically within the process flow, it is nevertheless important to specify, for example, the sender or receiver of a message event.

References

1. Adams, M.: The resource service. In: Hofstede, A., van der Aalst, W., Adams, M., Russell, N. (eds.) Modern Business Process Automation, pp. 261–290. Springer, Berlin (2010)
2. Awad, A., Grosskopf, A., Meyer, A., Weske, M.: Enabling resource assignment constraints in BPMN, [working paper BPT Technical Report 04-2009], Business Process Technology, Hasso Plattner Institute, Potsdam (2009)
3. Borgida, A., Brachman, R.J.:Conceptual modeling with description logics. In: Baader, F., Calvanese, D., McGuinness, D.L., Nardi, D., Patel-Schneider, P.F. (eds.) The Description Logic Handbook: Theory, Implementation and Applications, pp. 349–372. Cambridge University Press, New York (2003)
4. Colombetti, M.: A commitment-based approach to agent speech acts and conversations. In: Proceedings of the Workshop on Agent Languages and Conversation Policies, "Agents 2000" Conference, pp. 21–29. Barcelona (2000)
5. Dignum, F., Weigand, H.: Communication and deontic logic. In: Wieringa, R., Feenstra, R. (eds.) Information Systems: Correctness and Reusability, pp. 242–260. World Scientific, Singapore (1995)
6. Eiter, T., Mascardi, V., Subrahmanian, V.: Error-tolerant agents. In: Kakas, A., Sadri, F. (eds.) Computational Logic: Logic Programming and Beyond, pp. 83–104. Springer, Berlin (2002)
7. Fleischmann, A., Schmidt, W., Stary, C., Obermeier, S., Börger, E.: Subject-Oriented Business Process Management. Springer, Berlin (2012)
8. Governatori, G., Milosevic, Z.: A formal analysis of a business contract language. Int. J. Coop. Inf. Syst. **15**(4), 659–685 (2006)
9. Grossi, D., Royakkers, L., Dignum, F.: Organizational structure and responsibility: an analysis in a dynamic logic of organized collective agency. Artif. Intell. Law **15**(3), 223–249 (2007)
10. Hilpinen, R.: Deontic logic. In: Goble, L. (ed.) The Blackwell Guide to Philosophical Logic, Chap. 8, pp. 159–182. Blackwell, Malden (2001)
11. Hohwiller, J., Schlegel, D., Grieser, G., Hoekstra, Y.: Integration of BPM and BRM. In: Dijkman, R., Hofstetter, J., Koehler, J. (eds.) Business Process Model and Notation: Third International Workshop, BPMN 2011, Lucerne, pp. 136–141. Springer, Berlin (2011)
12. Korherr, B., List, B.: Extending the EPC and the BPMN with business process goals and performance measures. In: Filipe, J., Cordeiro, J., Cardoso, J. (eds.) Enterprise Information Systems: 9th International Conference, ICEIS 2007, Funchal, pp. 287–294. Springer, Berlin (2007)
13. Kossak, F., Illibauer, C., Geist, V., Kubovy, J., Natschläger, C., Ziebermayr, T., Kopetzky, T., Freudenthaler, B., Schewe, K.D.: A Rigorous Semantics for BPMN 2.0 Process Diagrams. Springer, Cham (2015)
14. Kunze, M., Luebbe, A., Weidlich, M., Weske, M.: Towards understanding process modeling – the case of the BPM academic initiative. In: Business Process Model and Notation. Lecture Notes in Business Information Processing, vol. 95, pp. 44–58. Springer, Berlin (2011)
15. Milanović, M., Gašević, D., Wagner, G., Hatala, M.: Rule-enhanced business process modeling language for service choreographies. In: Schürr, A., Selic, B. (eds.) Model Driven Engineering Languages and Systems. Lecture Notes in Computer Science, vol. 5795, pp. 337–341. Springer, Berlin (2009)
16. Minoli, D.: Enterprise Architecture A to Z: Frameworks, Business Process Modeling, SOA, and Infrastructure Technology. Auerbach Publications, Boca Raton (2008)
17. Natschläger, C.: Towards a BPMN 2.0 ontology. In: Dijkman, R., Hofstetter, J., Koehler, J. (eds.) Business Process Model and Notation. Lecture Notes in Business Information Processing, vol.95, pp. 1–15. Springer, Berlin (2011)
18. Natschläger, C., Geist, V.: A layered approach for actor modelling in business processes. Bus. Process Manag. J. **19**, 917–932 (2013)
19. Natschläger-Carpella, C.: Extending BPMN with Deontic Logic. Logos, Berlin (2012)
20. Object Management Group: Semantics of business vocabulary and business rules (SBVR), v1.0. http://www.omg.org/spec/SBVR/1.0 (2008). Accessed 25 Sep 2015

21. Object Management Group: Business Process Model and Notation (BPMN) 2.0. http://www.omg.org/spec/BPMN/2.0 (2011). Accessed 06 Oct 2015
22. Object Management Group: OMG Unified Modeling Language (OMG UML), version 2.5. http://www.omg.org/spec/UML/2.5 (2015). Accessed 06 Oct 2015
23. Recker, J.: BPMN modeling - who, where, how and why. Bus. Process Trends **5**(5), 1–8 (2008)
24. Recker, J., Indulska, M., Rosemann, M., Green, P.: How good is BPMN really? Insights from theory and practice. In: Ljungberg, J., Andersson, M. (eds.) 14th European Conference on Information Systems, pp. 1582–1593. Goeteborg (2006)
25. Rodríguez, A., Fernández-Medina, E., Piattini, M.: A BPMN extension for the modeling of security requirements in business processes. IEICE–Trans. Inf. Syst. E90-D(4), 745–752 (2007)
26. Russell, N., ter Hofstede, A., Edmond, D., van der Aalst, W.: Workflow Resource Patterns. BETA Working Paper Series WP 127. Eindhoven University of Technology, Eindhoven (2004)
27. Scheer, A.W.: ARIS - Business Process Frameworks. Springer, Berlin (1999)
28. Scheer, A.W.: ARIS - Business Process Modeling. Springer, Berlin (2000)
29. Scheer, A., Thomas, O., Adam, O.: Process modeling using event-driven process chains. In: Dumas, M., van der Aalst, W., ter Hofstede, A. (eds.) Process-Aware Information Systems: Bridging People and Software through Process Technology, pp. 119–146. Wiley, Hoboken (2005)
30. Tan, K., Crampton, J., Gunter, C.: The consistency of task-based authorization constraints in workflow systems. In: Proceedings of the 17th IEEE Workshop on Computer Security Foundations, CSFW'04, Pacific Grove, pp. 155–169. IEEE Computer Society, Washington, D.C. (2004)
31. van der Aalst, W.M., ter Hofstede, A.H.: Workflow patterns homepage. http://www.workflowpatterns.com. Accessed 25 Sep 2015
32. Wohed, P., van der Aalst, W., Dumas, M., ter Hofstede, A., Russell, N.: On the suitability of BPMN for business process modelling. In: Dustdar, S., Fiadeiro, J., Sheth, A. (eds.) Business Process Management. Lecture Notes in Computer Science, vol. 4102, pp. 161–176. Springer, Berlin (2006)
33. Wolter, C., Schaad, A.: Modeling of task-based authorization constraints in BPMN. In: Alonso, G., Dadam, P., Rosemann, M. (eds.) Business Process Management: 5th International Conference, BPM 2007, Brisbane, pp. 64–79. Springer, Berlin (2007)
34. Wooldridge, M.: An Introduction to MultiAgent Systems. Wiley, Chichester (2009)
35. Zachman, J.: A framework for information systems architecture. IBM Syst. J. **26**(3), 267–292 (1987)

Chapter 4
A Typed Approach to User Interaction Modelling

Flexibility in business process technology is becoming more and more important. Today's IT system architectures in enterprises are often experienced as inflexible, which makes them difficult to change or maintain. Preliminary scientific work revealed gaps, in particular, between workflow definitions and system dialogue programming, which can be traced back to gaps and tensions between modern business process tools and techniques [23, 28]. For example, business process modelling exists on its own; it is often used in a non-formal way to communicate ideas but not for executable specifications. Business process automation is composed of workflow definition and application programming. A workflow definition typically is a visual, high-level program that is interpreted by a workflow engine, whereas application programming concerns the realisation of the system dialogues. Problems arise due to a missing canonical mapping between the components that are under the control of workflow technology and the entities addressed by business process modelling [22]. This shortcoming is the result of absent integration capabilities, limiting the power of Business Process Management (BPM).

To mitigate these gaps and tensions, we propose a typed approach to business process specification that supports the integration of workflow definition and dialogue programming and is also open to business process modelling. The resulting key artefact is called *workflow chart* and still models the control flow of business processes but puts more emphasis on user interaction modelling by implementing a submit/response-style user interaction pattern [3, 4, 28]. Submit/response-style systems often occur in practice, ranging from legacy terminal/server-based systems, over form-based client–server systems to web applications, especially in the domains of enterprise computing and e-commerce. The interaction with a submit/response-style system consists in a continuous interchange of report presentations and form submissions. The concept of workflow charts relies on a methodology to model form-based applications that specifies submit/response-style dialogues as typed, bipartite state machines called *formcharts* [25].

However, although formcharts have their semantic specification based on Unified Modeling Language (UML) semantics, they lack a complete formal semantic specification. To meet the needs of workflow specification, formcharts are extended to

© Springer International Publishing Switzerland 2016
F. Kossak et al., *Hagenberg Business Process Modelling Method*,
DOI 10.1007/978-3-319-30496-0_4

workflow charts in due consideration of the worklist paradigm, parallelism, and users as well as roles. A formalisation of workflow charts using Abstract State Machines (ASMs) will provide a precise operational semantics. Workflow charts represent a technology-independent, conceptual modelling language and are at the same time designed for integrating workflow definitions and dialogue programming to create an executable specification language, providing a more flexible process technology [33].

In this chapter, we present and formalise the concept of workflow charts as a typed, strictly dialogue-based approach to user interaction modelling in a formal business process model. In Sect. 4.1, we first motivate the need for a seamless integration of workflow definition and dialogue programming and discuss its contribution. We then provide a survey of related work on dialogue modelling and user interaction modelling in business process and workflow management in Sect. 4.2, and give a very short overview of the theory that forms the basis of the suggested approach in Sect. 4.3. In Sect. 4.4, we present a formal description of the typed workflow chart and discuss the operational semantics of workflow charts using ASMs, including descriptions of the assumed environment, required nodes and associations, and miscellaneous rules and functions. We also provide an assessment of the concept by implementing a substantial workflow of a major Austrian social insurance company as proof of concept in Sect. 4.5. In Sect. 4.6, we sum our main findings up and also comment on future work.

4.1 Motivation

Today, BPM technology is successfully used in many existing enterprise application projects. The interplay of the applications is surveyed to identify certain rules which are automatically executed by a BPM product. However, often the design of the Human–Computer Interaction (HCI) is not obvious if a workflow-intensive system should be set up with BPM technology. Business process models currently define user tasks as atomic units which are not broken down any further. Additional relationships, e.g. to documents, other business processes, or roles, might be specified indeed, however, their refinement is not designated. BPM technology is simply able to control the workflow states but is not able to control the dialogues that span the workflow states. Hence, the internal states of enterprise applications, i.e. the system dialogues, form black boxes. There is only limited support for advanced BPM techniques, e.g. business process monitoring or simulation [22]. Thus, for implementing process-oriented enterprise applications, it is actually important to specify the user interaction in terms of forms and applied data.

Another challenging task is to determine a corresponding granularity of workflow states compared to dialogue states. Even though there exist some heuristics [67], there is no systematic approach available. For example, the simplest state unifying workflow and dialogue states consists of a report and its connected forms. Workflow engines provide facilities to manage workflow states and enable software developers to assign defined forms to the states. However, seamless integration is not yet solved by these workflow products. Furthermore, rapid development tools of several workflow management systems exactly support the development of "one-step" dialogues, i.e. a worklist leads to a client page consisting of a report and a form that leads back to the worklist upon the submission of data by calling a server action. In this case, every dialogue state belongs to a process state, resulting in a high number of states, with the meaning that workflow control always returns to the worklist after having submitted a form. However, there is no support to flexibly handle more complex dialogues. (In addition, a further problem is that common process definition languages do not distinguish between reports and forms, so there is no possibility to determine which type is associated with a node.)

Hence, we recommend to consider integration of both workflow and dialogue states in advance, i.e. to specify forms and data which are required for processing a user task already within the business process model. The suggested approach, on the one hand, establishes scientific added value for fully integrating business processes and system dialogues by applying a typed, implementation-independent approach that focuses on the type concept for dialogues [33]. On the other hand, this not only leads to significant improvements for developing process-oriented enterprise applications but also allows process designers to flexibly specify which parts of a process apply to workflow technology and which parts make up the system dialogues. In addition, it provides the opportunity to design the user's work with a system as efficiently as possible. The system dialogues become pervasive and thus all benefits of the BPM technology including support for advanced techniques are available. Furthermore, the structure of dialogues becomes changeable, which leads to a natural partition of business logic into services of appropriate granularity.

As a result, the concept of workflow charts will provide a more flexible process technology in order to support modern enterprises to answer to challenges of the new globalised and quickly changing markets. The enterprises are able to dynamically react to emerging demands, opportunities, and threats in their business environment, considering flexibility and adaptivity as important success factors. In this respect, the suggested approach will also accelerate the BPM life cycle and allow for low cost software development.

4.2 Related Work

This section provides an overview of the most relevant literature on dialogue modelling, workflow management, and BPM in the form of a brief historical summary. Please refer to [33] for a detailed discussion of related work on user interaction modelling in business processes.

After the development of relational databases and the accomplishment of the Structured Query Language (SQL), all issues surrounding data and activity management seemed to be solved [45]. The vision of Codd, Chamberlin, and Boyce [18, 19] was to design the database interface as a direct human–computer interface, so that it can become the single most important tool in enterprise computing by providing structured access to data in a generic and user-friendly way (expert systems). Subsequently, tools for generating complete dialogues, also web-based dialogues, from database schemas (Entity–Relationship (ER) models) have been developed in order to overcome the actually experienced unhandiness of the database interface and to free end users from applying SQL, e.g. [16, 49, 52]. Model-Based User Interface Development Environment (MB-UIDE) technology focuses on the design and generation of user interfaces using a set of declarative models for describing UI functionalities. Representatives of the second generation include ADEPT [44], BOSS [65], JANUS [5], MASTERMIND [69], and TRIDENT [7].

An object-oriented approach to provide an integrated model for conceptually designing both databases and user interfaces has been introduced by Schewe and Schewe in [63, 64]. The proposed approach dealing with dialogue objects and dialogue classes is a general and mature approach, whereas the class of form-oriented systems is primarily specialising in two-staged interaction and is thus rather specific. A further category of approaches are proposals for hypermedia and web design languages, e.g. the Hypertext Design Model (HDM) [32], Relationship Management Methodology (RMM) [37], Object-Oriented Hypertext Design Model (OOHDM) [58], and Web Modeling Language (WebML) [17]. A further approach that is closely related to WebML is the User Interface Markup Language (UIML) [1] for designing user interfaces by abstracting from appliance-specific details.

UML [51] might be a convenient candidate for designing user interfaces because the notation is the established standard for object-oriented application modelling. However, it is not obvious how user interface elements, e.g. user tasks and presentations, are supported in UML models [42]. Many proposals concern the design of user tasks, applying several different notations (e.g. [39]), or the design of user interfaces using declarative models (e.g. [68]). Also several UML profiles and extensions for modelling user interfaces were introduced (e.g. in [6, 55, 56]).

However, users expect more from enterprise information systems than is addressed by the listed approaches. They expect a clear guidance through the system, authorised data access, as well as support for data acquisition (HCI aspect) [58]. Thus, high-level task models [57] have been developed, which are also used to generate executable interface prototypes. Classical task models are considered as the basic models for ensuring learned design beyond hacking [75]. Related approaches are, amongst others, task-driven design techniques with hierarchically organised task structures to derive user interface models [54] and approaches that automate the derivation process [43] or expect designers to relate task models and user interface models [48].

An essential class of tools for UI development are CASE tools that typically follow the use case driven approach [38]. A new approach for designing user interfaces without a task modelling language constitutes the proposal for modelling business applications using the Business process Model and Notation (BPMN), Extensible Markup Language (XML), XML schema, and a hybrid dialogue modelling language based on interconnected, abstract interaction objects as well as UML statecharts called Diamodl [46, 71]. Other, more recent, approaches are presented, e.g. in [34] on model-to-code transformation and in [20] on the composition of distributed user interfaces.

Up to now, the approaches only concentrate on HCI aspects of a single user, whereas collaborative work involves multiple users and roles. Therefore, the introduction of the worklist concept is inevitable to support transcending dialogues of multiple participants. By means of a comprehensive investigation of advanced role model concepts in terms of patterns, the workflow community found a variety of distinct features in commercial workflow and BPM tools that recur quite frequently in the requirements of workflows [60, 73]. An abstraction of these requirements led to several workflow resource patterns [59]. The patterns describe how human resources distribute and execute task items in workflows. This way, an HCI viewpoint that refines the current global viewpoint of an overall action flow is created.

In fact, workflow technology incorporates worklists and advanced role models to allow for an executable specification of tasks. The subject of executable specification ranges from automatic programming [53] over Domain-Specific Languages (DSLs) [74] to Model-Driven Architecture (MDA). Two converging communities foster the trend to achieve executable business process specifications, i.e. the business process modelling community, taking BPMN [50] as a representative, and the workflow management community [35].

Automating business processes does not require special-purpose tools or technologies in fact [2]. Business process modelling can be supported by a general-purpose drawing tool, just as workflow-intensive applications can be developed without workflow management technology. However, there are specialised technologies available, supporting business process modelling on the one hand and business process automation on the other hand. Business process modelling tools typically offer support for many different modelling standards, covering also multiple aspects such as data, organisational structure, deployment structure, and strategic plans. Tools that support business process automation, i.e. BPM suites and workflow management systems, also offer a workflow definition tool to visually specify business process models. However, these tools do not offer the full range of features, e.g. support for different kinds of diagrams.

What is missing in current solutions is, thus, a clear interface for the integrated specification of user interaction. Current approaches do not fully integrate the application programs that constitute the dialogues of an enterprise application. This means that they focus on the process states but not on the dialogues that bridge the process states. On the one hand, this leads to a successful use of business process and workflow technologies in enterprise application projects in the sense that rules are identified in the interplay of existing enterprise applications and then automated. On the other hand, if a workflow-intensive system is to be built from scratch with business process and workflow technologies, it is not obvious how to design HCI aspects.

4.3   Foundations of the Theory

The suggested approach is based on the form-oriented analysis [25], which introduces a methodology to model form-based applications. This methodology specifies submit/response-style dialogues in terms of typed, bipartite state machines with clear semantics called *formcharts*. Formcharts represent a formal approach to user interaction modelling by specifying the dialogue model of a system. The interaction with the system appears to the user as a continuous interchange of report presentations and form submissions. In so-called client states, reports (pages) are presenting information to the user and are offering several options for entering and submitting user input. After the submission of data, the dialogue model changes to a server state. Server states use actions to process the submitted data and trigger the transition to the next client state, i.e. the server state is left automatically. Thus, submitting data is similar to calling a method, including user input as parameters.

Experiences in industrial projects have shown that modelling user interaction is important, especially during the analysis phase [3, 4, 28]. The submit/response-style interface clearly separates the client and server states and defines the interactions between the states, which has proved to be essential for users to understand the interaction process. At the same time, formcharts provide a formal means to develop process-oriented enterprise applications by following a typed approach, which is related to a layered data model, together with dialogue constraints to complete the concept.

However, formcharts show limitations regarding workflow execution as they only support single-user scenarios of two-staged HCI without parallelism. Therefore, formcharts need to be extended with workflow semantics by introducing a role concept, parallelism, and the worklist paradigm. The proposed key artefact is called *workflow chart*.

4.4   The Typed Workflow Chart

The key artefact of the dialogue-based approach to user interaction modelling in business processes is specified as a tripartite directed graph called *workflow chart* [2, 23, 33]. It represents a workflow definition that specifies the most detailed level in a hierarchy of business processes and is executable in the sense that it can be interpreted by a workflow management system that maintains the states using a worklist client. Workflow charts extend formcharts by introducing an additional interaction stage in order to meet the needs of workflow definition. Formcharts follow the two-staged interaction paradigm of submit/response-style systems, i.e. editing data in a form and submitting the data. In contrast, workflow charts include the worklist concept to enable the selection of the next page for editing and submitting data. Thus, workflow charts follow a three-staged interaction paradigm, supporting the management of users and roles, parallelism, and the identification of (complex) dialogues.

4.4.1 Specification Overview

The specification of the workflow chart consists of three types of nodes with signatures, i.e. client pages, immediate server actions, and deferred server actions, and different types of connectors in between (see Fig. 4.1). The alternation of nodes is strictly defined, i.e. a client page is only followed by (one or many) immediate server actions, an immediate server action is only followed by (one or many) deferred server actions, and a deferred server action is only followed by (one or many) client pages.

Each node is assigned with a type based on arbitrarily complex sum-of-product data types [23]. The workflow chart is also annotated with dialogue constraints needed for workflow specification (i.e. enabling conditions, activation conditions, and flow conditions) and with role assignment information. All components of the workflow chart specification are described in detail in the following. (The discussion is based on the level of abstract syntax, which means that the specification holds the data structure and is independent of any concrete representation, e.g. layout or colours.)

Node Types. *Client pages* represent computer screens that show information and provide forms for user input. They are specified using circles in workflow charts. Their type describes data that is displayed as a report to the user. *Immediate server actions* (A_1 to A_n) represent forms that appear on computer screens and are specified using rectangles. The type of an immediate server action describes data that the user can enter to modify the system state upon submission, which represents a user-editable function. *Deferred server actions* (B_1 to B_M) appear as references to client pages in the worklists of the corresponding users and are specified as rectangles with a gradient fill. As it is a common practice to show links in worklists, the type of a deferred server action is void.

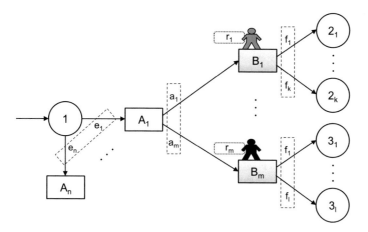

Fig. 4.1 Basic typed tripartite workflow chart

The concrete benefit of introducing deferred server actions in the tripartite work-flow chart is the split of business logic and task determination. In general, immediate server actions have side effects on the system. By adding an intermediate step, it is possible to perform potential side effects of business logic immediately and to delay the decision about which concrete client page is to be referenced in a user's worklist. Thus, tripartite workflow charts represent a smart approach for specifying an HCI, providing a design space with marginal error messages. The tripartite system structure also reveals advantages concerning the modelling of assignment information [33].

Transitions and Conditions. The transitions in the workflow chart have a twofold meaning. On the one hand, they communicate the flow of control through the graph and, on the other hand, they function as associations defining which data is to be presented to a user. The associations are usually guarded by different kinds of conditions: Client pages and their corresponding immediate server actions form a kind of meta-nodes (as they are not visited separately during workflow execution) and are associated via so-called *enabling conditions* (e_1 to e_n). If an enabling condition evaluates to true, the respective data input and edit opportunities available for the user according to the associated immediate server actions are presented to the user. Thus, enabling conditions can be used to extend or restrict the scope of options displayed to the user. However, even in the presence of multiple actions to choose from, the user can only submit data for one immediate server action. (After the completion of an immediate server action, the user is led to their worklist.) The edges from immediate server actions to deferred server actions are annotated with so-called *activation conditions* (a_1 to a_m) with the following semantics: If an activation condition evaluates to true, the corresponding deferred server action is activated, i.e. a new link to the next client page (represented by the deferred server action) is inserted into the worklist of the user who is associated with that deferred server action. The multiple choice of immediate server actions leads to parallelism in the execution of a workflow chart; the evaluation of the activation conditions connected to the outgoing transitions of an immediate server action determines the number of parallel tasks added to the worklist. (Parallelism in this context means that a user is able to influence how to process defined sequences of activities by selecting tasks from the worklist.) If the user chooses a worklist entry, the corresponding next client page (with its associated enabled immediate server actions) is presented to the user. This is determined by *flow conditions* (f_i in Fig. 4.1) between deferred server actions and client pages, whose evaluation must be unique.

Roles. Switching from the single-user scenario to a workflow scenario supporting multiple users or roles is enabled by the introduction of the worklist. In workflow charts, roles are attached to deferred server actions using stick figures with dotted rounded rectangles (labelled with r_1 to r_m). During workflow execution, for each activated deferred server action, a new entry is added to the worklist of the users belonging to the role which is attached to that deferred server action. Resource constraints are needed to ensure clear semantics of business process behaviour. For example, if no assignment restrictions are given, any authorised user may decide to select and process a task in their worklist. As a consequence, that task must be removed from all other worklists of users of the given role to avoid simultaneous selection of the same task. Other options are to use group worklists by defining an additional area within the worklist containing common tasks, to create multiple instances of the task, or to choose one concrete user from the set of users in advance.

Concerning several scenarios in workflows regarding resources, a survey on advanced role model concepts from a workflow perspective is important to close the gap between business process modelling and business process automation. In this context, a comprehensive discussion of workflow patterns in the workflow community resulted in the investigation and comparison of existing workflow technology, also considering resources in particular [59]. For example, a potential scenario might be the handling of responsibilities based on previous task execution. If a particular user starts a process instance by processing the first task of the process that is assigned to a role, the same user should perform a later task within the process instance that is also assigned to that role (*retain familiar*). Another scenario is the handling of common tasks within the dialogue model, e.g. a part of a workflow chart that does not contain parallelism but deferred server actions with the same role attached can be declared as "complex" dialogue (see Sect. 4.4.3) for the first user who enters that dialogue, or the user can be redirected to the worklist after the completion of each task, giving other users the chance to perform the subsequent tasks.

A general approach to realise such (and further) workflow scenarios is to support some kind of task assignment handler to be able to add any assignment information in order to achieve any workflow resource pattern (as it is proposed, e.g. in Chap. 3).

Data. For workflow charts, the required information that needs to be persisted are data concerning the management of users and roles, information about process specifications and process instances, description of task instances and their current states, assignment information, and process attributes. Process attributes are represented by the different kinds of node types, i.e. the type of an immediate server action defines the data provided by the user and the type of a client page defines the data displayed on a screen. These data are stored in the data model by recording the name, value, and type of each attribute. Finally, a parameter mapping approach is required to define the attributes and their relations, which is necessary to describe how the value of an attribute is obtained (cf. [33]). For example, the value could be available, determined by a method call, or retrieved by querying the data model. It is a feasible approach to store these data in tables of a relational data model, establish relationships between the data, and query/update the data model during workflow execution in order to retrieve/persist essential runtime information. Particular attention must be paid to consistency and currentness of entries in the users' worklists, especially if group worklists are supported (see also Sect. 4.4.2).

In a more profound way, user interactions need to be captured by means of operations on data views defined on top of a database schema [62]. That way, the data model results from view integration; however, global consistency has to be addressed, because a global database may infer dependencies between activities, which are not visible on the level of the control flow. Further issues that need to be addressed in a more conceptual sense concern the interrelationship of business (or domain) objects, which may be supported, e.g. by so-called *data objects* in BPMN, and process attributes specified by workflow charts, as well as advanced transaction concepts for supporting compensation, e.g. via rollbacks.

A sophisticated data approach based on local view generation and global view translation is currently being developed.

4.4.2 The Worklist Metaphor

The worklist is a central part of the workflow chart concept. Following the workflow requirements, it enables parallelisms in workflow charts as well as roles to perform multiple tasks at the same time by various users. The worklist is organised per user (local view) and divided into two areas, i.e. the process and the task area. The process area contains a list of all business processes that can be started by the user (start menu); the task area includes a list of all tasks that are ready to be executed. Starting a process instance leads to the appearance of a new task entry, which is represented by a deferred server action and displayed as link to a subsequent client page. Thus, the worklist is generally shown to the user after having called an immediate server action.

The organisation of the task area offers several display options. Some interesting HCI aspects for presenting the worklist are discussed in detail in [33], e.g. (i) reacting to upcoming tasks, (ii) the handling of out-of-date links, and (iii) the handling of complex dialogues. For example, addressing the first issue, there have been discussions about the convenient point in time for showing new tasks to the user. Basically, an upcoming task is to be shown to the user as soon as possible. However, this point in time depends on the HCI style of the workflow system [23]. In terminal/server-style systems, the worklist is only available when the user does not operate on a client page. After the submission of data, the user returns to the worklist containing all links that have been added in the meantime. In a window-style system, the worklist is always accessible to the user. For both implementations, terminal/server-style and window-style, the feasible strategy for updating the worklist is an issue, i.e. presenting new tasks immediately to the user or not. This issue is rather an HCI than a technological question. For example, if a worklist can suddenly be rearranged due to the insertion of new links in an ordered list, it might be confusing for the user looking at the worklist. Another undesired effect of an immediate update emerges if a link is added to the end of the list and the content of the worklist exceeds the computer screen, meaning that the user is not informed about the available task. A convenient solution might be to support the reload of the worklist whenever new tasks are available by notifying the user or to enable the user to manually refresh the worklist.

The second situation might occur if a task is assigned to more than one user of the same role. As a result, the link to the corresponding client page may be contained in multiple worklists. Problems arise if one user selects the link and starts working, and another user also tries to select that link without refreshing the worklist. Therefore, simultaneous selection of the same task must be detected. A possible way to prevent such a situation is to check on every selection if there exists a task that was included in a user's worklist and would disappear from the worklist after a reload but was not performed by the user (considering alternative flows). Thus, if it comes to a simultaneous selection of the same task, the worklist of the second user should be refreshed and an appropriate notification message should be shown.

Finally, a further situation that requires a special handling of the worklist is the identification of complex dialogues within workflow charts (see Sect. 4.4.3). This situation occurs if a user wants to continue work with several consecutive client pages before being redirected to the worklist, especially when working with legacy systems.

Another relevant topic regarding the worklist concept is the notion of parallelism and synchronisation within workflow charts. Sources of parallelism in workflow charts are in general immediate server actions; the evaluation of activation conditions connected to outgoing transitions determines the number of parallel tasks added to the worklist. By the opportunity to select the next task from the worklist, the user is able to influence how defined sequences of activities in a business process will be processed.

Naturally, parallelism may require synchronisation. Synchronisation, in the context of workflow charts, does not mean, however, that users are being blocked in performing their work, because they can always access their worklists. Thus, synchronisation only affects the question whether a task entry will be shown to the user in the worklist or not. A common practice might be to support a default synchronisation pattern with the following behaviour: a task entry is shown in the worklist only if all preceding tasks that are relevant for the synchronisation have been completed. In detail, before adding a new entry to the worklist, i.e. at the end of the preceding immediate server action, a check for synchronisation is required. Therefore, it must be recorded whether a client page was already visited and which corresponding immediate server actions were performed. If the deferred server action that follows the immediate server action has multiple predecessors, i.e. more than one transition point to that node, then synchronisation might be necessary. For the potential candidate, the chronological order of client pages and server actions from backward to forward within the workflow chart is observed. If the predecessors have a common source for which parallelism is given, the link to the next client page must not be shown in the worklist until all preceding client pages were visited and left via executing continuative immediate server actions that finally lead to the deferred server action in question.

The default synchronisation pattern applies to workflow charts following the principles of structured modelling [23]. For other models, it provides a suggestion. A major benefit is that the default behaviour can be replaced in order to realise any synchronisation pattern (cf. [60]) by adding the corresponding synchronisation information. Thus, also the issue of supporting inclusive merge (OR-join), i.e. if not all parallel flows of a fork have been activated, can be addressed in this way by providing an adequate join mechanism. Another issue is how to handle the situation if multiple task instances (tokens) that should be synchronised pass each other before being merged. To prevent such situations, many common workflow management systems do not support multi-instance loops. However, the issue can be solved by simply extending the default synchronisation pattern with an additional instance ID for tasks in order to be able to implement a ticketing system.

4.4.3 Identifying (Complex) Dialogues

Workflow charts follow the three-staged interaction paradigm of workflows, i.e. selecting a task from the worklist, editing input data, and submitting the data, whereas the preceding concept of formcharts do not have the worklist as an intermediate stage between server actions and client pages. Thus, workflow charts are interpreted by the interaction of two different kinds of clients, i.e. the *worklist client* representing the first stage of interaction and the *dialogue client* covering the second and third stage of interaction [2]. The worklist client presents the worklist to the user and enables the user to select a concrete link to a subsequent client page. After the task selection, the worklist client passes control to the dialogue client that renders the report on the client page and supports the submission of form data to the selected immediate server action. Afterwards, the dialogue client hands over to the worklist client by default. However, the worklist processing stage can be skipped, i.e. the user can continue working on multiple subsequent client pages without being redirected to the worklist. That scenario is possible if the completion of a client page unambiguously leads to a single succeeding client page that is attached to the same user. In the context of formcharts, this two-staged, single-user interaction is called a *dialogue*, only considering the interaction with a client page. Also certain parts of a workflow chart that neither include parallelism nor user changes can be considered as dialogues being interpreted by the dialogue client only. The power to interpret sub workflow charts as so-called *complex dialogues*, consisting of many different client pages and server actions wired together, overcomes the strict separation of workflow definition and application programming. Furthermore, the ability for users to perform multiple subsequent tasks in series allows for more efficient work, i.e. the number of visits of the worklist can be significantly reduced. Identifying (complex) dialogues within workflow charts can be exploited in various approaches. A static check is applicable if concrete users are attached to client pages and the system conditions can be evaluated without the need for runtime values. Another approach is the dynamic detection of dialogues. By applying this approach, it is possible to evaluate at runtime whether the submission of data to a server action by a user results in a single subsequent client page that is assigned to the same user. Based on that evaluation, the user is directed to the worklist or to the next client page dynamically.

The dynamic scheduling approach can be realised by including an intermediate step after each immediate server action that performs a dynamic check and directly redirects to the next client page if possible or by calling a dynamic checker at the end of each immediate server action (implicit inclusion of the intermediate step). The checker determines the next page shown to the user, i.e. the worklist or a concrete subsequent client page. In both cases, two kinds of information need to be considered for the dynamic check. First, activation conditions are used to check if the immediate server action exactly leads to a single subsequent client page, i.e. if the evaluation is unique. Secondly, the concrete user associated with the deferred server action referring to the client page on which the immediate server action was called must be the same as the user associated with the subsequent deferred server action. If these requirements are met, the worklist can be skipped and the user is directed to the next client page.

Comparing concrete users attached to client pages involves some considerations about the role model (see Sect. 4.4.1). The check is trivial using a single-user role model, but it becomes complex if more than one user is attached to a client page, e.g. if a role having assigned multiple users is associated or if multiple concrete users (of different roles) are associated with the client page. A possible solution would be to directly lead the user of the previous client page to the next page, implicating that the other assigned users will never be notified about the task. The other solution is to simply not declare the respective part of the workflow chart as a dialogue.

A point of criticism concerning the dynamic identification of dialogues might be a violation of an important dialogue principle, i.e. the conformity to user expectations [36]. A user might get confused due to a sudden redirect to a subsequent client page instead of the worklist [2]. Another risk of the dynamic scheduling approach is that users might miss the chance to select the next task themselves because, when declaring a part of the workflow chart as a dialogue, the users are restricted in their opportunity to process tasks in parallel. This is the case if they are led from one client page to the subsequent client page directly after the submission of data without having the chance to see or select another task from the worklist that might has arrived in the meantime. Despite its risks, the dynamic scheduling approach shows the significant potential of dialogues contained in workflow charts.

A further approach is to introduce a means to explicitly specify the dialogues in workflow charts, e.g. a graphical modelling element or a textual language construct. Marking an immediate server action that supports a unique evaluation of the connected conditions facilitates the identification of dialogues in a workflow chart, i.e. the identification of the parts that should be interpreted without the worklist client [2]. This opens a design space for system modellers who are now able to intentionally design the interplay of both worklist and dialogue client. Thus, this approach also requires some kind of validation if the explicitly specified part of the workflow chart is valid, which means that it must not span more than one user or contain any immediate server action that leads to more than one subsequent client page. However, various workarounds can be found. For example, if a part of a workflow chart that includes parallel flows is declared as a dialogue, the workflow system might detect the sequences of tasks without parallelism (via a static or dynamic check) and redirects to the worklist if necessary or define the order of tasks itself, whereby the second option would be less preferable from the user's perspective.

4.4.4   Formal Execution Semantics

In this section, we formalise the concept of workflow charts using ASMs. We base the specification of the operational semantics on a basic approach presented in [40]. The reason for creating such a formalisation is twofold. On the one hand, creating such a specification seems the prudent way to avoid problems (e.g. problems with OR-joins [14]) that arise due to a lack of a precise formal specification for common business process modelling languages [41], or unclarities in the semantics of those languages [30]). On the other hand, we want to be able to reason about workflow charts and, even further, provide the possibility to simulate models without needing to write a prototype in a conventional programming language.

The semantics of formcharts, the predecessor of workflow charts, have partly been specified using the semantics of UML class diagrams [26]. So it seems natural to draw from the specification of UML in ASMs, e.g. from Sarstedt and Guttmann [61] or Börger et al. [12, 13].

Another way to specify the operational semantics of workflow charts would be to use Petri nets [47], because they were also applied for specifying the formal semantics of BPMN by Dijkman et al. in [21]. The authors propose a mapping from BPMN to Petri nets that lacks features which coincide with the limitation of Petri nets, finally leading to the design of Yet Another Workflow Language (YAWL) [72]. YAWL is a workflow definition language that extends Petri nets with a number of high-level features. However, modelling with Petri nets can soon become very complex, as can be seen, e.g. in [70], where a relatively simple transaction in a travel agency's business process leads to a very complex Petri net representation. Finally, the operational semantics of workflow charts could also formally been described using Communicating Sequential Process (CSPs), which has been done for the semantics of BPMN by Wong and Gibbons in [76].

Additionally, the concept of ASMs has been successfully used to specify the semantics of BPMN as presented by Börger and Thalheim in [8, 10, 11]. Inspired by this underlying work, we already formally defined the semantics of an enhanced version of BPMN 2.0 (on which the Hagenberg Business Process Modelling (HBPM) method is based) with ASMs in [41]. In particular, we focussed on purifying the BPMN specification by investigating whether constructs of BPMN can be omitted, merged, or generalised. Now, as a further step, we specify an ASM agent that operates on a given workflow chart specification to provide a basis for supporting user interaction in business processes. For this purpose, we assume an environment in which this machine will operate. We further assume that there is a user interface component available which displays information to the user and receives input from them.

In the following, we introduce the necessary universes, rules, and proper functions (static, shared, monitored, controlled, and derived functions) for specifying the operational semantics of workflow charts using ASMs. Please refer to [41] for information on auxiliary functions and constructs used within a mathematical context that are not part of the standard ASM syntax.

The environment provides events a user can cause, i.e. those for selecting tasks from the worklist and for having completed them. We model *users* as *agents* and define the corresponding universes in an abstract, implementation-independent way. Thereby, users denote concrete individuals, whereas agents can be seen as kinds of programs that execute defined actions. We further define controlled functions for associating users with agents (i.e. one agent for workflow chart processing per user) and for storing all tasks available for user selection in the *worklist*. The tasks in the worklist are designated for a certain user (or rather agent) and represent a set of deferred server actions.

universe users, agents

controlled workflowChartAgent : users → agents

controlled user : agents → users

controlled worklist : agents → Set

The different kinds of nodes that form the tripartite graph of a workflow chart are also defined as new universes. These are (i) *clientPages* showing information for the user in terms of reports on a computer screen, (ii) *immediateServerActions* providing forms for user input, and (iii) *deferredServerActions* representing tasks in the worklists of the corresponding users. All kinds of nodes are aggregated to the abstract universe *nodes*.

universe clientPages, immediateServerActions,
    deferredServerActions

universe nodes := clientPages ∪ immediateServerActions ∪
    deferredServerActions

According to their responsibilities, nodes are defined by their *types* and proper *actions*. In addition to the new universe definitions, we define a static function *node*, which yields a unique identifier for each kind of nodes. The *type* of a node denotes relations described by n-ary tuples over attributes that assign both data type and attribute name. Thus, for a specific workflow, the type describes the actual signature of the node. For example, a node for creating a business trip application might require relations for the requested purpose, time frame, and route, whereby the latter one might be specified by the starting point, destination, and means of transport. Refining the signature based on relations involves structural aspects for grouping parameters, also indicating whether a relation may be updatable or not. In addition, order relations can be defined to affect the way parameter values are displayed. The *action* of a node is either a reporting action (client pages), an action modifying the system state (immediate server actions), or an action for unique task determination (deferred server actions). In a final system, an action refers to a piece of executable code that will be executed in the system context.

universe types, actions

static node : types × actions → nodes

Workflow charts define two types of associations, although they are displayed identically in the diagrams. Associations from deferred server actions to client pages or from immediate to deferred server actions respectively are triggered by the user, whereas associations from client pages to immediate server actions have a more structural aspect. Both types are defined by the universe *associations*. We could partition that set according to the types of their related conditions given in Sect. 4.4, but for our purpose the unpartitioned set suffices. We define a static function called *association*, where the first parameter represents the *source* of the association, the second parameter represents the *target* node, and the third parameter is a Boolean expression which guards the association from source to target. *Guards* may evaluate information available in the environment as well as the available input data and correspond to the different kinds of conditions in the workflow chart.

```
universe associations, guards

static association : nodes × nodes × guards ⇸ associations
```

For the parameters given for each kind of node and association, we specify derived functions of the form *param(id)*, which applied to the related elements yield the corresponding parameter. For example, the derived function *action* yields the action associated with the given node, *guard* yields the guard of the given association, and so on. The result of the *choose* statement is deterministic in all cases, because the given identifier is unique. (This means that a node can be unambiguously identified by its type and action, and an association is clearly defined by its source, target, and guard.)

```
derived action : nodes ⇸ actions
derived action(id) =
  return a in
    choose a in actions, t in types with node(t, a) = id

derived guard : associations ⇸ guards
derived guard(id) =
  return g in
    choose g in guards, s in nodes, t in nodes with
        association(s, t, g) = id
```

In addition, we define a controlled function *assignedUser* to store which node (i.e. which deferred server action) is associated with which user. (Since we assume a single-user role model at this point, the assigned user corresponds to the user responsible for performing the given item.)

```
controlled assignedUser : nodes ⇸ users
```

The ASM agent, which we call *WorkflowChartAgent*, operates on a workflow chart diagram from a user's perspective. The corresponding control states and basic operations of the *WorkflowChartAgent* are represented by nodes in the state machine in Fig. 4.2. The transitions between the nodes are labelled by events and, if required, by guards that together condition the firing of the (so-called triggered) transitions [9].

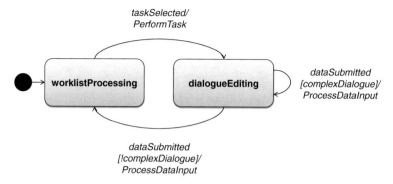

Fig. 4.2   Basic states and operations of the *WorkflowChartAgent*

By being an ASM agent, the *WorkflowChartAgent* is also associated with a special function *self*, denoting the currently active agent. (Note that multiple agents can process multiple items of the global worklist.)

The basic control states of the *WorkflowChartAgent* are (i) a state for selecting a worklist item (task) (*worklistProcessing*) and (ii) a state for editing data in a form and submitting the data (*dialogueEditing*). The agent will typically start in the *worklistProcessing* state.

universe controlStates := {" worklistProcessing ",
    " dialogueEditing "}

controlled controlState : agents → controlStates

Associated with these states are the *events* for having selected a task of the worklist and for having submitted data input. We further define a user-controlled 0-ary monitored function *event*, which is assumed to contain the actual occurrence of an event (i.e. a trigger, refer to the communication concept proposed in Chap. 5).

universe events := {"taskSelected ", " dataSubmitted "}

monitored event : → events

In addition, we define two more monitored functions which are to contain required information about the selected node and the submitted data. The function *selectedNode* provides the deferred or immediate server action respectively, which corresponds to the selection of a task from the worklist or which has been activated by providing data input in a form on a screen. Upon the submission of data by the user, the function *dataInput* will contain the associated data.

monitored selectedNode : agents → nodes

monitored dataInput : agents → Data

Now we can define the main rule of the *WorkflowChartAgent*. According to the basic state machine shown in Fig. 4.2, the rule *PerformTask* is called to execute the selected entry of the worklist in the *worklistProcessing* state, and the rule *Process-DataInput* is called for updating the system state based on the provided user input in the *dialogueEditing* state. After each step, the proper control state is switched respectively.

Referring to the described interpretation of workflow charts by the interaction of two different kinds of clients, i.e. the worklist and the dialogue client, the worklist client is responsible for state *worklistProcessing*, whereas the dialogue client is responsible for state *dialogueEditing*. However, supporting complex dialogues represents an exception to that mutual interpretation of the two clients, because the worklist processing stage can be skipped if a client page unambiguously leads to a single succeeding client page that should be handled by the same user (as described in Sect. 4.4.3).

```
rule WorkflowChartAgent
rule WorkflowChartAgent =
parblock
  if controlState(self) = " worklistProcessing " and
      event = " taskSelected " then
    parblock
      controlState(self) := " dialogueEditing "
      PerformTask(selectedNode(self))
    endparblock
  if controlState(self) = " dialogueEditing " and
      event = " dataSubmitted " then
    let isComplexDialogue =
        interpretByDialogueClient(selectedNode(self)) in
      parblock
        if isComplexDialogue then
          controlState(self) := " dialogueEditing "
        else
          controlState(self) := " worklistProcessing "
        ProcessDataInput(selectedNode(self), isComplexDialogue)
      endparblock
endparblock
```

Performing the task determined by the selected deferred server action is basically done by identifying and displaying the proper client page, which is implicitly selected with that deferred server action. The rule *PerformTask*, therefore, takes a deferred server action node as its parameter and calls the rule *ShowDialogue*. In order to wait for any effect of the executed deferred server action on task determination to be settled before a user interface is presented (e.g. multiple selection of group tasks or selection of out-of-date tasks [33]), the statements of this rule are executed in sequential order.

The *choose* statement is deterministic in this case (refer to the nature of flow conditions in Sect. 4.4.1). Note that the last two parameters in the call of *enabledNodes* refer to the universes of (all potential) source and target nodes respectively. This is admissible because a universe is a special kind of a set in ASMs (see [9]) and has the advantage of being able to provide a generic function for delivering the subsequent enabled nodes for any starting node by calling it with different parameters in

different places (see below). Furthermore, all enabling conditions for the corresponding immediate server actions must be evaluated in order to show the ambient client
page. Subsequently, the given selected deferred server action is to be removed from
the worklist of the corresponding user.

```
rule PerformTask: nodes
rule PerformTask(deferredServerAction) =
seqblock
  Action(deferredServerAction))
  let clientPage = choose clientPage ∈
        enabledNodes(deferredServerAction, deferredServerActions,
        clientPages) in
    ShowDialogue(clientPage, enabledNodes(clientPage,
        clientPages, immediateServerActions))
  remove deferredServerAction from
    worklist(workflowChartAgent(assignedUser(
    deferredServerAction)))
endseqblock
```

We do not specify the refinement of data operations for the abstract *Action* in
this place. We introduce new universes as abstract representations for data *views* and
transactions, and assume that the abstract rule *Action* executes the action on the type
of the given node. In the case of a client page, the action would refer to generating
a readable view on the basis of the node's signature describing a certain extract of
global data for the user. This would mean to include each location that defines a value
for the given parameters. In the case of an immediate server action, the action may
involve update, insert, and delete statements, yielding an updated view on the basis
of user input specified through the signature of that immediate server action. (As
deferred server actions are side effect free, they can be disregarded for addressing
global consistency in the global data model.)

```
universe views, transactions
```

```
abstract rule Action : nodes → views
```

The identification of the implicitly selected client page is done by an auxiliary
function. The derived function *enabledNodes* yields the succeeding, enabled nodes of
a given selected node in a workflow chart, i.e. all successors whose guards (enabling
conditions for client pages, activation conditions for immediate server actions, and
flow conditions for deferred server actions) evaluate to true. In the case of the client
page to be performed, the function *enabledNodes* is called with the currently selected
deferred server action, the set of all (originating) deferred server actions, and the
set of all (targeting) client pages. We can reuse the function to determine which
immediate server actions are enabled by their conditions as well (for presenting the
actual dialogue; see above) by calling it with the currently active client page and the
sets of all client pages and immediate server actions as the parameters.

```
derived enabledNodes : nodes × Set × Set → Set
derived enabledNodes(currentNode, sources, targets) =
  { target | target ∈ targets and currentNode ∈ sources and
      forsome association ∈ associations holds
```

```
source(association) = currentNode and
target(association) = target and
guard(association) }
```

The rule *ShowDialogue* is responsible for supplying the user interface displayed to the user in terms of (one-step) dialogues with the required data. Therefore, the reporting action of the given client page to be shown is used for view generation *v(_report)*. By means of form generator capabilities, which are not described in more detail here, the resulting dialogue is displayed to the user who is intended for performing the related task. The dialogue contains reporting information as well as forms providing the input fields corresponding to the data types of the enabled immediate server actions.

```
rule ShowDialogue : nodes × Set → Boolean
rule ShowDialogue(clientPage, enabledImmediateServerActions) =
  return res in
  seqblock
    let v_report = Action(clientPage) in
      res := Display(v_report)
    forall immediateServerAction ∈ enabledImmediateServerActions
        do
      res := (res and Display(type(immediateServerAction)))
  endseqblock
```

The abstract rule *Display* uses the given data views (logical relations, also in terms of node signatures) for user interface generation.

```
abstract rule Display : views → Boolean
```

In the second state of the *WorkflowChartAgent*, we need to process the data provided by the environment, or more precisely by the user. Assuming that the environment provides the selection of the node in the location *selectedNode*, which refers to an immediate server action, and the submitted data in the location *dataInput*, we capture user interaction by means of operations on data views. More precisely, by applying the action of the given immediate server action node to its signature, we receive a new (updatable) view *v_submit* (cf. ASM transducers [66]). The rule *SubmitData* evaluates this view in order to transmit any modifications, insertions, and deletions from the local dialogue perspective to the global data model.

```
rule SubmitData : nodes × transactions → Boolean
rule SubmitData(immediateServerAction, transactionId) =
  return res in
    let v_submit = Action(immediateServerAction) in
        res := Submit(v_submit, transactionId)
```

The abstract rule *Submit* is responsible for translating changes from the local to the global view, i.e. it represents a coupling mechanism for views and the physical data model. We abstract from the actual implementation and leave refinements of view composition as well as a proper transaction concept subject to a comprehensive data concept.

abstract rule Submit : views × transactions → Boolean

After data submission, the rule *ProcessDataInput* either triggers the next dialogue or the worklist to be shown to the user, depending on the existence of a complex dialogue. In the first case, we need to identify the next client page and, in the latter case, we need to know which activation conditions are enabled. We can use the function *enabledNodes* for both purposes by calling it with the parameters given below. (Note that in the case of a complex dialogue, choosing the deferred server action is unique.)

Afterwards, all resulting deferred server actions are added as tasks to the worklist of the corresponding user. (Note that we again specify a sequence for performing the data action and subsequent operations, in particular, the insertion of task items into the worklist. Thus, we guarantee that the action is completed before new items are added to the worklist. The insertion of worklist items can happen in parallel again.)

```
rule ProcessDataInput : nodes × Boolean
rule ProcessDataInput(immediateServerAction, isComplexDialogue) =
seqblock
  SubmitData(immediateServerAction)
  if isComplexDialogue then
    let deferredServerAction = choose deferredServerAction ∈
        enabledNodes(immediateServerAction,
        immediateServerActions, deferredServerActions) in
    let clientPage = choose clientPage ∈
        enabledNodes(deferredServerAction,
        deferredServerActions, clientPages) in
      ShowDialogue(clientPage, enabledNodes(clientPage,
          clientPages, immediateServerActions))
  else
  seqblock
    forall deferredServerAction ∈
        enabledNodes(immediateServerAction,
        immediateServerActions, deferredServerActions) do
      add deferredServerAction to worklist(workflowChartAgent(
          assignedUser(deferredServerAction)))
    ShowWorklist(self)
  endseqblock
endseqblock
```

In addition, we state the declaration of the abstract rule *ShowWorklist*, which lists all processes that are permitted to be launched as well as all tasks that are ready to be performed by the given user or agent respectively.

abstract rule ShowWorklist : agents → Boolean

Finally, the derived function *interpretByDialogueClient* checks if it is possible to skip the worklist processing stage, i.e. if certain conditions are met to allow a user continuing their work on multiple, subsequent client pages without being redirected to the worklist. This only applies if the given immediate server action evaluates to a unique succeeding deferred server action and if the same user is intended to perform both tasks.

```
derived interpretByDialogueClient : nodes → Boolean
derived interpretByDialogueClient(immediateServerAction) =
  | enabledNodes(immediateServerAction, immediateServerActions,
      deferredServerActions) | = 1 and
      forsome deferredServerAction in
      deferredServerActions with
      deferredServerAction ∈ enabledNodes(immediateServerAction,
      immediateServerActions, deferredServerActions) holds
        assignedUser(deferredServerAction) = user(self)
```

4.5   Assessment

The proof of concept for the approach described in Sect. 4.4 is given by surveying and realising a substantial workflow of a major Austrian social insurance company using the typed workflow chart. First, we present a prototypical implementation of the concept. The implementation uses a formal language specification to define the DSL based on workflow charts. It translates the input specification, consisting of client pages and server actions, to an intermediate system model and generates a web application, which is then used to execute the workflow and to illustrate various application scenarios in terms of screen diagrams. Alternatively, we rely on the formal execution semantics defined in Sect. 4.4.4 to be able to simulate the workflow without writing a prototype in a conventional programming language. The implementation with CoreASM [29] enables us to do that in a short and concise way. Finally, we discuss the major findings of this assessment.

4.5.1   Application Scenario: A Business Trip Workflow

An illustrative example of the workflow chart is given in Fig. 4.3. The workflow chart presents a workflow for conducting a business trip that deals with the tasks of business trip application, review, approval, support, and reporting (cf. Sects. 2.5 and 3.5). The workflow is one of the scientific outcomes of an industrial project conducted in association with the Austrian Social Insurance Company for Occupational Risks (AUVA) [24]. To cover all aspects considered in the concept, the workflow is slightly modified and extended. A detailed description of the business trip workflow and its tasks is given in [33].

Before conducting a business trip, a consultant needs to create an application that is reviewed, accepted, approved, rejected, or cancelled. For some consultants with sufficient permissions, review is not required (specified by activation conditions) and the application is directly passed to the approver. Furthermore, flow conditions determine for which consultants an application can be rejected or cancelled, and for which consultants the application cannot be dismissed but sent back to the applicant for revision. (Revision is supported by enabling conditions, representing a further

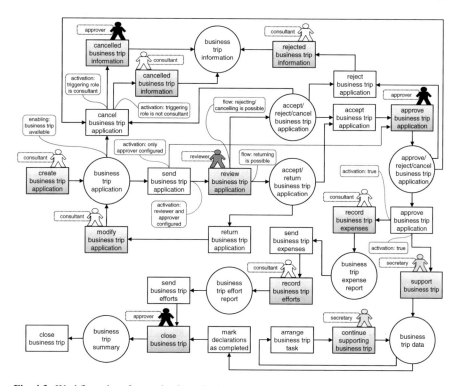

Fig. 4.3 Workflow chart for conducting a business trip

option on the business trip application page.) In the further course of the business trip workflow, if the approver authorises the application, the consultant may travel. In parallel, a secretary starts to support the business trip of the consultant with arrangements and further administrative tasks (extension to the original workflow). After having performed the business trip, the consultant needs to declare both the business trip expenses and efforts. Finally, provided that the secretary has marked the declarations as completed before, the approver is notified that the business trip can be closed.

So the workflow chart in Fig. 4.3 shows quite well the respective responsibilities, available actions, and required data.

4.5.2 Proof of Concept

To evaluate the practical application of the approach described in Sect. 4.4, we developed a prototypical implementation [33]. The implementation uses the compiler generator tool ANTLR 3 [15] to realise a formal language description called a grammar for the system specification of a process-oriented enterprise application based on workflow charts. (It is based on a basic bipartite dialogue model, which is more reductionistic but covers all important phenomena of workflow definition and dialogue programming.)

The grammar provides basic rules for recognising the system structure containing client pages and server actions. All elements can define parameters; in addition to primitive types, also list-style types as well as custom record types are supported. A further interesting feature is the possibility of choosing between various display options for parameters, such as plain text fields, checkboxes, or drop-down lists. Parallelism and role assignment are indicated by special keywords. Figure 4.4 shows an excerpt of the formal language description and the system specification of the business trip workflow.

The grammar, in a first step, constructs an intermediate-form tree data structure called an Abstract Syntax Tree (AST) for internal representation. This AST is walked in multiple ways by tree grammars to perform semantic checks and produce a translation based on embedded grammar actions. The system specification (with organisational knowledge regarding the role model) is then translated to a resulting JavaServer Faces (JSF) application.

Another basic issue of the implementation is the realisation of the worklist. The worklist also represents the entry point to the web application. At any time, it shows a start menu to activate the execution of a new business trip workflow instance and a list of pending tasks per user. The implementation also includes a value-binding mechanism to define relationships between the node signatures and their mapping to a physical data store (data views). Additionally, a default synchronisation pattern is implemented, which searches backwards in history for common sources of parallel branches in the workflow chart before showing links to subsequent client pages in a user's worklist. A dynamic algorithm for dialogue detection, which identifies regions that do not include parallelism nor user changes, is used for improvement in efficiency.

In an intermediate step, the implementation offers the opportunity to modify generated artefacts of the web application or to add supplementary code. This allows to implement any complex synchronisation pattern, to provide code for business logic or branching conditions, and to adjust the web application's look and feel. Please refer to [33] for details of the implementation.

With respect to the application scenario described in Sect. 4.5.1, the web application is used to execute the business trip workflow and to illustrate various application scenarios in terms of screen diagrams. A screen diagram [25] represents a special kind of page diagram, i.e. a very lightweight state transition diagram that supports coarse-grained state transitions in opposite to common user interface modelling. The application scenarios are designed to cover as many aspects as possible of the typed workflow chart (i.e. multiple and unique choice of attached conditions, synchronisation, and dialogue detection).

By way of example, Fig. 4.4 shows the beginning of the business trip workflow in the notation of screen diagrams based on the generated web pages of the implementation. After successful login, the worklist of the executing consultant provides a link to create a new business trip workflow in the process area. Thus, the consultant first

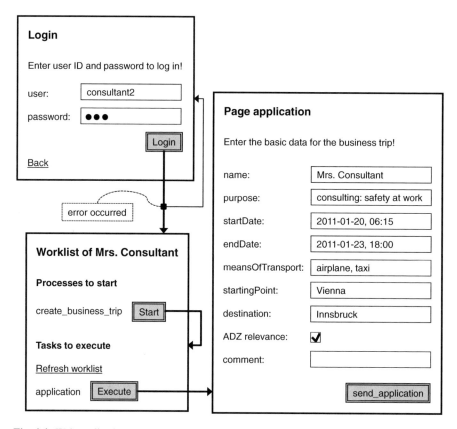

Fig. 4.4 Web application: creating a business trip application

starts a new instance of the workflow and then executes the task *application* in the worklist in order to create a business trip application. Then the consultant can enter data of the business trip application, which is intended to improve safety at work in terms of a consulting workshop, and sends the application for further processing.

We also implemented the specified semantics using CoreASM [29]. Based on the simulation capabilities of CoreASM, we are able to analyse and reason about the workflow chart specification already in early design phases, which helps in validating the resulting model. The implementation is divided into two major parts: (i) one part simulating users and user input—the *UserEmulatorAgent* (which simply makes a random selection of an element from the worklist of the active user, on the one hand, and randomly chooses an immediate server action to submit user input, on the other hand), and (ii) the other part being the workflow chart interpreter—the *WorkflowChartAgent*. Both parts are modelled as ASM agents, which are already supported by CoreASM via a plug-in.

4.5.3   Discussion

The evaluation addresses the research questions regarding relevant HCI aspects of integrating business processes and system dialogues. We now summarise and discuss the basic findings of this assessment.

A user's interaction with an enterprise application is characterised by passing inputs to the application and receiving responses from the system. The concrete workflow, i.e. which user is responsible to perform which task at which point in time to achieve a certain objective, needs to be extracted from the application in order to make processes more transparent by omitting the actual realisation. Thus, a technology- and platform-independent platform for executing business process specifications is developed. The minimal requirement for the platform is a formal description of the workflow including the client pages and server actions, assignment information, and runtime conditions. The core element is the typed workflow chart that defines an alternating sequence of actions and pages with parameters, enabling conditions, activation conditions, flow conditions, and user interaction.

The gap between components that are under the control of workflow technology and entities addressed by business process modelling is closed by applying typed workflow charts and the interplay of two clients, i.e. the dialogue and the worklist client. The interplay defines the meaning of user changes within business process specifications. The dialogue client handles the presentation of reports and transfers user input to the server, using actions. Afterwards, it passes control to the worklist client, which determines the next task(s) that will be shown in a user's worklist. Parallelism is accomplished by introducing users and roles instead of following the single-user scenario. Activation conditions give rise to parallelism, considering side effects of actions. Synchronisation is supported provided that users are not being blocked in performing their work because they always reach their worklists. Users and roles are supported by assigning them to deferred server actions and defining a user specification containing their basic properties. Worklists are handled per user and divided into a process and a task area. The forms of dialogues are considered as task items, which are updated based on the system specification each time the worklist is shown. The update strategy of the worklist is affected by the defined alternative and parallel flows as well as by the default synchronisation pattern, which checks for common sources of parallelism for deferred server actions that have more than one incoming transition before showing the worklist. A comprehensive data model keeps track of the current state of process and task instances. It also facilitates detecting and preventing simultaneous execution if a task is assigned to more than one user. Last but not least, users are supported to perform their work with the system as efficiently as possible by identifying regions of the workflow chart that are assigned to the same user and do not exhibit parallelism. Such regions can be handled exclusively by the dialogue client and, thus, the user does not need to be redirected to the worklist on every completion of a task.

4.6 Summary

While most business process modelling languages focus on the control flow of the process, such as BPMN or YAWL, there are also languages which put their emphasis on different aspects, e.g. Subject-Oriented Business Process Management (S-BPM) [31] is more focused on the subjects and their tasks. Modelling user interaction is usually not in the focus of those languages.

In this chapter, we presented *workflow charts* as a convenient way to describe business processes and a way of putting more emphasis on HCI. Workflow charts [2, 23, 33] follow a strictly dialogue-based approach to business process specification in order to improve flexibility in business process technology by proposing a concept for integrating workflow definition and application programming that is also open to business process modelling. They are specified as tripartite graphs and describe an alternative sequence of typed nodes for showing information and providing forms for user input. One of the fundamental metaphors of workflow charts is the worklist metaphor to present users with their currently enabled tasks. The worklist is the one point where users in a workflow choose the next step in a workflow to execute. Each user has their own worklist, respectively their own view of the global worklist. The simple design of workflow charts and the clear separation of content and layout by abstracting from client pages significantly enhance intelligibility, which has also become evident in several industrial projects (see, e.g. [3, 4, 28]).

Workflow charts can be used as a technology-independent, conceptual modelling language for system planning and documentation. Hence, they represent a platform-independent model and add value by grasping the essential structure of a workflow system. By elaborating a programming language for specifying dialogue constraints, side effects, and the type system, workflow charts can be exploited as a domain-specific language, i.e. a high-level programming language that overcomes the artificial separation of workflows and dialogues in modern BPM suites. An integrated development environment based on workflow charts provides a full design space for dialogues in workflow-intensive systems and may significantly improve principles of software engineering, such as reuse, maintainability, or testability.

The formalisation using ASMs contributes to a precise operational semantics for reasoning about workflow charts [40]. Considering other languages, such as BPMN, which lacks a precise formal specification [41], or UML, which has unclarities in its semantics [30], and the evidence of the problems to which that may lead, such a specification seems the prudent way to avoid those problems. Furthermore, the activity on formalising workflow charts enables us to simulate models (as it can be done with CoreASM in a short and concise way) and allows generating executable code from formal descriptions of process-oriented enterprise applications. Evaluation is shown on the basis of a substantial workflow for conducting a business trip of a social insurance company [24].

Future work will address the semantics of sub-workflows and synchronisation. As workflow charts relay the responsibility for synchronising different execution paths to the interplay of side effects and activation conditions that need to be specified by the process designer, no general synchronisation semantics is currently given in [23, 33]. In addition, the semantics of sub-workflows is currently not clearly specified and will be addressed later on.

A survey on visual programming interfaces is intended to define a proper visual front-end to the proposed specification. A convenient choice might be the adaptive modelling tool for metamodels and their instances called AMMI [27] to develop a comprehensive metamodel for workflow charts.

Finally, issues that need to be addressed upon the integration of the dialogue model with traditional activity-oriented approaches, such as BPMN, will primarily concern the interplay of the dialogue client and workflow client, as well as the associated identification of complex dialogues (dynamic detection vs. explicit specification) (see Chaps. 6 and 7).

References

1. Abrams, M., Phanouriou, C., Batongbacal, A.L., Williams, S.M., Shuster, J.E.: UIML: an appliance-independent XML user interface language. In: Proceedings of the 8th International Conference on World Wide Web, WWW'99, pp. 1695–1708. Elsevier North-Holland, Inc., New York (1999)
2. Atkinson, C., Draheim, D., Geist, V.: Typed business process specification. In: Proceedings of the 14th IEEE International Enterprise Distributed Object Computing Conference, EDOC'10, pp. 69–78. IEEE Computer Society (2010)
3. Auer, D., Geist, V., Draheim, D.: Extending BPMN with submit/response-style user interaction modeling. In: Proceedings of CEC'09, pp. 368–374. IEEE Computer Society (2009)
4. Auer, D., Geist, V., Erhart, W., Gunz, C.: An integrated framework for modeling process-oriented enterprise applications and its application to a logistics server system. In: Proceedings of the 2nd International Symposium in Logistics and Industrial Informatics, LINDI'09, pp. 166–171. eXpress Conference Publishing (2009)
5. Balzert, H., Hofmann, F., Kruschinski, V., Niemann, C.: Application development environment – generating more than the user interface. Computer-Aided Design of User Interfaces, pp. 183–206 (1996)
6. Blankenhorn, K., Jeckle, M.: A UML profile for GUI layout. In: Weske, M., Liggesmeyer, P. (eds.) Object-Oriented and Internet-Based Technologies, pp. 110–121. Springer, Berlin (2004)
7. Bodart, F., Hennebert, A., Leheureux, J., Provot, I., Sacre, B., Vanderdonckt, J.: Towards a systematic building of software architectures: the TRIDENT methodological guide. In: Designing, Specification and Verification of Interactive Systems, pp. 262–278. Springer, Vienna (1995)
8. Börger, E., Sörensen, O.: BPMN core modeling concepts: inheritance-based execution semantics. In: Embley, D.W., Thalheim, B. (eds.) Handbook of Conceptual Modeling: Theory, Practice and Research Challenges, pp. 287–335. Springer, Berlin (2011)
9. Börger, E., Stärk, R.: Abstract State Machines: A Method for High-Level System Design and Analysis. Springer, Berlin (2003)
10. Börger, E., Thalheim, B.: A method for verifiable and validatable business process modeling. In: Börger, E., Cisternino, A. (eds.) Advances in Software Engineering, vol. 5316, pp. 59–115. Springer, Berlin (2008)
11. Börger, E., Thalheim, B.: Modeling workflows, interaction patterns, web services and business processes: the ASM-based approach. In: Börger, E., Butler, M., Bowen, J., Boca, P. (eds.) Abstract State Machines, B and Z. Lecture Notes in Computer Science, vol. 5238, pp. 24–38. Springer (2008)

12. Börger, E., Cavarra, A., Riccobene, E.: Modeling the dynamics of UML state machines. In: Gurevich, Y., Kutter, P., Odersky, M., Thiele, L. (eds.) Abstract State Machines – Theory and Applications. Lecture Notes in Computer Science., vol. 1912, pp. 167–186. Springer, Berlin (2000)
13. Börger, E., Cavarra, A., Riccobene, E.: On formalizing UML state machines using ASMs. Inf. Softw. Technol. **46**(5), 287–292 (2004)
14. Börger, E., Sörensen, O., Thalheim, B.: On defining the behavior of OR-joins in business process models. J. Univers Comput. Sci. **5**(5), 30–32 (2009)
15. Bovet, J., Parr, T.: ANTLRWorks: an ANTLR grammar development environment. Softw.: Pract. Exp. **38**, 1305–1332 (2008)
16. Carey, M.J., Haas, L.M., Maganty, V., Williams, J.H.: PESTO: an integrated query/browser for object databases. In: Proceedings of the 22th International Conference on Very Large Data Bases, VLDB '96, pp. 203–214. Morgan Kaufmann Publishers Inc., San Francisco (1996)
17. Ceri, S., Fraternali, P., Paraboschi, S.: Web modeling language (WebML): a modeling language for designing web sites. In: Proceedings of the 9th International World Wide Web Conference, pp. 137–157. Elsevier (2000)
18. Chamberlin, D., Boyce, R.: SEQUEL: a structured English query language. In: FIDET '74: Proceedings of the 1974 ACM SIGFIDET (now SIGMOD) Workshop On Data Description, Access and Control, vol. 1, pp. 249–264 (1974)
19. Codd, E.: The Relational Model for Database Management: Version 2. Addison-Wesley Longman Publishing Co. Inc, Boston (1990)
20. Daniel, F., Soi, S., Tranquillini, S., Casati, F., Heng, C., Yan, L.: From people to services to UI: distributed orchestration of user interfaces. In: Proceedings of the 8th International Conference on Business Process Management, BPM'10, pp. 310–326. Springer, Berlin (2010)
21. Dijkman, R.M., Dumas, M., Ouyang, C.: Formal semantics and analysis of BPMN process models using petri nets. Technical report 7115, Queensland University of Technology, Brisbane, Australia (2007)
22. Draheim, D.: Towards seamless business process and dialogue specification. In: Proceedings of the 19th International Conference on Software Engineering & Knowledge Engineering, SEKE'07, Knowledge Systems Institute Graduate School, Boston, Massachusetts (2007)
23. Draheim, D.: Business Process Technology - A Unified View on Business Processes, Workflows and Enterprise Applications. Springer, Berlin (2010)
24. Draheim, D., Natschläger, C.: A context-oriented synchronization approach. In: Electronic Proceedings of the 2nd International Workshop in Personalized Access, Profile Management, and Context Awareness: Databases in Conjunction with the 34th VLDB Conference, PersDB'08, pp. 20–27 (2008)
25. Draheim, D., Weber, G.: Form-Oriented Analysis – A New Methodology to Model Form-Based Applications. Springer, Heidelberg (2004)
26. Draheim, D., Weber, G., Lutteroth, C.: Finite state history modeling and its precise UML-based semantics. In: Advances in Conceptual Modeling – Theory and Practice. Lecture Notes in Computer Science, vol. 4231, pp. 43–52. Springer, Berlin (2006)
27. Draheim, D., Himsl, M., Jabornig, D., Küng, J., Leithner, W., Regner, P., Wiesinger, T.: Concept and pragmatics of an intuitive visualization-oriented metamodeling tool. J. Vis. Lang. Comput. **21**, 157–170 (2010)
28. Draheim, D., Geist, V., Natschläger, C.: Integrated framework for seamless modeling of business and technical aspects in process-oriented enterprise applications. Int. J. Softw. Eng. Knowl. Eng. **22**(5), 645–674 (2012)
29. Farahbod, R., Gervasi, V., Glässer, U.: CoreASM: an extensible ASM execution engine. Fundamenta Informaticae **77**(1), 71–103 (2007)
30. Fecher, H., Schönborn, J., Kyas, M., de Roever, W.P.: 29 new unclarities in the semantics of UML 2.0 state machines. In: Proceedings of the 7th International Conference on Formal Methods and Software Engineering, ICFEM'05, pp. 52–65. Springer, Berlin (2005)
31. Fleischmann, A., Schmidt, W., Stary, C., Obermeier, S., Börger, E.: Subject-Oriented Business Process Management. Springer, Berlin (2012)

32. Garzotto, F., Paolini, P., Schwabe, D.: HDM - a model-based approach to hypertext application design. ACM Trans. Inf. Syst. **11**, 1–26 (1993)
33. Geist, V.: Integrated Executable Business Process and Dialogue Specification. Dissertation, Johannes Kepler University, Linz (2011)
34. Guerrero, J., Vanderdonckt, J., Gonzalez, J.M., Winckler, M.: Modeling user interfaces to workflow information systems. In: Proceedings of the 4th International Conference on Autonomic and Autonomous Systems, pp. 55–60. IEEE Computer Society, Washington (2008)
35. Hollingsworth, D., et al.: The workflow reference model: 10 years on. In: Fujitsu Services, UK; Technical Committee Chair of WfMC (2004)
36. International Organization for Standardization: International standard ISO 9241-10. Ergonomic requirements for office work with visual display terminals (VDTs) – part 10: dialogue principles (1991). ISO
37. Isakowitz, T., Stohr, E.A., Balasubramanian, P.: RMM: a methodology for structured hypermedia design. Commun. ACM **38**, 34–44 (1995)
38. Jacobson, I., Booch, G., Rumbaugh, J.: The Unified Software Development Process. Addison Wesley, Reading (1999)
39. Johnson, P.: Human computer interaction: psychology, task analysis and software engineering. McGraw-Hill, Maidenhead (1992)
40. Kopetzky, T., Geist, V.: Workflow charts and their precise semantics using abstract state machines. In: EMISA. Lecture Notes in Informatics, pp. 11–24. Gesellschaft für Informatik e.V. (2012)
41. Kossak, F., Illibauer, C., Geist, V., Kubovy, J., Natschläger, C., Ziebermayr, T., Kopetzky, T., Freudenthaler, B., Schewe, K.D.: A Rigorous Semantics for BPMN 2.0 Process Diagrams. Springer (2015)
42. Kovacevic, S.: UML and user interface modeling. In: Selected Papers from the 1st International Workshop on The Unified Modeling Language: Beyond the Notation, UML'98, pp. 253–266. Springer, London (1999)
43. Luyten, K., Clerckx, T., Coninx, K., Vanderdonckt, J.: Derivation of a dialog model from a task model by activity chain extraction. In: Proceedings of DSV-IS'03. Lecture Notes in Computer Science, vol. 2844, pp. 191–205. Springer (2003)
44. Markopoulos, P., Pycock, J., Wilson, S., Johnson, P.: Adept – a task based design environment. In: Proceedings of the 25th Hawaii International Conference on System Sciences, pp. 587–596. IEEE Computer Society Press (1992)
45. McJones, P.: The 1995 SQL reunion: people, projects and politics (1997), sRC Technical Note 1997-018, Digital Systems Research Center
46. Molina, P., Trætteberg, H.: Analysis and design of model based user interfaces – an approach to refining specifications towards implementation. In: Proceedings of the 5th International Conference on Computer-Aided Design of User Interfaces, CADUI'04 (2004)
47. Murata, T.: Petri nets: properties, analysis and applications. Proc. IEEE **77**(4), 541–580 (1989)
48. Navarre, D., Palanque, P., Paterno, F., Santoro, C., Bastide, R.: A tool suite for integrating task and system models through scenarios. In: Proceedings of DSV-IS'01. Lecture Notes in Computer Science, vol. 2220. Springer, Berlin (2001)
49. Nguyen, T., Srinivasan, V.: Accessing relational databases from the World Wide Web. In: Proceedings of the 1996 ACM SIGMOD International Conference on Management of Data, SIGMOD'96, pp. 529–540. ACM, New York (1996)
50. Object Management Group: Business Process Model and Notation (BPMN) 2.0. http://www.omg.org/spec/BPMN/2.0. Accessed 06 Oct 2015 (2011)
51. Object Management Group: OMG Unified Modeling Language (OMG UML), version 2.5. http://www.omg.org/spec/UML/2.5. Accessed 06 Oct 2015 (2015)
52. Papiani, M., Dunlop, A., Hey, J.: Automatically generating World-Wide Web interfaces to relational databases (1997), British Computer Society Seminar Series on New Directions in Systems Development: Intranets The Corporate Superhighway, University of Wolverhampton
53. Parnas, D.L.: Software aspects of strategic defense systems. Commun. ACM **28**, 1326–1335 (1985)

54. Paterno, F., Mancini, C., Meniconi, S.: ConcurTaskTrees: a diagrammatic notation for specifying task models. In: Proceedings of Interact'97, pp. 362–369. Chapman & Hall, Sydney (1997)
55. Pinheiro da Silva, P., Paton, N.: UMLi: the unified modeling language for interactive applications. In: Proceedings of the UML'00, York. Lecture Notes in Computer Science, vol. 1939, pp. 117–132. Springer (2000)
56. Pinheiro da Silva, P., Paton, N.: User interface modelling with UML. In: Proceedings of the 10th European-Japanese Conference on Information Modelling and Knowledge Bases (2000)
57. Reichart, D., Forbrig, P., Dittmar, A.: Task models as basis for requirements engineering and software execution. In: Proceedings of the 3rd Annual Conference on Task Models and Diagrams, TAMODIA'04, pp. 51–58. ACM, New York (2004)
58. Rossi, G., Schwabe, D., Lyardet, F.: Web application models are more than conceptual models. In: Proceedings of the Workshops on Evolution and Change in Data Management, Reverse Engineering in Information Systems, and the World Wide Web and Conceptual Modeling, ER'99, pp. 239–253. Springer, London (1999)
59. Russell, N., ter Hofstede, A., Edmond, D., van der Aalst, W.: Workflow Resource Patterns. BETA Working Paper Series WP 127, Eindhoven University of Technology, Eindhoven (2004)
60. Russell, N., ter Hofstede, A., van der Aalst, W., Mulyar, N.: Workflow Control-Flow Patterns: A Revised View. Technical report, BPMcenter.org (2006)
61. Sarstedt, S., Guttmann, W.: An ASM semantics of token flow in UML 2 activity diagrams. In: Proceedings of the 6th International Andrei Ershov Memorial Conference on Perspectives of Systems Informatics, pp. 349–362. Springer, Novosibirsk (2007)
62. Schewe, K.D.: Horizontal and vertical business process model integration. In: Decker, H., Lenka, L., Link, S., Basl, J., Tjoa, A. (eds.) Database and Expert Systems Applications. Lecture Notes in Computer Science, vol. 8055, pp. 1–3. Springer, Berlin (2013)
63. Schewe, K.D., Schewe, B.: View-centered conceptual modelling – an object-oriented approach. In: Proceedings of the 15th International Conference on Conceptual Modeling ER'96, pp. 357–371. Springer, London (1996)
64. Schewe, K.D., Schewe, B.: Integrating database and dialogue design. Knowl. Inf. Syst. 2, 1–32 (2000)
65. Schreiber, S.: The BOSS system: coupling visual programming with model based interface design. In: Proceedings of DSV-IS'94, Focus on Computer Graphics, pp. 161–179. Springer (1995)
66. Spielmann, M.: Verification of relational transducers for electronic commerce. J. Comput. Syst. Sci. 66(1), 40–65 (2003)
67. Stegmaier, B., Ebbers, M., Begovac, T.: Image and workflow library: flowmark v2.3 design guidelines. Technical report, IBM International Technical Support Organization (1998)
68. Szekely, P.: Retrospective and challenges for model-bases interface development. Computer-Aided Design of User Interfaces, pp. xxi–xliv (1996)
69. Szekely, P., Sukaviriya, P., Castells, P., Muthukumarasamy, J., Salcher, E.: Declarative interface models for user interface construction tools: the MASTERMIND approach. Engineering for Human-Computer Interaction, pp. 120–150 (1996)
70. Takemura, T.: Formal semantics and verification of BPMN transaction and compensation. In: Proceedings of the 2008 IEEE Asia-Pacific Services Computing Conference, APSCC'08, pp. 284–290. IEEE Computer Society, Washington, DC (2008)
71. Trætteberg, H., Krogstie, J.: Enhancing the usability of BPM-solutions by combining process and user-interface modelling. In: Stirna, J., Persson, A. (eds.) The Practice of Enterprise Modeling. Lecture Notes in Business Information Processing, vol. 15, pp. 86–97. Springer, Berlin (2008)
72. van der Aalst, W.M.P., ter Hofstede, A.H.M.: YAWL: yet another workflow language. Inf. Syst. 30, 245–275 (2005)
73. van der Aalst, W., Barros, A., ter Hofstede, A., Kiepuszewski, B.: Advanced workflow patterns. In: Proceedings of the 7th International Conference on Cooperative Information Systems CoopIS'00. Lecture Notes in Computer Science, vol. 1901. Springer (2000)

74. van Deursen, A., Klint, P., Visser, J.: Domain-specific languages: an annotated bibliography. ACM Sigplan Not. **35**, 26–36 (2000)
75. Wilson, S., Johnson, P.: Bridging the generation gap: From work tasks to user interface designs. Computer-Aided Design of User Interfaces, pp. 77–94 (1996)
76. Wong, P.Y., Gibbons, J.: A process semantics for BPMN. In: Liu, S., Maibaum, T., Araki, K. (eds.) Formal Methods and Software Engineering. Lecture Notes in Computer Science, vol. 5256, pp. 355–374. Springer, Berlin (2008)

Chapter 5
An Enhanced Communication Concept

In this chapter, we propose a generalisation of the event concept of the Business Process Model and Notation (BPMN) [20] which can, amongst others, increase flexibility for users in matters of communication. Parts of this chapter have previously been published in [11] (reuse with kind permission of the Gesellschaft für Informatik).

In business process management, communication via events serves different purposes:

- A new process instance can be started by the environment;
- A process may notify its environment of the termination of an instance, as in "I have finished, now you can continue with my results";
- The default workflow can be changed, as in the case of an error or in the case of changed circumstances which require abortion and maybe compensation (undoing preliminary results) of a process instance;
- Synchronisation between different processes, or between a process and its environment, requires communication, for which events are well suited; and
- Data can be exchanged via events (in particular via *messages*), for instance if no common database access is available; the exchange of data may also be combined with one of the other purposes, e.g. a new process instance may be initialised with certain data or a process instance may have to wait for data (a message) at some synchronisation point.

BPMN offers a predefined set of named event types, or *trigger types* (as called in [13]), including "Message", "Signal", "Error", "Cancel", "Terminate", "Compensation", "Escalation", "Conditional", "Timer", and "Link". Thereby "Conditional" and "Timer" differ from the other types in which such events are not thrown by some event node or by the environment but are triggered automatically when a condition—in the case of "Timer", a certain time of the clock—becomes true; as the BPMN standard calls it, "Conditional" and "Timer" event triggers are only "implicitly thrown" [20, p. 234].

© Springer International Publishing Switzerland 2016
F. Kossak et al., *Hagenberg Business Process Modelling Method*,
DOI 10.1007/978-3-319-30496-0_5

A "Link" event is atypical in that it does not serve any of the communication purposes stated above but only allows for a graphical "gap" within the workflow for reasons of geometry or overview; the intended behaviour is that the workflow ending at the throwing "Link" event node is simply continued at the corresponding catching event node as if there had been a sequence flow in between. As this does not actually serve a communication need in a closer sense, we will largely ignore link events in this place.

In the following, we will speak of a *trigger* to refer to an object representing an occurrence at a particular time which usually would, in common parlance, be called an "event". The reason is that in BPMN, the word "event" usually (though not always) refers to an *event node*, that is, a flow node which either throws or catches such a trigger. We will usually write *event node* instead of "event" to avoid ambiguity. The word "trigger" is also used in BPMN to refer to such a "runtime event object", but only when such an object is caught; when thrown, such an object is called a "result" in the BPMN standard (see e.g. [20, p. 233]). Note that the word "trigger" is often also used in the BPMN standard to denote the type of an event, which we explicitly call a *trigger type* (such as "Message" or "Signal", see above). In order to have a single name for a single type of object, we will use "trigger", and only "trigger", to denote a runtime event object. With these deviations from BPMN notation, we intend to avoid ambiguity. To summarise our notation:

> An *event node* either throws or catches *triggers* at certain points in time. Every trigger is of one particular *trigger type*, and an event node can throw or catch triggers of one or several different trigger types, which are defined in its *event definitions*.

The specific event trigger types named above can be distinguished by different purposes, as the names suggest. However, more generally, most of them can also be distinguished by different properties, mostly properties concerning the distribution of triggers, answering questions like the following:

- Is the trigger intended for a particular process or may it be interesting for different processes (like a fire alert is relevant for employees of different companies in a single office building)?
- Is the trigger intended for a particular process *instance*, e.g. for a particular business case (concerning a particular order number), or may it be caught by any instance of the process in question (like a call to a help desk may be answered by *any* employee concerned with that help desk)?
- If there is no particular recipient (no particular process instance) addressed, is it sufficient that *just one* process and process instance deals with the trigger or should more or even all of the potential recipients deal with it (as in the case of a fire alert)?
- Is it obligatory that someone deals with the trigger (as in the case of a help desk call), or is it optional (as in "There is a special offer today in the canteen")?
- Can the trigger only be caught instantly, or is it valid for some time (or even indefinitely)?

(In these considerations, we were considerably aided by the work of Lachlan Aldred, see [1].)

When we define respective properties for triggers, we can use them to identify a signal as a trigger which should be broadcast to all processes (of a given set) and to all process instances and which should be sustained even when some actor has already reacted to it.

However, all the possible combinations of possible values for different properties (reduced by possible constraints) offer more scope for communication than the above-mentioned set of named BPMN event trigger types would allow, and it might make sense to offer all these possibilities to the designers and actors of business processes. The *triggerType* with the predefined set can still be used, first of all to provide for additional distinctions (as we will see later, e.g. "Error" triggers are not distinguishable from "Signal" triggers by the proposed new properties alone), but also for the sake of simplicity.

The proposed trigger properties define, most importantly, how a trigger shall be forwarded or distributed. But we may also give users (actors) some scope for deciding which events (which triggers) they are interested in and in what order they want to react to different triggers.

There are certainly triggers which *have* to be delivered to a particular recipient, like a mail service has an obligation to deliver a letter at a given address. But people may opt out of receiving certain kinds of messages (like spam mail), and at the same time, they may opt-in to get certain notifications in which they are particularly interested in, as this is possible through RSS feeds.

Furthermore, actors may get many messages or other triggers at once, or faster than they can react to them. They may also get messages "in absence" (when they are not active). Some triggers may be more important than others, but this is not necessarily for the senders to decide and should, in most cases, be left to the recipient to decide.

A number of different *event pools* can make both kinds of user choice possible: a user can subscribe to pools of choice, and a user can pick triggers out of pools in any chosen order. We thereby use a pool concept influenced by that proposed for S-BPM (see [7, esp. Sects. 5.5.3 and 5.5.4]), as S-BPM lays a special focus on the viewpoint of actors (or "subjects"). At the same time, event pools can also facilitate different types of trigger delivery.

In summary, on the following pages, we propose

- To generalise event trigger types by a combination of different *properties* of event triggers (see Sect. 5.4) and
- To use different types of *event pools* to increase flexibility in the distribution and selection of event triggers (in Sect. 5.5).

In the rest of this chapter, after a motivation for our approach in Sect. 5.1, we give an overview of related work in Sect. 5.2. In Sect. 5.3, we present some preliminaries. Subsequently, we specify a generalisation of event trigger types by a combination of different properties of event triggers in Sect. 5.4. Then in Sect. 5.5, we specify different types of event pools which enable increased flexibility in the distribution and selection of event triggers. Next we discuss the scope of communication which these concepts enable (Sect. 5.6) and show how the named trigger types of BPMN can be related to those concepts (Sect. 5.7). Furthermore, we consider changes to the ASM ground model proposed in [13] required for the enhanced communication concept, which is summarised in the chapter on eP^2 in Sect. 7.5.3. Finally, we summarise the results of this chapter in Sect. 5.8.

5.1   Motivation

In case business processes are modelled individually, simple communication patterns usually suffice for communication within a process and with a conceptually modelled environment. Nevertheless, frequently we also have to model interactions between different processes, mostly even between very heterogeneous systems. Because of growing requirements for integrating different processes in several organisations, simple communication patterns like "Messages" or "Signals" are usually not satisfactory.

Furthermore, following the goals of the European "Industry 4.0" initiative, which was initialised by the German government [3], will require modelling of heterogeneous processes transcending individual organisations, and thus more complex communication patterns. "Industry 4.0" intends to apply new trends from information and communication technology to production systems in order to secure Europe's position as an attractive location for industry in the age of globalisation and to establish Europe as a global technological leader. The specific goal of the "Industry 4.0" initiative is to create intelligent machines, logistic systems, and equipment which independently communicate with each other—mostly via the Internet—and that are further able to trigger suitable events, and are even capable of mutually controlling each other [10] These networked and communicating systems, which can be arbitrarily complex, are called CPS, and when they are used in production, CPPS [18], respectively.

An extension of those production systems to so-called "Smart Factories" is further intended by including even the supply chain (sourcing and delivery), which additionally widens the range of communication to external partners. Within "Industry 4.0", further domain-specific keywords like "Smart Product", "Smart Grid", "Smart Buildings", "Smart Logistics", and "Smart Mobility" all entail communication needs between IT and software technologies with electronic parts [10].

The advantage of simple communication patterns, as those provided by the BPMN 2.0 standard [20], is that they are relatively simple and easy to depict in diagrams, as they use quite intuitive symbols. However, for a fully integrated method like the H-BPM method, which includes automated processes, human actors (see Chap. 3), and user interactions (see Chap. 4), it requires more flexibility and customisation, particularly with respect to communication. Moreover, those simple communication patterns are no longer satisfying today's and especially future requirements of communication and hardly meet the needs of the "Industry 4.0" initiative.

We claim that our communication concept—proposed in this chapter—provides a considerably greater scope for serving all these purposes than currently available concepts, which we review in Sect. 5.2. This review shows that a general concept for addressing various ways of communication in BPM, which at the same time is concrete enough for being integrated directly in tools, is obviously missing.

5.2 Related Work

BPMN provides "different strategies to forward a *trigger* to catching **Events**: publication, direct resolution, propagation, *cancellations*, and *compensations*" [20, p. 234] and uses correlation to address a certain process instance. The relation of our work to BPMN is detailed in Sects. 5.6 and 5.7.

The event pools of S-BPM [7] are customised for actor convenience. However, they are not embedded in a wider delivery concept. Furthermore, S-BPM allows some additional configuration for input pools, whose most important application seems to be an enforcement of synchronous communication. Nevertheless, the pools of S-BPM have inspired our communication concept (cf. Sect. 5.6).

Aldred suggests "process integration patterns" [1], in the context of YAWL, which have substantially influenced our concept, as described in Sect. 5.6. However, some "dimensions" of Aldred's communication refer more to process design than to communication issues. Aldred does not translate the proposed patterns into formal mechanisms.

The workflow patterns of van der Aalst et al. [21]—a basis of YAWL—consider various perspectives which are relevant for event handling. In the view of the control-flow patterns, events are especially involved in *deferred choice*, *implicit termination*, and in some *cancellation* patterns. Furthermore, two patterns explicitly describe the conception of *triggers*. Triggering work execution and external data interaction patterns are only partly supported.

Mendling et al. [17] define an extension to EPC to improve the support for workflow patterns by adopting the concept of YAWL. For supporting *cancellation* patterns, they introduce cancellation areas. However, the core area of EPC is semi-formal process documentation rather than formal process specification.

WS-BPEL [19] supports propagation, correlation as well as the definition of timeouts (by *message* and *alarm* events). Nonetheless, deficiencies exist in event consumption as well as in the generality of specifying event handlers.

Etzion and Niblett present common event-driven patterns in [5]. The authors look at BPM as a technology related to event processing and show current trends (e.g. asynchronous BPM and event-driven architecture) as well as future directions. They propose basic and dimensional patterns including common temporal patterns. Further parallels to our approach regarding pattern policies exist (e.g. consumption or cardinality policies).

A framework for generic event and error handling in business processes is proposed by Lucchi and Mazzara [15]. They reduce the amount of different methods for event, exception, and compensation handling in WS-BPEL to a single mechanism, which is based on the concept of event notification. The resulting specification helps to simplify BPEL models and implementations in the realm of Web service orchestration.

Weske proposes a set of service interaction patterns in [23]. These patterns primarily apply to the service composition layer. Nevertheless, the classification according to the number of involved participants is a subject common to our communication concept.

Ferreira et al. [6] introduce the WED-flow approach, which proposes data states for integrating event processing into workflow management systems. Information which is required for event handling is stored in these data states, whereby forward and backward recovery options are increased as well. The WED-flow approach does not define control flow but triggers over attribute values (wed-states), and hence handles the flow as a consequence of satisfied conditions.

So-called *process events* are proposed by Herzberg et al. [9]. These process events enrich events—occurring during process execution—with context data, with intent to create events that are correlated to the proper process descriptions. Correlation is the main issue of their processing platform. However, they focus on business process monitoring and analysis rather than modelling.

The Complex Event Processing (CEP) discipline [16] is an emerging technology and deals with event-driven behaviour. Its combination with BPM is an important issue [2] and applied to *Event-Driven Business Process Management* [22] to detect and react to possible errors in processes. It is further used in business process exception management [14] as well as to support dynamic business process adaptation [8].

The communication concept of BPMN is not always sufficient, yet we use it as a starting point for our concept as it is an international standard, well known, and supported by many tools. S-BPM defines event pools, which have inspired our concept, but focuses more on the viewpoint of actors. Also the patterns of Aldred have influenced our concept, but these patterns lack a formal basis. Events are involved in some of the workflow patterns, of which two describe the concept of *triggers*. WS-BPEL supports propagation and correlation as we do, but event consumption is only partly dealt with. Similar to our approach, Etzion and Niblett propose common temporal patterns and use policies. Lucchi and Mazzara simplify BPEL models in the realm of Web service orchestration in a way similar to our improvements in BPM. Weske classifies the number of involved participants, which is common to our communication concept. The WED-flow approach handles control flow as a consequence of satisfied conditions, which is completely different to our approach. Contrary to our communication concept, the CEP discipline deals with event-driven behaviour.

5.3   Preliminaries

The following concepts build on the ASM ground model for a semantics of (a modified version of) BPMN 2.0 introduced in [13, Chap. 4], on which H-BPM is based. (An uncommented summary of the ground model is available at [12].) We briefly recapture the most important bits from the ground model which are relevant here (from Sect. 4.7 on *Events* of the quoted book).

In the ground model, there are **universes** (basic data types) for, amongst others:

- *triggers* and
- *eventTriggerTypes*.

Triggers are thrown and caught by event nodes. The respective rule for throwing and the derived function for catching are left abstract in the ground model.

The abstract rule *ThrowEvent* creates a new trigger. The first parameter identifies the trigger type, the second parameter the target node, the third parameter the process instance which *triggers* the event (in whose course the trigger is created), and the fourth parameter the event node which throws the event trigger. We state the signature with the universes of the parameters:

```
abstract rule ThrowEvent : eventTriggerTypes ×
    flowNodes × instances × flowNodes
```

The shared function *availableTriggers* stores, for a given event node, all the relevant event triggers which are currently available.

```
shared availableTriggers : flowNodes → Set
```

Note that the derived function *givenTriggerOccurred*, which was also used in [13] and left abstract there, can be easily specified by means of *availableTriggers*, which has subsequently been done in [12].

In the following, we will refine the original ground model by, amongst others, specifying the rule *ThrowEvent* and transforming the shared function *availableTriggers* into a derived function.

Caught triggers may or may not have to be removed. This is done in the rule *RemoveTrigger*, which is employed in the *EventOperation* of the rule *CatchEvent-Transition*. In [13], this rule was left abstract, but we will specify it as well in this chapter.

```
abstract rule RemoveTrigger : triggers
```

5.4 Properties of Event Triggers

We now consider different properties to characterise different types of event triggers.

We need to consider a system in which several communicating processes are running concurrently. For instance, according to the BPMN standard, messages are exchanged between different processes, or potentially between the environment and a process, but never within a single process [20, p. 234].

Consequently, we need to identify, for a given trigger, one or more processes which shall receive it. For messages (with one recipient), the receiving process may be identified via a message flow (in a diagram represented by a broken line between two event nodes of different processes), but for a generalised model, we cannot rely on the existence of such a flow object. (However, when such a message flow exists, we need to assure consistency!) We thus introduce the property *recipientProcesses* as a shared function which identifies a set of recipients (processes) of a trigger.

```
shared  recipientProcesses  :  triggers  →  Set
```

This function is **shared** (i.e. both the process in question and the environment can change its value) because both a process and its environment have to be able to set this property for triggers which they, respectively, create, as well as to read the value of this property of a trigger which they receive. Note that the universe *processes* overlaps with the universe *flowNodes* as both contain sub-processes; we treat sub-processes like top-level processes wherever possible, as we did in [13] (see the respective discussion there, in particular in Sect. 4.1).

If no recipient process is identified (i.e. *recipientProcesses* is either **undef** or empty), all processes running on the workflow engine (or visible to the workflow engine) shall receive the trigger, except if a particular public event pool is specified (see below).

Next, we may want to identify a particular event node of the target process. For instance, there may be alternative start nodes and the environment may want to determine where exactly the process shall start. Again, in the case of messages, the recipient node *may* be identified by a message flow, but if the sender of the message is not visible (not within the scope of the diagram), such a message flow will be absent, and more generally, we cannot rely on the presence of such a connecting object. We therefore define the property *recipientNode*. Again, the value may be **undef**, in which case any suitable event node within a targeted process may catch the trigger (if no further constraints apply).

```
shared  recipientNode  :  triggers  →  flowNodes
```

Of course, there is a dependency between *recipientNode* and *recipientProcesses*. If no particular process is identified, or more than one process identified, then it is not possible to identify a particular node, which we formalise by an assertion:

```
assert
   forall trigger ∈ triggers holds
      if recipientProcesses(trigger) = undef or
         |recipientProcesses(trigger)| ≠ 1 then
      recipientNode(trigger) = undef
```

(Above, the vertical bars denote the cardinality of the enclosed set.)

If a *recipientNode* is defined, then the only member of *recipientProcesses* (see above) must be the parent of the *recipientNode* (note that *parentNode* is also defined if the parent is a top-level process). Thereby we also make sure that only event nodes that are direct children of a given process can be addressed; this means that event nodes within sub-processes can only be addressed (from outside) indirectly, via the mechanism of propagation (see below).

```
assert
  forall trigger ∈ triggers holds
      if recipientNode(trigger) ≠ undef then
        forall process in recipientProcesses(trigger)
          holds
            process =
                parentNode(recipientNode(trigger))
```

Note that in combination with the previous assertion, we can derive that when a recipient node is defined, then *recipientProcesses* must be defined and the cardinality of *recipientProcesses* must be 1 (just apply modus tollens and de Morgan to the previous assertion); thus **forall**, above, actually ranges over a single process.

If a recipient process but no particular recipient node is specified, we may still want to specify whether some event node directly within the recipient process shall react to the trigger or whether the trigger may be *propagated* into sub-processes of the recipient process (recursively, i.e. potentially also into sub-processes of those sub-processes, etc.). This corresponds to the distinction between the two concepts of *direct resolution* and *propagation* in BPMN (see [20, p. 234f]).

```
shared mayBePropagated : triggers → Boolean
```

If a *recipientNode* is specified, then propagation is obviously not desired; we lay this down as an assertion:

```
assert
  forall trigger ∈ triggers holds
    if recipientNode(trigger) ≠ undef then
      mayBePropagated(trigger) = false
```

Next, we consider process *instances*, which are of particular interest for messages (though not necessarily *only* for messages). For instance, when a customer has placed an order and subsequently asks when they can expect delivery, then this request must be linked with the process instance associated with the respective order number. The association with the correct process instance can work like this: In response to a new order, a new process instance of the respective business process is created, together with a unique order number which is firmly linked with the new process instance. The customer receives an order confirmation which contains the order number. When the customer sends a request message by replying to the order confirmation, or if the customer manually includes the order number in a request, this order number can be used to identify the respective process instance.

An order number is an example of *correlation information*. In general, correlation information can be any piece of information through which a particular process instance can be identified. In BPMN, correlation is not only used to associate a message with a particular instance, but also to link several start event nodes with each other such that several triggers with the same correlation information will trigger only a single new process instance ("**Start Events** that share the same correlation information", see e.g. [20, p. 426] and [13, Sect. 4.7.4]). To make correlation between an event trigger and a process instance possible, the same *correlationInfo* must be shared by a respective property of both trigger and instance. As we do not want to restrict the possible form of correlation information, we define an own universe whose implementation is left open, be it a string or whatever. Note that we leave it open whether correlation information should be a unique identifier for a particular instance, as this is not necessary for our concept. (The term "correlation information" is also used in BPMN. Also compare with the *correlation sets* of WS-BPEL [19, Sect. 9], which can be arbitrarily complex.)

universe correlationInfo

shared correlationInfo : triggers → correlationInfo

controlled correlationInfo : instances →
    correlationInfo

Note that the identifier *correlationInfo* is overloaded: it denotes a universe as well as two different functions; however, from the presence or absence and the type of the parameter (and usually also from the context), it is always well defined which is spoken of in a particular place. As process instances are internal to the process engine, the *correlationInfo* of an instance is **controlled**, that is, it can only be modified by the process engine.

The universe *correlationInfo* as well as the respective functions for triggers and instances have already been defined in [13], where also the correlation information of a trigger which starts a new process instance is already passed to that instance to enable correlation with following triggers.

In the next section, we will introduce *event pools*, and some of these event pools may be directly addressed by a trigger. To this end, we introduce the property *recipientPool*, for which we will need yet another universe for *eventPools*.

universe eventPools

shared recipientPool : triggers → eventPools

The property *recipientPool* is chiefly interesting for what we will call *public event pools*. In other cases, however, it may be that other properties already determine a particular event pool associated with a particular process, in which case we have to guarantee consistency. In such a case, either *recipientPool* shall be **undef** or identify the correct pool; see the next section for details.

Another important property of a trigger shall indicate whether it suffices that one actor reacts to it or not. This can also be expressed by the following question: Shall the trigger be deleted once it has been caught by some event node or shall it be sustained so that other event nodes can catch it as well?

shared deleteUponCatch : triggers → Boolean

Next we want to specify whether a trigger is supposed to be caught instantaneously or whether, alternatively, it shall be sustained for some time, and in the latter case, for how long. To this end, we specify a *timeout*. There are at least three possible ways to define a timeout:

- in terms of an absolute point in time, as in "there will not be any Internet connection until 1 February, 2015, 15:00"; or

- in terms of a time span from the creation of the trigger, as in "the examinees shall have 15 min to answer the questions"; or
- in terms of a particular hour and/or day of the week and/or week, etc. after the creation of the trigger, as in "requests for change may be entered until *the following Friday by 14:00*" (i.e. the Friday after the respective notification was sent).

More exotic variants are imaginable, but those at least should be supported, which will require the following properties:

- The first variant requires a simple time property, which we will call *timeout*.
- The second variant requires a duration, which we will call *lifetime*, in combination with a *timestamp* of the time of creation of the trigger.
- The third variant also requires a *timestamp*, but additionally we have to be able to define a (semi-)relative time potentially containing a time of the day, day of the week, day of the month (as in "the 5th of the following month"), month (as in "November of the same year"), terms for "this day/week/month/year" and "following day/week/month/year", and possibly more. We abstract from a possible, concrete specification of such a relative time by means of a new, general universe which we call *RelativeTime*. We call the respective trigger property *relativeTimeout*.

Consequently, we define the following, additional properties for event triggers:

```
shared timestamp : triggers → Time

shared timeout : triggers → Time

shared lifetime : triggers → Time

shared relativeTimeout : triggers → RelativeTime
```

In the case of the *lifetime*, the given time will be simply added to the *timestamp*, which is obligatory if a *lifetime* is defined. A *timestamp* is also obligatory when a *relativeTimeout* is defined. Furthermore, at most one of the functions *timeout*, *lifetime*, and *relativeTimeout* may be defined for a particular trigger:

```
assert
  forall trigger ∈ triggers holds
    if lifetime(trigger) ≠ undef or
        relativeTimeout(trigger) ≠ undef then
      timestamp(trigger) ≠ undef

assert
  forall trigger ∈ triggers holds
    (timeout(trigger) = undef and
        lifetime(trigger) = undef) or
    (timeout(trigger) = undef and
        relativeTimeout(trigger) = undef) or
    (lifetime(trigger) = undef and
        relativeTimeout(trigger) = undef)
```

If neither *timeout* nor *lifetime* nor *relativeTimeout* are defined, then either the process engine has defined a default lifetime which will come into effect or the trigger *does not expire* as long as a potential recipient process is running.

If the *lifetime* is set to a value corresponding to zero (e.g. 0 seconds), then we assume that the trigger will expire *after the next step of the ASM*, corresponding to the time required by the process engine such that it is possible for a relevant catching event node to catch the trigger in question; that is, we assume that throwing and catching of a particular trigger *cannot* happen within a single step.

Finally, in many cases, the process that sent a given trigger is of interest. For instance, we would like to know which process sent an "Error" or "Escalation" trigger. (Note that a sender instance can be derived from the sender process in combination with *correlationInfo*.) Even the throwing flow node may be of interest, and as the process can be derived from that (as *parentNode(flowNode)*), we define the *senderNode* as a trigger property.

shared senderNode : triggers $\rightarrow$ flowNodes

We summarise the properties of triggers by which different trigger types can be distinguished:

shared recipientProcesses : triggers $\rightarrow$ Set

shared recipientNode : triggers $\rightarrow$ flowNodes

shared mayBePropagated : triggers $\rightarrow$ Boolean

shared correlationInfo : triggers $\rightarrow$ correlationInfo

shared recipientPool : triggers $\rightarrow$ eventPools

shared deleteUponCatch : triggers $\rightarrow$ Boolean

shared timestamp : triggers $\rightarrow$ Time

shared timeout : triggers $\rightarrow$ Time

shared lifetime : triggers $\rightarrow$ Time

shared relativeTimeout : triggers $\rightarrow$ RelativeTime

shared senderNode : triggers $\rightarrow$ flowNodes

Additionally, we retain the property *triggerType*, with values like "Message", "Signal", "Error", etc., for the following reasons:

- The BPMN trigger types "Signal", "Error", and "Escalation" cannot be distinguished by the newly defined trigger properties, yet "Error" and "Escalation" have algorithmic significance for the workflow.
- The relatively small set of trigger types defined by BPMN, reflecting the most common communication needs, renders a diagram much easier to understand and

those types can be represented by symbols which are relatively easy to identify and to remember.

- We want to remain compatible with the BPMN standard as far as possible.

shared triggerType : triggers → eventTriggerTypes

However, we must be aware that there is a certain redundancy of information shared between the *triggerType* and other properties, and that we must assure consistency. We will discuss the relations between classical trigger types and the trigger properties introduced above in Sect. 5.7.

For the following considerations, we further stipulate that triggers are unique (uniquely identifiable) and that duplication always leads to *different* (i.e. distinguishable) triggers.

5.5   Event Pools

5.5.1   Overview

If we want to enable users to choose in which order to process messages (and possibly other event triggers), we have to give them a kind of "pool" into which event triggers are delivered and from which users can pick. This concept is well known and established in the form of the "inbox" of an email client but has also an analogy in the older snail-mail letterbox. The pool concept we are going to introduce is also influenced by that proposed for S-BPM (see [7, esp. Sects. 5.5.3 and 5.5.4]), as S-BPM lays a special focus on the viewpoint of actors (or "subjects").

We not only want users to be able to choose the order in which to process triggers but also to be able to opt-in for additional, non-obligatory trigger sources, like certain kinds of news (like RSS feeds). This can be enabled by giving users access to certain additional event trigger pools, i.e. pools not directly associated with a particular process.

Furthermore, there are certain kinds of event triggers, like signals, errors, or compensation triggers, which may be supposed to be caught by more than one actor, or by more than one process or sub-process. One way to handle this is to duplicate such events for every potential recipient, and this is how it is usually handled by the email system and similar communication systems, at least on the physical layer and on lower layers of abstraction. Another possibility, at least for the conceptual level, is to deposit such a trigger in a pool which is not associated with a particular process but which is generally accessible or "public"; to make sure that more than one process—and also more than one instance per process—can catch the trigger, it must be marked such that it is *not* removed when caught (i.e. *deleteUponCatch(trigger)* = **false**).

So the general idea is to have not only one *event pool*, as we will call it, per process or sub-process but additionally also more generally accessible event pools. However, a user might want to have only a single view on all the pools accessible to them. Thus we *virtually* collect all the triggers from all the pools relevant for a particular process in a virtual (or derived) pool which we call the process's or sub-process's *inbox*, in analogy to the familiar email "inbox".

It shall be possible to restrict the visibility or accessibility of event pools. Moreover, we will predefine one *private event pool* for each top-level process or sub-process, plus one *group event pool* for each top-level process or sub-process which shall be visible for all sub-processes within this (sub-) process, recursively. The private event pool will be used for triggers intended to start a new instance, for example, while the group event pool makes sense for error handling which a process designer might want to hide in a special (event-based) sub-process or, more generally, for the propagation of triggers.

A further aspect concerns the *throwing* of a trigger: a process (or the respective event node) might not want to care for all the event triggers which it throws exactly to which recipients those triggers should be delivered. The process *may* specify a particular process, flow node, and/or instance as addressee (see the trigger properties proposed in the previous section), but for broadcasts, the sender need not know or need not want to know whom exactly they may concern.

It should be possible to derive the appropriate pools for delivering such triggers from the triggers' properties. Consequently, we can abstract the throwing procedure from a process's point of view by means of an *outbox*: For the throwing (sub-) process, it suffices to put a new event trigger (with the relevant properties set) in the course of throwing into this abstract outbox, and we assume that some mechanism behind this outbox (like a mail server) will find the appropriate event pools to deliver the trigger.

To summarise, we propose the following types of event pools (cf. Fig. 5.1):

- A *private* event pool for each process or sub-process for triggers which are only visible for event nodes that are directly within this (sub-) process (this corresponds to "direct resolution" in BPMN);
- A *group* event pool for each process or sub-process for triggers which are visible also within sub-processes of this (sub-) process, recursively, to enable propagation;
- *public* event pools to which processes can subscribe or to which several processes can be mandatorily subscribed (by the process designer);
- A virtual *inbox* for each process or sub-process which makes all relevant event triggers for that (sub-) process visible in a single view; and
- An abstract *outbox* for each process or sub-process which hides the details of delivering triggers thrown within this (sub-) process in accordance with the triggers' properties.

So we have four different types of input pools (of which *inbox* is only "virtual" or derived) and one type of output pool.

A particular user can probably be identified via a respective process *instance*. When we associate an event pool or an inbox with a process, the respective instance—possibly corresponding to a user, but alternatively maybe also to a particular business

Fig. 5.1 Event pools of a
(sub-) process

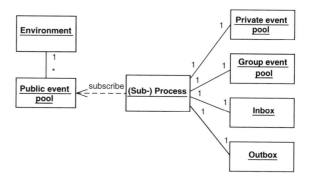

case, etc.—can be identified by means of *correlation information* as explained in the
previous section.

A few more comments may be in order before we address the details. One possible
argument against the use of "public" pools for signals and similar event triggers is
that we have to remember whether a particular instance of a particular activity has
already processed a certain trigger or not.

One way in which this can be solved is by means of the workflow: After the
trigger has been caught, the workflow moves on and does not pass a suitable catching
event node any more. But we cannot rely on this; nor can we rely on the trigger
being invalidated by a timeout before it is caught again. We will solve this problem
by introducing a controlled function, *hasBeenCaughtByInstance*, which is **false** by
default and set to **true** for the respective process instance when the trigger is caught.

This problem could alternatively be solved by duplication of triggers for each
recipient, as already mentioned; a recipient could then delete the trigger upon catching
and thus we need not remember whether they already processed it or not. Such a
solution may seem easier or more intuitive at first sight.

A drawback of the duplication concept, however, is that the sender, or at least
some agent in between (like a mail server), has to know in advance exactly who the
recipients shall be, while with a pool concept, this can be left open, at least to some
degree—the sender or distributing agent only needs to know to which pool or pools
to deliver and not who will actually look at those pools. In this way, we can model
blackboard-style (many-to-many) communication as well as webpage-style (one-to-
many) communication, both with dynamically changing participants or readers, in
an intuitive way.

A further advantage of handling also broadcasts by means of pools (at least on
an abstract level) is that we can use a single concept for all types of communication.
User choice leads us to a pool concept as an obvious solution, and if all other sorts
of communication issues can be easily and intuitively supported by that concept, the
better.

However, for the special case in which a trigger has to be delivered to several
different pools, it will still have to be duplicated. For instance, the sender might want
to make sure that all members of a certain group (think of a mailing list) really get the

trigger, so the trigger has to be duplicated for the private or group event pool of each recipient process, or duplicates with different correlation information for different process instances have to be sent to the same event pool.

If not all triggers are automatically removed from an event pool when caught, we may expect clogging of pools after a while. This can be solved by means of the *timeout* properties of triggers defined in the previous section, for which either process designers or maybe even tool vendors might set a maximum or a default. This is a purely technical issue, however, and would not deserve treatment in this place if timeout would not also be of more principal importance as a characteristic and necessary property for certain types of triggers.

5.5.2   Refining the Ground Model with Event Pools

Having explained the basic ideas, we now specify the event pool concept formally.

Intuitively, we define an *event pool* as a set containing triggers. Thereby "set" is meant not in a purely mathematical sense with an extensional notion of identity, but in the more technical sense of a container to which triggers can be added and from which triggers can be removed again. As we want to leave a concrete implementation open, we define a new universe:

universe eventPools

We can add triggers to an event pool and remove triggers from an event pool; in both cases, we might want to know whether the operation succeeded, for which we give a Boolean return value.

abstract rule AddTrigger : triggers × eventPools → Boolean

abstract rule RemoveTrigger : triggers × eventPools → Boolean

We can also check whether a given trigger is available in an event pool or not:

abstract derived containsTrigger : eventPools × triggers → Boolean

We omit the obvious axioms for the operations on such a container.

An event pool may or may not be associated with a particular process or sub-process, which we model by a static function, *ownerProcess*. Every private or group event pool is associated with a particular (sub-) process.

A public event pool will be associated with the *environment*. Furthermore, also the environment will need to receive triggers from a process, for instance, from an end event node. Therefore, we treat the environment as a kind of special process. In contrast to a process in the closer sense, however, we cannot make assumptions like it having instances or an internal lifecycle, etc.; hence, we simply add a constant *environment* to the ASM, thought to be the only member of a respective universe (which is then simply the set containing just *environment*), and assumed to be able to mix with processes in certain circumstances (see below).

For the sake of simplicity, we assume that there is a fixed number of event pools in a given run of a process engine, and that also the association with a particular (sub-) process is fixed; hence, we define the function *ownerProcess* as **static**, i.e. its value is fixed for all locations (after initialisation at the start of a run of the ASM). In the context of a more dynamic setting, this might be changed to **monitored**, but possible implications may have to be considered.

```
static ownerProcess : eventPools → processes ∪ {
    environment }
```

A derived function can be specified which identifies all event pools owned by a particular (sub-) process or by the environment:

```
derived eventPools : processes ∪ { environment } →
    Set
derived eventPools(process) =
    { pool | pool ∈ eventPools and ownerProcess(pool) =
        process }
```

An event pool associated with a particular (sub-) process may be *private* or a group event pool; in the latter case, it is simply not *private*. If an event pool associated with the environment is *private*, it is supposed to receive triggers for the environment for whose further processing we make no assumptions. If an event pool associated with the environment is *not private*, this is a public event pool to which processes can subscribe or can be subscribed. (In this chapter, we will not specify the subscription process and, in particular, not specify any access restrictions.)

```
static private : eventPools → Boolean
```

We can then define the following:

- a *private event pool* as a *pool* with *ownerProcess(pool)* ∈ processes and *private(pool)* = **true**,
- a *group event pool* as a *pool* with *ownerProcess(pool)* ∈ processes and *private(pool)* = **false**,
- a *public event pool* as a *pool* with *ownerProcess(pool)* = environment and *private(pool)* = **false**, and
- the environment's event pool (for triggers addressed to the environment) as a *pool* with *ownerProcess(pool)* = environment and *private(pool)* = **true**.

In terms of BPMN, a private event pool serves the concept of *direct resolution*, a group event pool that of *propagation*, and a public event pool that of *publication* (cf. [20, p. 234f]).

Additionally, we stipulate that there is a *default* public event pool to which signals can be distributed if their destination is not further specified and which is visible for all processes:

```
static defaultPublicEventPool : → eventPools

assert
  ownerProcess(defaultPublicEventPool) = environment
    and private(defaultPublicEventPool) = false
```

Additional public event pools may be defined by the business process designer.

We may want an event pool, and in particular a public event pool, to have further properties such as access rights. We do not consider access rights in this place, but we remark that introducing them might require to refine the function *private* with a more complex data type.

We assert that every process has exactly one private event pool and one group event pool:

```
assert
  forall process ∈ processes holds
      |{ pool | pool ∈ eventPools and
          ownerProcess(pool) = process and
          private(pool) = true }| = 1
      and
      |{ pool | pool ∈ eventPools and
          ownerProcess(pool) = process and
          private(pool) = false }| = 1
```

The environment has one unique private event pool:

```
assert
  |{ pool | pool ∈ eventPools and
      ownerProcess(pool) = environment and
      private(pool) = true }| = 1
```

For a process which does not have sub-processes, a group event pool might seem superfluous. However, we do not want a sender or delivery service need to care whether a recipient process has a group event pool or not. Certain kinds of event triggers shall always be delivered to a group event pool, and the *inbox*, which we will discuss soon, will offer a single view to all relevant event pools anyway.

We can then identify the unique event pools of a given process by derived functions:

```
derived privateEventPool : processes → eventPools
derived privateEventPool(process) =
  choose pool in eventPools(process) with
      private(pool) = true do
    return pool

derived groupEventPool : processes → eventPools
derived groupEventPool(process) =
  choose pool in eventPools(process) with
      private(pool) = false do
    return pool
```

We also need to know which public pools are visible for a particular process. We define the *visiblePublicEventPools* of a process as monitored to enable users to add (or remove) pools from this set. Adding and removing pools from *visiblePublicEvent-Pools* is outside the scope of this chapter, so we also ignore the issue of access rights here.

monitored visiblePublicEventPools : processes → Set

The *defaultPublicEventPool* must be visible for all processes:

assert
  forall process ∈ processes **holds**
      defaultPublicEventPool ∈
          visiblePublicEventPools(process)

The *visibleEventPools* of a process are then the *visiblePublicEventPools* plus the private and group *eventPools*.

derived visibleEventPools : processes → Set
derived visibleEventPools(process) =
    eventPools(process) ∪
    visiblePublicEventPools(process)

We can now define the *inbox* of a process as a view showing all triggers available in any of the *visibleEventPools*.

derived inbox : processes → Set
derived inbox(process) =
  { trigger | **forsome** pool ∈
      visibleEventPools(process) **holds**
      containsTrigger(pool, trigger) }

One might want to additionally apply different filters to the contents of the *inbox* by adding respective derived functions; we leave this option open in this place.

For throwing a trigger, from a process's point of view, it shall suffice to put it into an *outbox*. Each process shall have an own *outbox*.

shared outbox : processes → eventPools

The process puts new triggers into the *outbox* and some delivery service takes them out to distribute them (like a snail-mail post service emptying mailboxes in regular intervals). As the delivery service may be outside the scope of the process engine in order to service the environment (including foreign process engines) as well, this function needs to be **shared**.

A possible *outbox* of the environment is outside the scope of this specification.

An alternative to one *outbox* per process would be a common outbox for all processes (within the scope of a given process engine), but this might preclude delivery algorithms which do as much as possible locally, like not taking intra-process triggers outside and back in. If one would like to have a common outbox, the *outbox* of a process could simply be redefined as a proxy for that common outbox (e.g. **derived** outbox(process) = commonOutbox).

The delivery service must distribute the collected new triggers to private, group, and public event pools according to the properties of those triggers. For any *trigger,*

- If *recipientProcesses(trigger)* is **undef** or empty, then the *trigger* shall be delivered to a public event pool; if additionally *recipientPool(trigger)* = **undef**, then the *trigger* shall be delivered to *defaultPublicEventPool*.
- If there is some *process* in *recipientProcesses(trigger)* and *mayBePropagated(trigger)* = **true**, then the *trigger* shall be delivered to the group event pool of each specified process.
- If there is some *process* in *recipientProcesses(trigger)* and *mayBePropagated(trigger)* = **false**, then the *trigger* shall be delivered to the private event pool of each specified process.
- If *environment* ∈ *recipientProcesses(trigger)*, then the *trigger* shall (also) be delivered to the environment's (private) event pool.

We have already mentioned that a trigger in a public event pool may or may not be removed from this pool once it has been caught by some event node, depending on the value of the trigger's *deleteUponCatch* predicate. If it is not removed, then we must remember that the process instance for which the trigger was caught has already reacted (see the discussion in the previous subsection).

The controlled function *hasBeenCaughtByInstance* indicates whether a particular trigger has already been caught by a particular process instance or not. It is **false** by default and set to **true** for the instance in question once is has been caught by that instance. Note that the process in question can always be identified via the instance (which is unique).

```
controlled hasBeenCaughtByInstance : triggers ×
   instances → Boolean
```

Removal of triggers from event pools according to timeout properties must be performed by some service of the process engine; this is an implementation-related detail which we do not consider further in this place.

Now we can refine the rule *ThrowEvent*, which was left abstract in the original ground model (see [13]). We create a new trigger, set the properties as far as known, and add the new trigger to the outbox of the sender process or sub-process. Note that the given *senderNode* is an event node, thus the sender process is the parent of *senderNode*.

```
rule ThrowEvent(triggerType, recipientNode,
    senderInstance, senderNode) =
  let newTrigger = new(triggers) in
  seqblock
    triggerType(newTrigger) := triggerType
    recipientNode(newTrigger) := recipientNode
    senderNode(newTrigger) := senderNode
    correlationInfo(newTrigger) :=
        correlationInfo(senderInstance)
    SetTypeDependentTriggerProperties(newTrigger,
        triggerType)
    AddTrigger(newTrigger,
        outbox(parentNode(senderNode)))
  endseqblock
```

We rely upon a service to collect triggers from all outboxes. How different trigger types translate to other trigger properties will be considered in Sect. 5.7, whereupon we can specify the subrule *SetTypeDependentTriggerProperties*.

We also have to adapt the shared function *availableTriggers*. In [13], this was defined as a *shared* function, that is, we expected direct environment input via this function. By means of the pool concept, however, we can easily map this function to the *inbox* (thereby making it a derived function instead of a shared function and changing its type from *Set* to *eventPools*):

```
derived availableTriggers : flowNodes → eventPools
derived availableTriggers(eventNode) =
  inbox(parentNode(eventNode))
```

The type change from *Set* to *eventPools* also requires changes wherever the function *availableTriggers* is called. Wherever we had

```
trigger ∈ availableTriggers(flowNode)
```

we now have

```
containsTrigger(availableTriggers(flowNode),
    trigger)
```

What is left to do is wherever a trigger is actually caught, we need to add a check whether *deleteUponCatch* is **true** and if so, remove the trigger from its pool. If *deleteUponCatch* is **false**, we have to set *hasBeenCaughtByInstance* to **true** for the given trigger and process instance.

In the ground model in [13], an abstract rule *RemoveTrigger* (with a trigger being the only argument) is defined and used in the appropriate places in *CatchEventTransition* (see e.g. *EventOperationDefault*). We can now refine this rule, but we have to add the process instance under which the trigger was caught as an additional argument. We check if the property *deleteUponCatch* is **true** for the given trigger, and if so, we employ the function *RemoveTrigger* with the pool from which to remove as a second argument (as declared further above; we can now see that, unfortunately, the naming of the original *RemoveTrigger*, as used in [13], was a bit misleading).

```
rule RemoveTrigger : triggers × instances
rule RemoveTrigger(trigger, instance) =
  if deleteUponCatch(trigger) then
    RemoveTrigger(trigger, poolOfTrigger(trigger))
  else
    hasBeenCaughtByInstance(trigger, instance) := true
```

The derived function *poolOfTrigger* returns the event pool in which the given trigger is located. We assume that triggers are unique (e.g. duplication leads to *different* triggers) and that every trigger resides in some (proper) event pool.

```
derived poolOfTrigger : triggers → eventPools
derived poolOfTrigger(trigger) =
  return pool in
    choose pool in eventPools with
        containsTrigger(pool, trigger)
```

This basically concludes the refinements of the original ground model required to employ the enhanced communication concept. These refinements will be summarised and supplemented in the Chapter on the eP^2 architecture, in Sect. 7.5.3.

Unfortunately, we cannot take advantage of the *whole* power of the presented communication concept without major changes in the original ground model. In particular, we must still rely on the property *triggerType* to find suitable event nodes within a process. Furthermore, we cannot make use of most of the introduced trigger properties when throwing a new trigger; we would require additional interfaces to let actors set all these properties. Note that required changes might adversely affect compatibility with BPMN.

We leave a wider exploitation of the concept to future work and considerations. However, triggers sent from the environment to processes run by a given process engine can already make use of all the trigger properties.

In subsequent sections, we will discuss what scope of communication our concept enables and how the trigger types of BPMN relate to the trigger properties which we have introduced. But before that, we briefly look at the special issue of "indirectly thrown" triggers.

5.5.3   *"Indirectly Thrown" Triggers*

According to the BPMN standard, "**Timer** and **Conditional** *triggers* are implicitly thrown. When they are activated they wait for a time-based or status-based condition, respectively, to trigger the *catch* **Event**" [20, p. 234]. Note that a "Timer" event is just a special "Conditional" event in which the condition is that a certain time has been reached.

In [13, Sect. 7.4], a concept for such "implicitly thrown" triggers is introduced where the Workflow Interpreter registers all such conditions and explicitly throws respective triggers when the conditions become true. Advantages of this concept are that the events can be logged by the workflow interpreter and that we do not need to care about data required to fulfil the condition (or access to a clock) at the level of the event node. A drawback is that an extra service of the environment is required and that many unnecessary triggers may be thrown when the respective event nodes are not enabled. An alternative solution would be to evaluate the conditions in situ. In this case, wherever we have an expression of the form

```
containsTrigger(availableTriggers(eventNode),
    trigger)
```

we might use another derived function, e.g.

```
givenTriggerOccurred(eventDefinition, eventNode)
```

with the following specification:

```
derived givenTriggerOccurred(eventDefinition,
    eventNode) =
  return result in
```

```
let triggerType =
    getTriggerTypeFromEventDef(eventDefinition) in
  if triggerType ="Conditional"then
    result = evaluate(condition(eventDefinition))
  else if triggerType ="Timer" then
    result = (evaluate(timeDate(eventDefinition))
        or
         evaluate(timeCycle(eventDefinition)) or
         evaluate(timeDuration(eventDefinition)))
  else
    result = forsome trigger ∈
        availableTriggers(eventNode)
      holds triggerType(trigger) = triggerType
```

If logging should be possible, we might turn *givenTriggerOccurred* into a rule where a respective log entry is performed as a side effect. Anyway, both the original and the above given solution are valid refinements of the ground model.

An additional and independent question is whether we want to allow for a certain duration for which the event trigger should be sustained *after* a given time has been reached. In BPMN, only one of the three possible attributes *timeDate*, *timeCycle*, and *timeDuration* may be set, and it is not clear whether *timeDuration* includes such a possibility. If we would include, in a "TimerEventDefinition", attributes corresponding to the timeout attributes which we proposed in the previous section, we could enhance also the possibilities for "Timer" events and would also achieve consistency with other trigger types.

5.6   The Scope of Possible Communication

Let us now look at the scope of communication which the proposed event trigger properties and the event pool concept together enable.

Let us start with the BPMN standard, which describes "different strategies to forward the *trigger* to catching **Events**: publication, direct resolution, propagation, *cancellations*, and *compensations*" [20, p. 234]. Cancellation and compensation do not actually constitute different ways of delivering triggers (see also Sect. 5.7 below), but all the different delivery strategies can be handled by our proposal:

- **Publication** within a process can be achieved by specifying a recipient process of the trigger and leaving the recipient node undefined; publication across processes can be achieved by specifying a public event pool as the recipient pool.
- **Direct resolution** can be achieved by specifying a recipient node.
- **Propagation** can be achieved by setting *mayBePropagated* to **true** (whereby the trigger will be put into the respective group event pool).

The BPMN standard also says that "**Events** for which publication is used are grouped to **Conversations**. Published **Events** MAY participate in several

Conversations" [20, p. 234]. This can be handled by public event pools by subscribing all members of a conversation to the same pool.

Lachlan Aldred defines "process integration patterns" in [1], many of which are relevant for our communication concept. Aldred distinguishes the following "dimensions" of communication:

- **Participants**: 1–1, 1–many, or many–many; the first two can basically be covered by setting *deleteUponCatch* to **true** for 1–1 and **false** for 1–many, and also by choosing a suitable event pool, e.g. a public event pool for 1–many. The case of many–many can be handled by allowing different senders to send triggers to a particular public event pool (with *deleteUponCatch* set to **false**).
- **Unidirectional/bidirectional**: this is a matter of process design (though a public event pool could aid in bidirectional communication).
- **Synchronous/asynchronous**: this can be supported via the *timeout/lifetime* properties of triggers.
- **Thread coupling**: this is a matter of process design.
- **Time** (whether two participants need to both be participating in an interaction at the exact same moment): this can be supported via the *lifetime* property, which is set to zero (or a respective minimum) for immediate communication.
- **Direct/indirect contact**: direct contact is straightforward by defining a recipient (process/node/instance); indirect contact between communication partners that need not know each other can be supported by public event pools.
- **Duplication**: in our concept, duplication *can* be (but need not be) replaced by setting the trigger property *deleteUponCatch* to **false** and possibly using a public event pool.

Patterns of process instantiation, however, as discussed in [4], are a matter of process design and not of trigger design.

Thus, our concept obviously covers a wide range of different and important communication patterns.

It should be mentioned that S-BPM provides some extra "configuration parameters" for input pools, i.e. maximum numbers of messages in general and of messages from particular senders (subjects) and/or with specific identifiers [7, p. 75]. One important application of this appears to be the enforcement of synchronous communication by setting the maximum number of messages (from a certain sender and/or of a certain type) to zero. In H-BPM, we can enforce synchronous communication (and similar restrictions) by means of *trigger* properties, in particular by timeout properties. We thereby do not need to worry about what should happen with extra triggers if a pool is "full" (cf. [7, p. 76]). In H-BPM, the concept of an *outbox* allows to assume that the sender is never blocked just because an event trigger could not be delivered. If a block is desired, this can be modelled by explicit synchronisation mechanisms.

S-BPM also provides for the possibility of "alternative" messages: if one message to a particular addressee is blocked, an alternative message can be sent to another addressee to prevent blocking of the workflow [7, p. 76f]. We think that the resulting "subject interaction diagrams" are difficult to understand at first sight. In H-BPM, we strive to clearly separate control-flow issues (represented by gateways) from other issues such as communication.

5.7   Standard Event Trigger Types

We now explain how the standard event trigger types defined in the BPMN standard [20] relate to the trigger properties defined in Sect. 5.4.

The BPMN standard defines the following trigger types: "Message", "Signal", "Error", "Escalation", "Cancel", "Compensation", "Terminate", "Conditional", "Timer", and "Link" (cf. Fig. 5.2 and the overview in [20, p. 32]). We will not consider "Link" triggers here as they just serve for the continuation of normal workflow.

Conditional and **Timer** triggers, if explicitly thrown, concern a particular event node; the service that throws such a trigger will have to know the process and event node and can thus set the *recipientProcesses* and *recipientNode* properties. As the recipient node is known, *mayBePropagated* shall be **false**. As more than one instance may be waiting for a condition to become **true** or a time to be reached, *correlationInfo* shall be **undef**. The *recipientPool* is already determined by *mayBePropagated* being **false** to be the private event pool of the recipient process, thus the property *recipientPool* is redundant in this case and may or may not be **undef**. The property *deleteUponCatch* shall be **false**, as more than one instance may be interested. We cannot determine the timeout properties for Conditional triggers, though, without specifying additional settings in the *eventDefinition* of the respective event node. A timeout for a timer trigger can only be set if the *timeDuration* of the *eventDefinition* is defined.

Messages "typically describe B2B communication between different **Processes**" [20, p. 234]. In this case, *recipientProcesses* will be defined. If there exists a respective

Fig. 5.2 Supported event trigger types

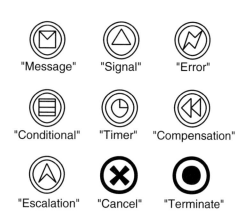

message flow, also the *recipientNode* will be defined by the *targetRef* of the message flow, but it *may* also be defined if there is no message flow. If no *recipientNode* is defined, then *mayBePropagated may* be **true**, else it must be **false**; we assume that a message usually shall *not* be propagated. A specific process instance *may* be addressed using *correlationInfo* (cf. [20, p. 234]). The respective event pool is already defined by *recipientProcesses* and *mayBePropagated* and thus also *recipientPool may* be **undef**. Usually, *deleteUponCatch* will be **true**, and a process designer may define this as the default or even as obligatory. We can also expect that no timeout is specified (or that the *lifetime* is set to a rather high value, as messages—think of letters or email—usually do not decay anytime soon).

Signals "are typically used for broadcast communication within and across **Processes**" [20, p. 234]. It is further hinted that a message, *in contrast to a signal*, "has a specific target for the **Message**" [20, p. 241]; thus we may assume that we do not have a particular recipient, and that there will typically be more than one recipient (which is the nature of a broadcast). Thus at least *recipientNode* shall be **undef**, but likely also *recipientProcesses*. We may assume that a signal may be caught in an event sub-process, so *mayBePropagated* shall be **true** (at least by default). Correlation is obviously not applicable, so *correlationInfo* shall be **undef**. A particular *recipientPool* may be given, especially to make the signal visible for all, or for a certain group of subscribers, in a public event pool (which was designed as a means for broadcasting). The property *deleteUponCatch* shall be **false** by default, as a broadcast will have several potential recipients. A timeout *may* be specified.

Error triggers are characterised by the BPMN standard as "critical and suspend[ing] execution at the location of throwing" [20, p. 235]. But the suspension of the throwing instance does not affect the properties of the trigger (except the *triggerType*). As for recipients, there is the restriction that "the **Error Start Event** is only allowed for triggering an in-line **Event Sub-Process**" [20, p. 243]. But the recipient may be within the throwing process—e.g. the start event of an event sub-process designed for this purpose—or outside, as an end event may inform the environment about the associated problem. We further read in the BPMN standard that "if no catching **Event** is found for an error or escalation *trigger*, this *trigger* is unresolved" [20, p. 235]; this confirms that at least *recipientNode* shall be **undef**. The paragraph from which the previous quotation was taken speaks of propagations, so *mayBePropagated* shall obviously be **true**. We may thus see an error trigger as a specialised signal, only distinguished by the *triggerType*.

Escalation triggers are similar to error triggers just that "**Escalations** are non critical and execution continues at the location of throwing" [20, p. 235] (though a few pages on, we read that an escalation event sub-process can be interrupting as well [20, p. 243]). However, criticality or interruption of the throwing process instance does not affect trigger properties, so like error triggers, we can also see escalation triggers as specialised signals. (One might add a *priority* property for triggers to express, amongst others, criticality, but we do not consider this essential for the proposed communication concept and leave such a property optional.)

Cancel triggers "are directed towards a **Process** or a specific **Activity** *instance*" [20, p. 235]. Thus a recipient process shall be defined. Cancellation is discussed

in the BPMN standard together with propagation, thus *mayBePropagated* shall be
true and *recipientNode* shall be **undef** (note that a *recipientNode* is always an event
node and not an activity). It is obviously intended that only a particular instance
shall be cancelled, thus *correlationInfo* shall be defined. A *recipientPool* need not
be specified as it is already fixed by *mayBePropagated* as the group event pool of
the specified recipient process; to avoid inconsistencies, the *recipientPool* is best
left **undef**. The property *deleteUponCatch* shall be **false** as all sub-processes of the
process in question must react to it. Cancellation is supposed to happen instantly,
thus a minimum (or "zero") timeout should be set.

Compensation triggers have the same properties as cancel triggers (the semantic
information that compensation shall be performed is given by the *triggerType*).

Terminate triggers are also discussed in the BPMN standard together with propagation; they indicate "that all **Activities** in the **Process** or **Activity** should be immediately ended. This includes all *instances* of *multi-instances*" [20, p. 235]. There is
no difference to cancel or compensation triggers relevant for the properties proposed
in this work. The fact that no "*compensation* or *Event handling*" is to be done is only
relevant for the recipient's reaction to such a trigger but not for the distribution of
the trigger.

To summarise, we can distinguish different trigger types, or at least groups of
trigger types, by the trigger properties we have defined in the following way (some-
what simplified, under certain reasonable assumptions, and not taking into account
the special cases of "Conditional" and "Timer" triggers):

- A "Message" trigger has a single, defined recipient process, *deleteUponCatch* is
  true, and there is no timeout.
- A "Signal" trigger has *deleteUponCatch* (at least typically) set to **false** and *may-
  BePropagated* (at least typically) is **true**.
- An "Error" trigger is in effect a special-purpose "Signal" trigger.
- An "Escalation" trigger is in effect a special-purpose "Signal" trigger.
- A "Cancel" trigger has defined *recipientProcesses*, *mayBePropagated* is **true**,
  deleteUponCatch is **false**, and timeout is minimal.
- A "Compensation" trigger has the same properties as a "Cancel" trigger (except
  for *triggerType*).
- A "Terminate" trigger has the same properties as a "Cancel" trigger (except for
  triggerType).

5.8 Summary

While BPMN [20] provides a few specific event trigger types (more than other notations), serving some standard communication patterns, this is not always sufficient.
For example, Aldred describes much more sophisticated communication patterns for
business process modelling [1].

We have proposed a combination of two concepts to open up a wide scope of possibilities to model different communication needs within and between business processes. First, we have introduced a set of different *trigger properties* which can be combined, with a few constraints, to define a large number of different (unnamed) trigger types. And second, we have introduced an *event pool* concept with three different basic pool types, which enables flexibility in delivery methods for event triggers as well as flexibility in the *collection and selection* of event triggers by users, even beyond the vision of S-BPM [7].

We have shown how many important "dimensions" of communication [1] are covered by our proposal, and how "standard" event types (as defined by BPMN) can be mapped to our proposal.

Not all aspects of communication can be modelled this way. Aspects like synchronous versus asynchronous communication are largely left to the business process modeller, although our concept may give some aid also there. The same holds for protocols for bidirectional communication and similar aspects.

One might want to add still more trigger properties, e.g. a priority and/or criticality property, or add security/access properties to event pools. However, as desirable as such properties may often be, they do not actually add to the scope of communication *strategies*, and we leave it to future work to consider such aspects as well (with due consideration of other BPM dimensions such as actor and user interaction modelling).

References

1. Aldred, L.: Process integration. In: ter Hofstede, A.M., van der Aalst, W.M.P., Adams, M., Russell, N. (eds.) Modern Business Process Automation: YAWL and its Support Environment, pp. 489–511. Springer, Heidelberg (2010)
2. Barros, A., Decker, G., Grosskopf, A.: Complex events in business processes. In: Business Information Systems, pp. 29–40. Springer, Heidelberg (2007)
3. Bundesministerium für Bildung und Forschung: Zukunftsprojekt Industrie 4.0. http://www.bmbf.de/de/9072.php. Accessed 30 Sept 2015
4. Decker, G., Mendling, J.: Process instantiation. Data Knowl. Eng. **68**(9), 777–792 (2009)
5. Etzion, O., Niblett, P.: Event Processing in Action. Manning Publications, Greenwich (2011)
6. Ferreira, J., Wu, Q., Malkowski, S., Pu, C.: Towards flexible event-handling in workflows through data states. In: SERVICES-1, pp. 344–351. IEEE, New Jersey (2010)
7. Fleischmann, A., Schmidt, W., Stary, C., Obermeier, S., Börger, E.: Subject-Oriented Business Process Management. Springer, Heidelberg (2012)
8. Hermosillo, G., Seinturier, L., Duchien, L.: Using complex event processing for dynamic business process adaptation. In: Proceedings of the 2010 IEEE International Conference on Services Computing, pp. 466–473. IEEE, New Jersey (2010)
9. Herzberg, N., Meyer, A., Weske, M.: An event processing platform for business process management. In: Proceedings of the 2013 17th IEEE International Enterprise Distributed Object Computing Conference, pp. 107–116. IEEE, New Jersey (2013)
10. International Controller Association (ICV): Industrie 4.0—Controlling in the Age of Intelligent Networks (2015), http://www.icv-controlling.com/fileadmin/Assets/Content/AK/Ideenwerkstatt/Files/Dream_Car_Industrie_4.0_EN.pdf, Accessed 23 Dec 2015
11. Kossak, F., Geist, V.: An enhanced communication concept for business processes. In: Kolb, J., Leopold, H., Mendling, J. (eds.) Proceedings of the Enterprise Modelling and Information

Systems Architectures—EMISA 2015. Lecture Notes in Informatics, vol. 248, pp. 77–91. Gesellschaft für Informatik (2015)

12. Kossak, F., Illibauer, C., Geist, V., Kubovy, J., Natschläger, C., Ziebermayr, T., Kopetzky, T., Freudenthaler, B., Schewe, K.D.: A rigorous semantics for BPMN 2.0 process diagrams: The ground model in detail. http://www.scch.at/en/HagenbergBPM (2014). Accessed 12 Oct 2015

13. Kossak, F., Illibauer, C., Geist, V., Kubovy, J., Natschläger, C., Ziebermayr, T., Kopetzky, T., Freudenthaler, B., Schewe, K.D.: A Rigorous Semantics for BPMN 2.0 Process Diagrams. Springer, Heidelberg (2015)

14. Linden, I., Derbali, M., Schwanen, G., Jacquet, J., Ramdoyal, R., Ponsard, C.: Supporting business process exception management by dynamically building processes using the BEM framework. In: Decision Support Systems III, LNBIP, vol. 184, pp. 67–78. Springer International Publishing, Heidelberg (2014)

15. Lucchi, R., Mazzara, M.: A pi-calculus based semantics for WS-BPEL. J. Logic Algebraic Program. **70**(1), 96–118 (2007)

16. Luckham, D.: The Power of Events: An Introduction to Complex Event Processing in Distributed Enterprise Systems. Addison-Wesley Professional, Boston (2002)

17. Mendling, J., Neumann, G., Nüttgens, M.: Yet another event-driven process chain. In: Business Process Management, pp. 428–433. Springer, Heidelberg (2005)

18. Monostori, L.: Cyber-physical production systems: roots, expectations and R&D challenges. Procedia CIRP **17**, 9–13 (2014)

19. OASIS: Web services business process execution language version 2.0. http://docs.oasis-open.org/wsbpel/2.0/wsbpel-v2.0.html (2007). Accessed 12 Oct 2015

20. Object Management Group: Business Process Model and Notation (BPMN) 2.0. http://www.omg.org/spec/BPMN/2.0 (2011). Accessed 6 Oct 2015

21. van der Aalst, W.M., ter Hofstede, A.H.: Workflow patterns homepage. http://www.workflowpatterns.com. Accessed 25 Sept 2015

22. von Ammon, R., Emmersberger, C., Ertlmaier, T., Etzion, O., Paulus, T., Springer, F.: Existing and future standards for event-driven business process management. In: Proceedings of the 3rd ACM International Conference on Distributed Event-Based Systems, pp. 24:1–24:5. ACM, New York (2009)

23. Weske, M.: Business Process Management: Concepts, Languages, Architectures. Springer Science and Business Media, Berlin (2012)

Chapter 6
Horizontal Model Integration

Until now, we proposed several extensions to the core process description of common business process modelling languages such as the Business Process Model and Notation (BPMN). These extensions represent different models and cover important aspects for workflow management. In this chapter, we give an overview on the models and their interfaces, and we describe how the different models are related and how they can work together—the core process description language as described in [16], the actor model (Chaps. 2 and 3), the user interaction (dialogue) model (Chap. 4), and the enhanced communication model (Chap. 5), co-ordinated at runtime by means of the enhanced Process Platform (eP^2) (Sect. 6.4 and Chap. 7).

We base our work on previous research on formal process description languages. In [16], we started with the basic business process model describing the control flow (including activities, gateways, and events) in an abstract way and presented a complete formal semantics for BPMN 2.0 process diagrams in a way which is precise yet easily understandable using Abstract State Machines (ASMs). Thereby, we also eliminated well-known inconsistencies and ambiguities in the BPMN standard (see e.g. [6, 7]). We now concentrate on horizontal model integration of business process models to refine the basic specification to our so-called Hagenberg Business Process Modelling (H-BPM) method, which supports the extensions detailed above with a strictly formal integration.

Additional support for standardised tools is given in this chapter by a reference architecture for a business process management system. This kind of improvement allows for more consistency in the interpretation of comprehensive models as well as for real exchangeability of models between different tools. In particular, we show how the abstract, platform-independent semantic business process model can be reliably refined towards a concrete implementation of a suitable workflow engine.

This chapter is structured as follows. Section 6.1 provides the motivation for integrating the proposed extensions, which are represented by different models. Related work is presented in Sect. 6.2. In Sect. 6.3, we first give an overview of the general picture of horizontal model integration, including concise descriptions of the different models. We discuss our four-step integration approach and show the usability of the suggested method by an example scenario for ordering supplies. Afterwards,

© Springer International Publishing Switzerland 2016   147
F. Kossak et al., *Hagenberg Business Process Modelling Method*,
DOI 10.1007/978-3-319-30496-0_6

Sect. 6.4 describes the eP^2 architecture, which brackets all modelling aspects treated in this book, including its components, the provided interfaces, and their operations. To facilitate model integration in general and user interaction in particular, we add some interfaces to the ground model of the core process description language presented in [16]. We conclude the chapter with a summary in Sect. 6.5.

6.1 Motivation

Due to different aspects of business processes, such as functionality, actors, user interaction, data, and communication, modelling information systems is a complex and challenging task [30]. Each aspect in general calls for its own model, which has to be integrated in the overall system model. In addition, those models are generally related to different abstraction layers, easily leading to discrepancies when integrating them.

Several of our industrial projects (see [9, 19]) have motivated the development of a comprehensive modelling method proposing a design for Business Process Management (BPM) systems which comprise much more than just process modelling. Process modelling is often considered as a first possible step in BPM, typically including control flow definitions as well as message and event handling. However, much more is needed for full-scale software support. By then, at the latest, *actors* will have to be added to the model and integrated with issues from *user interaction* and *communication* modelling.

We consider those extensions to a traditional core process description language as important aspects which are obviously needed in business process modelling and execution due to the following reasons. First of all, according to [35], BPMN provides good support for the control flow perspective, medium support for the data perspective, but only low support for the resource perspective. Also, in Chap. 3, the limited support for actor modelling provided by rigid swimlane concepts is discussed. In addition, business analysts and software developers often struggle with redundancies and inconsistencies in system documentations due to missing integration mechanisms for user interaction modelling [9]. Last, simple communication patterns, such as those provided by common modelling languages like BPMN, often do not suffice for modelling the interplay between different processes, especially between very heterogeneous systems [14]. In particular, when human actors and user interaction are included, more flexibility and customisation are demanded.

While different approaches and views on business processes represented by different models have been described before, formal integration of these different models is missing. However, only their interplay makes them useful in practice, and this interplay is not trivial. Therefore, the H-BPM method, as a novel approach for designing BPM systems, uses *horizontal model integration* to support successive enlargement of the core process language to integrate all those different models in a formal way. As a result, this new modelling method is capable of seamlessly integrating process, actor, user interaction, data, and communication models on all levels of abstraction. The different abstraction levels and integration steps provide an accurate guidance for process modellers and analysts to holistically model business processes.

6.2   Related Work

Already in 1977, the Standards Planning and Requirements Committee (SPARC) of the American National Standards Institute (ANSI) published the *three schema approach* for the design of database schemata, which consists of three levels (the *external schema* for user views, the *conceptual schema*, integrating the external schema, and the *internal schema*, defining physical storage structures) [5]. Although this approach considers integration as we do, it considers rather uneligible aspects for business processes.

Since 1980s, different views are used in software and information system architecture for abstraction to comprehend the complexity of such systems. Enterprise architecture frameworks [17] like ARIS, the Zachman Framework, and TOGAF bring systematisation to the plethora of models and views, or more generally to the plethora of related artefacts which show up during the life-time of systems.

The business process framework *Architecture of Integrated Information Systems* (ARIS) [27] comprises five views. The views are symbolically presented in the form of a house, the so-called ARIS house with the *Organisation View* as the roof, the *Data*, *Control*, and *Function View* as the three pillars, and the *Output View* as the basis of the house. A detailed comparison between ARIS and our approach would not be conducive, because ARIS is a framework for overall enterprise architecture, whereas H-BPM aims at seamlessly supporting different aspects in the domain of business process modelling. Nevertheless, three views of the ARIS concept are similar to our approach. The *Function View* supports goals and defines processing rules for application software. According to A.-W. Scheer, the designations "function", "process", and "activity" are used synonymously, thus this view is similar to our process model. In addition, the *Data View* comprises the data processing environment including messages, and is, therefore, similar to our data model. Furthermore, the *Organisation View* of ARIS comprises a hierarchical organisational model with organisational units and concrete instances [27], and resembles the homonymous view of our actor model.

The *Zachman Framework* [37] consists of six rows for viewpoints (*Scope*, *Enterprise* (or *Business*) *Model*, *System Model*, *Technology Model*, *Detailed Representations*, and *Functioning Enterprise*) and six columns for aspects (*Data*, *Function*, *Network*, *People*, *Time*, and *Motivation*). The aspect *Data* includes the logical and physical data model, the data definition, and the actual data; thus it is similar to our data model. The aspect *Function* contains the business process model and resembles our process model. Furthermore, the aspect *People* contains the workflow or organisational model with organisational units and hierarchical dependencies defined between them and correlates to our actor model. However, missing are detailed descriptions of user interactions.

Besides established enterprise architecture frameworks, which address aspects for describing whole enterprises, various approaches propose views suitable for automating business processes, e.g. by Hofmeister et al. [12], Clement et al. [8], or Rozansky and Woods [26]. All of them propose—at least—kinds of (i) a static view (also called *Conceptual Architecture View* or *Module Viewtype*) for describing the static structure of the system, (ii) a dynamic view (also called *Component-Connector Viewtype* or *Operational View*) for describing the runtime level, and (iii) an allocation view (also called *Execution Architecture View* or *Allocation Viewtype*) for describing the mapping of software components to the environment. Additional views of the individual approaches are, e.g. the *Code Architecture View* [12], focusing on development and deployment, the *Concurrency View* [26], describing the concurrency structure of the system, or the *Context View* [26], where the system is observed from outside. Similarly, the H-BPM approach provides the eP^2 architecture as the static view and then describes the operational semantics using ASMs, thereby focusing on parallel specifications and classified functions to reflect different kinds of visibility.

The eP^2 architecture is also related to the *Workflow Reference Model* published by the Workflow Management Coalition (WfMC), which covers the structure of workflow management systems including the main components, interfaces, and information interchange between them, among others. In detail, the *Workflow Reference Model* includes the runtime environment (process instantiation and activation and interaction with external resources)—which corresponds to our *Workflow Transition Interpreter*, process definitions (the business processes)—as addressed by our process model, workflow client functions (worklists to interact with end-users)—as supported by our dialogue model, and role management—corresponding to our actor model. However, the *Workflow Reference Model* is mainly focused on technology (tools and standards) [11] and workflow operability (to pass work items between different workflow systems), while the focus of the eP^2 architecture is rather on horizontal and vertical model integration from a conceptual point of view.

Beyond this, concrete BPM tools that support enterprise or software architecture frameworks may (explicitly or implicitly) define balancing rules between different kinds of supported artefacts. Such balancing rules target, e.g. the unique naming and unique place of definition of modelling elements or traceability features to materialise the conceptual relationships between the elements of several kinds of artefacts. However, the tools and frameworks do not elaborate domain-specific guidelines for concrete models as we do in H-BPM for actor and user interaction modelling. The approach presented in this work can be characterised as orthogonal to enterprise architecture framework approaches. It concentrates on the definition of process-oriented systems and proposes specific guidelines for this application domain, obviously lacking important enterprise dimensions. The models that are defined and integrated in our approach show up naturally and are provided to reduce complexity. However, the proposed H-BPM method goes beyond the definition of models or views; it is designed as an integrated method for seamless support of different aspects in business process modelling based on different abstraction levels and integration guidelines.

The more concrete guidelines, e.g., the tripartiteness of typed workflow charts or the powerful yet understandable deontic classifications of user tasks that are considered by our approach, can also be re-used or re-elaborated in the realm of other enterprise architecture frameworks.

Regarding the integration of actor modelling concepts in business processes, several evaluations and studies revealed the lack of completeness and clarity regarding this perspective, see e.g. [24, 35]. To address this problem, several approaches have been suggested, such as various extensions to BPMN to express task-based allocation and authorisation constraints using OCL [3, 36] or a rule-based extension of the BPMN metamodel based on the REWERSE Rule Markup Language (R2ML) [25]. Also some other business process modelling languages provide task-based assignment of resources to integrate actor modelling, e.g. UML Activity Diagrams [22], Event-Driven Process Chains (EPCs) [28], and Yet Another Workflow Language (YAWL) [34]. However, some approaches still use the pool and lane concepts to express the role hierarchy, resulting in a mixture of different resource definitions. In addition, it is not possible to specify generic restrictions (e.g. every business travel must be approved by the corresponding manager), dependencies between tasks concerning the executing roles, or to signify general permissions or obligations of users. In H-BPM, we consider such constraints and modalities when integrating the process and actor models and further extend the life-cycle of a classical BPMN activity by introducing two new life-cycle states, i.e. "Rejected" and "Skipped", to be able to handle tasks that are classified as permissible or alternative in the user interface of a *worklist*, which represents a new and innovative concept that is not yet realised in existing tools.

In addition, integrating dialogues into the activity-centred language represents a novel approach for refining business process models, and user tasks in particular, by dialogues and data views. Beyond existing approaches to user interface modelling [13, 23, 32] and integrating user interfaces and databases [29, 31], we specified how typed dialogues can be laid behind (or be graphically embedded in) the deontically classified user tasks of the process model, with designated entry points to the dialogue. As a result, the structure of dialogues becomes changeable, which leads to a natural partition of business logic into services of appropriate granularity. It further allows process designers to flexibly specify which parts of a business process apply to workflow technology and which parts make up the system dialogues, using an intuitive framework with defined modelling steps.

6.3 The General Picture

In this section, we provide the general picture of H-BPM regarding the different models that work together in order to cover relevant aspects in addition to core process modelling for workflow management. They also serve as input for the eP^2 architecture described in Sect. 6.4. One possibility to look at H-BPM is to start with the *Workflow Transition Interpreter* specified in [16], which is able to interpret process models that are closely based on BPMN 2.0. Another possibility is to start with the viewpoint of users and their interaction with the BPM system. In this case, we can start modelling with *workflow charts* as described in Chap. 4.

Basically, the dialogue model, which is defined in the notion of typed workflow charts (see Sect. 4.4), describes the same behaviour as the process model being interpreted by the *Workflow Transition Interpreter*. However, the viewpoint is different. Whereas the process model emphasises the control flow between activities, the dialogue-oriented approach focuses more on users and their interaction with applications based on editable forms and data. Thus, workflow charts abstract from purely activity-centred approaches and allow for realising more flexible business processes (see Sect. 4.1). In particular, they support a flexible choice of activity granularity [10] and improve efficiency regarding a user's work with data-intensive applications. We rely on these features of the dialogue approach and apply them to the proposed integration approach, thereby considering the interplay of the process client and the dialogue client (see Sect. 4.4.3).

The integration of the dialogue model into H-BPM, while retaining the advantages of modelling with workflow charts, requires the assignment of tasks (i.e. activities) of the process model to dialogues. The decision whether to organise the dialogue model as a whole (including actor information and "task-spanning" transitions to enable a comprehensive, form-based view on the system) or as fragments refining proper tasks, respectively, is up to the responsible process designer. Nevertheless, in both cases, a mapping is required that defines a kind of synchronisation points in terms of interfaces between tasks and dialogues based on state transitions, data, and user constraints.

As the execution level is dictated by the *Workflow Transition Interpreter*, the dialogue model will be laid "behind" the tasks of the process model. (Note that this kind of integration is only applicable for user tasks!) Thereby, the view of the process model is a global one, i.e. it includes the graph of activities and exchanged information entities in the overall business process. In contrast, workflow charts have a local view with regard to Human–Computer Interaction (HCI) and the worklist paradigm for processing workflows [10].

The connection between the different viewpoints is established via the eP^2 architecture. The eP^2 architecture describes how human resources distribute and execute task items in processes. This way, the HCI viewpoint that refines the current global viewpoint of the overall control flow is created. Considering dialogues as task items that move between the worklists of human participants enables the generalisation of clearly defined semantics of a single-user session of submit/response-style systems towards a dialogue-oriented workflow definition language. Dialogues, as a refinement of a certain task, specify the data and operations available to the user. The task is considered finished if all specified client pages and immediate server actions have been successfully processed. Thereupon, the *Workflow Transition Interpreter* is notified about the completion of that task and, depending on the specification of the process model, enables new tasks.

Some further integration issues also deserve a more detailed treatment and will be specified in the following sections and in Chap. 7, respectively.

- First, we need to integrate the existing *Workflow Transition Interpreter* in the eP^2 architecture.
- Secondly, we have to adapt the *Workflow Transition Interpreter* to incorporate deontic classifications and actors as well as the enhanced communication concept.
- Thirdly, we have to specify how user interaction modelling by means of workflow charts is to be integrated in the eP^2 architecture.

6.3.1 The Process Model

The *process model* basically follows the syntax of BPMN 2.0, with some deviations as specified in [16] as well as supplements for deontic classification and modelling as specified in Sect. 7.5.2 and for the enhanced communication concept as specified in Sect. 7.5.3. The process model is one possible starting point for modelling. In the following, we assume some familiarity with BPMN 2.0 as we describe deontic and actor modelling and the relation to other models.

In a first step towards actor modelling, the business process modeller can associate a set of *roles* with each user task or manual task—those roles which shall be obliged or permitted to perform that task. Additionally, a *deontic expression* can be associated with a user task or manual task by which rules can be enforced—for instance, that *Task B* must be performed by the same user as *Task A* (see Chap. 3 for details).

When a user or manual task is reached by a token, the users currently belonging to the associated roles are determined (with the help of the *actor model*, see below) and for each such user, the task is deontically classified—that is, it is classified as obligatory, permitted (optional), alternative, or forbidden for the user. Possible inputs are, amongst others, the deontic expression (if it exists) and the history of the encompassing activity.

The *Task Server* component (which represents the environment of the process model) is notified that the task is waiting to be performed by a user. The notification includes, for each user who may perform the task, the deontic classification and possible alternative tasks. Then the *Workflow Transition Interpreter*, which interprets the process model, waits for a notification from the environment (*Task Server* component) that the task was performed—or, alternatively, rejected (if there are alternatives) or skipped (if the task was optional).

The *Task Server* serves to connect the process model with the *dialogue model* (see below) by supporting the user with the performance of tasks.

The *Task Server* also manages communication between the process model and its environment (including other processes) by means of exchange of event triggers. To this end, *event pools* are added to the process model (see Chap. 5). The environment can put event triggers into event pools of the process model, and there is at least one other event pool associated with the environment where the process can leave event triggers for the environment (represented by the *Task Server*).

The process model also needs access to the *data model*. Specifically, when a token reaches an activity and the process modeller has defined required input data for this activity, we have to check whether such required data are currently available before we can activate the activity. In the case of a task, the environment (*Task Server*) will only be notified that the task can be performed once the required data are available. In the case of data related to user tasks and manual tasks, the process model only needs *read* access; any data *manipulation*, as well as more detailed reading of data, is to be specified in the context of the *dialogue model*.

As mentioned above, the process model largely follows the specification in [16]. The main differences are:

- The integration of *roles*, which can be associated with tasks, and *users* associated with these roles;
- An evaluation of the deontic classification of tasks at runtime, using deontic expressions associated with tasks and the (also newly introduced) history of the encompassing activity (amongst others);
- Interface functions for notifying the environment of tasks to be performed and of the deontic classification of those tasks, and for listening to the environment to learn when a task was completed, rejected, or skipped;
- Event pools for communication, additional properties of event triggers, and a refinement of event catching and event throwing.

6.3.2   The Actor Model

The layered approach for actor modelling presented in Chap. 3 comprises several views and layers that must be considered in horizontal model integration. The main view of the actor model is called the *process view* and comprises the process flow as described in the previous section. Important concepts of this view are task-based assignment of roles and concatenation of several roles that can execute an activity either together (only in case of non-atomic activities) or alternatively (first and second layer).

After assigning roles to tasks, the next step is to determine the users belonging to the associated roles. Therefore, the actor model provides the *organisational view* which comprises an organisation chart with all roles, a role hierarchy, and the individuals. The *organisational view* is realised by the *Actor Management* component of the eP^2 architecture, which implements the role hierarchy as escalation paths (see Sect. 6.4.6). An escalation can either be allowed under certain circumstances, e.g. if no permitted user is currently available, or by default, which means that in addition to the specified roles, all higher roles are implicitly permitted to execute the task as well.

The last view of the actor model is called the *rule view* and comprises further rules that specify dependencies between different tasks (e.g. to support patterns like *separation of duties* or *retain familiar*). These rules are managed within a global rule set and each rule is associated with one or more corresponding task(s). Sometimes, the evaluation of rules requires to extract information of already completed tasks, as e.g. the executing actor. This information is then provided by the *Workflow Transition Interpreter* (see Sect. 7.5.2 for further details).

The last missing concept of the actor model is that of speech acts, which are introduced as fourth layer of the actor modelling approach. Speech act theory treats communication (e.g. to inform, request, commit, or declare) as action and is used to support communication, coordination, and cooperation between users. In our process flow, the deontic classification of a task can be extended with speech acts, but this implies that the task performs a special action. Currently, the required actions are not supported by the *Task Server* component, so the implementation of speech acts is left for future work.

After evaluating the deontic classification with possible deontic expressions and determining the permitted users, the *Task Server* component is notified that the task is waiting to be performed by one of the users. The notification includes the deontic classification and possible alternative tasks for each user who may perform the task. Note that the deontic classification also depends on the executing user, e.g. in our application scenario (see Sect. 4.5.1 for the workflow chart), reviewing a business trip is optional if it was created by a consultant with reviewer permission, but obligatory for all other consultants. Finally, the *Workflow Transition Interpreter* waits for a notification of the *Task Server* component that the task was performed, rejected, or skipped.

6.3.3 The Dialogue Model

In this section, we propose a hierarchical approach for refining activity-centred business process modelling languages like BPMN by dialogues and related data. More precisely, we discuss how the typed approach for user interaction modelling presented in Chap. 4 can be integrated with the holistic framework of H-BPM and, in particular, with the eP^2 architecture described in Sect. 6.4.

Based on preceding considerations regarding the different viewpoints, we define the hierarchical approach for refining user tasks by dialogues, which consists of several refinement steps, as follows. According to the BPMN specification, a user task represents an activity that is assigned to a human workflow participant (i.e. an actor) and shall be performed with the aid of an IT-system, thereby excluding automatic or manual tasks. A dialogue, in this context, refers to a single-user HCI fragment. This means that a dialogue consists of an alternating sequence of client pages and server actions, only reflecting rendering and submission of forms. In its simplest form, a dialogue represents a *one-step dialogue*, i.e. a single client page with its connected server actions, or a *complex dialogue*, consisting of multiple client pages and server actions wired together. Special attention needs to be paid to user rights, i.e. that the user who is assigned to a task is authorised to perform all data operations included in the refining dialogue. The suggested approach considers the following steps, addressing the data related to a task, dependencies between dialogues, and technical refinement towards implementation. Optionally, also layout and usability can be considered.

1. *Definition of pre- and postconditions.* First, the view of required data related to a task (corresponding to consumption and production rules) from a business perspective needs to be defined. This includes (informally) describing both the artefacts required for task execution and the artefacts being produced, representing a simple set of data objects.
2. *Notation of dialogues.* Then, the dialogue that lies behind a user task needs to be determined. This refinement step mainly addresses the structuring of a set of forms with related data operations in terms of dialogue control (regarding ordering as well as dependencies). The focus of attention lies on supporting the assigned user in performing the task, which enables local decisions on how to provide certain data without affecting external visibility. An important issue is to ensure that the dialogue neither includes user changes nor parallel paths.
3. *Technical refinement.* As a further step, the dialogues can be refined from a technical perspective, e.g. regarding data (physical sources and targets, or intermediate persistence mechanisms for restoring data, maybe using the approach of *auto-commits* and *savepoints*).
4. *Layout and usability (optional).* The final step might address arrangement or appearance of data and is out of the scope of this book.

This means that coherent client pages and server actions should be identified from a business perspective and, vice versa, subject-related tasks should be refined by dialogues. For example, the task of making a bidding call may be divided into multiple, subsequent data entry forms without needing to change the corresponding user task (see the order placement process in Fig. 6.4). This enables flexible modelling of tasks by means of dialogues. A prerequisite for establishing a connection between the nodes of both models, i.e. the user tasks in the process model and the client pages and server actions in the dialogue model, is to be able to identify parts of a dialogue model without user changes and parallel paths (corresponding to one-step or complex dialogues).

The mapping must be based on state transitions. A dynamic approach may be realised by the interplay of dialogue client and worklist client, using the dynamic identification of complex dialogues based on synchronisation points and dialogue constraints (as described in Sect. 4.4.3). Alternatively, a static mapping can be defined. In this case, it is recommended to make knowledge about unique choices explicit, i.e. to label immediate server actions whose attached conditions evaluate uniquely per user, in order to facilitate the identification of dialogues in a workflow chart [1]. In other words, the dialogues must not span more than one user nor contain server actions with multiple choice of subsequent nodes. These parts should be processed only by the dialogue client, dealing with rendering and submitting forms.

Therefore, introducing an explicit construct for identifying certain parts of the dialogue model that can be interpreted as dialogues would be most suitable. They can be graphically highlighted in the workflow chart diagram using surrounding dashed lines (refer, e.g., to the BPMN group element) or by additional key words in the textual specification. This provides process designers with an extended design space for dialogue models, providing advantages for re-design and enabling tool support by proposing different, possible dialogues to the user. Of course, the approach requires some kind of validation to check whether the explicitly specified dialogues are valid. This can be done by applying a proper static check, e.g. as given by the derived function *interpretByDialogueClient* in Sect. 4.4.4 (provided that all required conditions can be evaluated at design time).

6.3.4   The Data Model

BPMN proposes *Data Objects* as the primary constructs for modelling items that are produced, manipulated, and consumed during process execution [21]. They are visually displayed in a process diagram and connected to activities via (directional) *Data Associations*. Tasks can define data inputs to describe their requirements and data outputs to describe their results in terms of so-called *InputOutputSpecification* elements. We already specified the execution semantics for data in [16], as far as detailed information has been available in the BPMN specification. Due to the importance of correct process models, several scientific works have addressed different notions of correctness also for data modelling (refer to, e.g. Awad et al. who introduce an approach for diagnosing and repairing data anomalies in business process models [4]).

In this place, we want to elaborate on the correlation between user tasks and dialogues regarding data. In H-BPM, user tasks in business processes are refined by dialogues and their displayed and editable data. Obeying the BPMN specification, required input data for an activity must be available when a token reaches the activity to activate it. Accordingly, required output data must be set before the activity is completed.

Whereas data in business processes are a global issue, data in dialogues are considered local, because only a certain subset of information is needed to satisfy the user. Therefore, in client pages, data is requested (which corresponds to a *read* operation) and manipulated in immediate server actions (which corresponds to *update*, *insert*, and *delete* operations). Deferred server actions are regarded as side effect free and can be neglected when addressing global consistency. Thus, in the dialogue model, we basically apply operations, causing changes of data, to data views and in turn receive new (updatable) views (cf. ASM transducers [33]). In other words, we capture user interactions by means of operations on data views. The abstract data operations in Sect. 4.4.4 (i.e. generating data views based on global data and translation of changes from a local perspective to the global one) are refined in the eP^2 architecture using the corresponding operations of the *Data Management* component.

In this context, it must be ensured that the input data specification of a user task fulfils the type specification of the first client page contained in the refining dialogue. In addition, the type specification of the final immediate server action(s) must correspond to the output data specification of the user task. We define the input data as $\Sigma(i)$, the output data as $\Sigma(o)$, the type of the client page as $\Sigma(cp)$, and the type of the immediate server action as $\Sigma(isa)$. Then, the following relations must apply: (i) $\Sigma(cp) \subseteq \Sigma(i)$ and (ii) $\Sigma(o) \subseteq \Sigma(isa)$. Of course the availability of input and output data in the corresponding data sets must be ensured (see [16]).

We further define transactions at the level of activities, i.e. a transaction is opened at the beginning of an activity and closed before the activity is completed, unless a transaction sub-process is given (see Sect. 7.5.8.6).

We do not investigate the handling of unexpected situations here but will address exception handling in business process models (in close connection to process adaptability) in future work (refer to Chap. 8).

6.3.5   A Four-Step Integration Approach

As the presented models have strong interdependencies and should not be considered in isolation from one another, we now show how these most relevant aspects of H-BPM can be integrated. The suggested approach utilises different levels of abstraction to define integration in a formal, unambiguous way. The *Workflow Transition Interpreter* plays a central role for the integration by controlling the interaction of all eP^2 components. It has been refined from the specification in [16] in order to integrate the enhanced communication concept as well as deontic classification, actor modelling, and user interaction modelling, in particular for user tasks, which, in contrast to a "classical" task, are marked as "obligatory", "optional", "alternative", and/or "forbidden".

These tasks are displayed in a *worklist*, which represents the core of a worker's view. The worklist is the one point where users in a business process select the next step to execute. Each user has their own worklist or rather their own view of the global worklist. The worklist is divided into two areas, i.e. the process and the task area. The process area (start menu) contains all registered business processes that can be started by the user. The entries in the task area are related to dialogues consisting of reports and forms, through which the users are led in order to complete the selected tasks.

In H-BPM, we distinguish between four steps which are required to achieve seamless integration of selected models for defining holistic business processes. All steps are illustrated by a concrete example model in Sect. 6.3.6.

Step 1 is dedicated to classical process modelling, including a set of activities, gateways, events, etc., using common modelling languages or notations such as BPMN.

Step 2 is to extend the model with *deontic classifications*, task-based assignment of actors, and data objects. The core deontic concepts are obligation (O), permission (P), and prohibition (F for "forbidden") extended with a derived operator for alternative (X). The inserted data objects illustrate the flow of data at a high level of abstraction and will be refined within the next step. The deontic classification allows to remove alternative empty paths and several surrounding (exclusive) gateways, with the advantage of reducing the structural complexity of the diagram and leading to increased understandability (see Chap. 3).

Step 3 includes the specification of user interaction and data using the particularly suitable *workflow chart* notation. A workflow chart is specified as a tripartite graph consisting of typed nodes for (i) rendering reports (*client pages*), (ii) providing forms for user input (*immediate server actions*), and (iii) representing task items of users' worklists (*deferred server actions*). Basically, the resulting dialogue model describes the same behaviour as the previously defined process model but includes considerably more details on the users' actual work within the defined process. This is because its viewpoint focuses more on users and their interaction with applications by specifying the data and operations available, which will be used to refine user tasks.

Step 4 is finally designed for integrating the dialogue model with the deontic process model in order to refine user tasks by dialogues and data (as shown in Sect. 6.3.6). This integration is made by groups of client pages and server actions that are assigned to a user task (according to the notion of a *dialogue*, which only includes immediate server actions with unique choice (see Chap. 4). Different kinds of workflow chart nodes refine the user tasks of the process model based on their types by also integrating the *data model*. The type of a client page describes data that is displayed as a report to the user. The type of an immediate server action represents a user-editable function, i.e. it describes data that the user can enter and submit. The type of a deferred server action is void (as deferred server actions are typically displayed as links in worklists). The types of both the client page and the immediate server action are defined by data views denoting lists of relations. The relations are described by n-ary tuples over data attributes that assign data type and attribute name.

6.3.6   An Illustrative Example

We demonstrate the usability of the model integration approach by means of the *order placement process*, a scenario for ordering supplies, as an illustrative example. We first model the process in BPMN-style, i.e. as a conventional process model. We then add deontic classifications and actors and describe required data by dialogues consisting of typed nodes (reports, forms, and links). Finally, we show how the deontically classified process model can be integrated with the actor modelling approach and workflow charts in H-BPM.

In Fig. 6.1, we show the classical process model, which primarily comprises user tasks. Somebody in the company signals a *demand* for supplies by sending a respective message. Now a purchaser in charge of ordering supplies must first turn this message into a proper *product specification* of the desired goods or services. The purchaser then has to decide whether to use a given *standard supplier* or, alternatively, to issue a *bidding call* to several possible suppliers. In the first case, the purchaser needs to check the *current offer* and general terms of shipment—a rather simple task.

A call for bidding, however, requires more work, which we show in the refined process model in Fig. 6.4. After a sufficient number of offers has been collected, there is the option to try to improve prices and conditions through *further negotiations* with a few selected trading partners. Finally, a *supplier is chosen* and the process continues in the same way as if a standard supplier had been chosen; the *order is placed* and our simplified process ends.

The next step is to extend the model with *deontic classifications* and task-based assignment of actors as shown in Fig. 6.2 (O for obligation, P for permission, F for prohibition, and X for alternative). The diagram is also augmented with data objects to illustrate the flow of data.

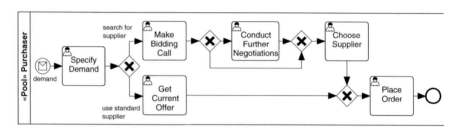

Fig. 6.1 Order placement process: classical process model in BPMN (step 1)

After the demand for supplies is signalled, the task *specify demand* must be performed within every process instance (i.e. there is no alternative to it) and is, thus, marked as obligatory. The execution of the task produces the data output *product specification*, which is used as data input object for the two alternative tasks *make bidding call* and *get current offer*. Task *make bidding call* further receives as data input possible *suppliers* and *general terms* of our company. Similarly, the alternative task *get current offer* receives as data input the standard *supplier*.

Both alternative tasks produce as data output one or more *offer(s)*. If the purchaser has chosen to search for further suppliers, then the optional task *conduct further negotiations* can be executed, but the completion of task *make bidding call* is specified as precondition (i.e. this ensures that the upper path has been taken). The precondition is mandatory, if the process flow is not explicitly given (e.g. in a work list). However, in the given example, the preconditions can also be omitted, which makes the deontic classification much easier to understand (pragmatic approach). Based on the deontic classification, the surrounding exclusive gateways and the alternative empty path can then be removed. Note that all data objects produced by an optional task are also optional, so if a data object is required as input for a subsequent task, then there must be an alternative source, e.g. in our case the original *offers*.

The last task on the upper path is to *choose a supplier*, which is classified as obligatory under the precondition that possible previous tasks are completed (i.e. the precondition can again be omitted). This task receives as data input all *suppliers* with their *offers* and produces as data output one selected *supplier* and one selected *offer*. The two alternative paths are then merged and the last, obligatory task *place order*

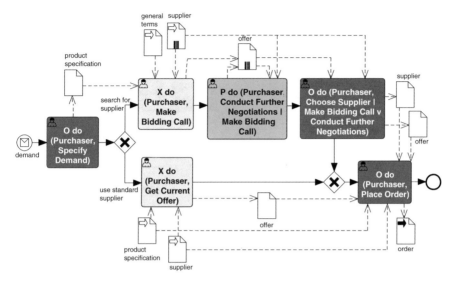

Fig. 6.2 Order placement process: deontic classification and data objects (step 2)

is executed. Since the task *place order* is performed within every process instance, it is marked as obligatory without preconditions. This task receives the three data input objects *product specification*, *supplier*, and *offer* and produces an *order* as data output. Finally, we can extend the deontic classification and specify permitted roles for every task. In our case, we assign the role *Purchaser* to each task and remove the corresponding pool shown in the classical process model.

In Fig. 6.3, we present the order placement process in *workflow chart* notation, which corresponds to the third step of the integration approach. *Client pages*, specified as circles in workflow charts, present information to the user and provide forms for user input. The forms are represented by *immediate server actions*, which are displayed by white rectangles. *Deferred server actions* appear as links to client pages in the worklists of the corresponding users and are specified as rectangles with a gradient fill. Actor information is attached to deferred server actions.

Regarding the order placement process, only one role, i.e. the purchaser, is concerned with ordering supplies, starting from *specifying a demand* to *placing the order*.

The final step is to integrate the dialogue model with the deontic process model. In doing so, user tasks of the process model are refined by dialogues and data as shown in Fig. 6.4.

For example, the task *Place Order* will be refined by the homonymous deferred server action (assigned to the role *Purchaser*), client page *order overview*, and immediate server action *send order*. In the following, an exemplary notation is given for defining the concrete types of these nodes.

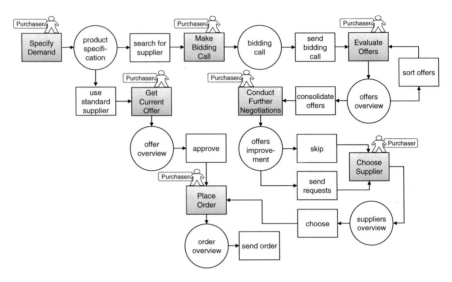

Fig. 6.3 Order placement process: workflow chart (step 3)

```
client page order_overview: (product_specification, supplier,
    offer)
immediate server action send_order: (order)

relation product_specification: (product_name:String ×
    description:String × quantity:Integer)
```

As there exists no universal way of business process and dialogue modelling, a proposed correlation of the process model to the dialogue model might influence modelling decisions but also opens up design space for the designer. In any case, appropriate choice of granularities must be considered; for example, it would make no sense to refine a process model which is already defined with correspondingly fine-grained tasks so that solely a single client page or a single immediate server action would lie behind a user task.

However, some recommendations for integration can be given. If multiple immediate server actions are defined for a client page, the user's choice shall be expressed explicitly in the worklist and, therefore, separate subsequent dialogues shall be defined. Also, if a deferred server action has multiple incoming transitions, it may be beneficial to start a new dialogue for the subsequent client page(s). Further considerations concern optionality in business processes; for example, an immediate server action labelled with *skip* indicates that a separate dialogue shall be defined.

Corresponding to explicitly defined dialogues with unique evaluation of immediate server actions per user in Fig. 6.4, selected deferred server actions represent entry points to the dialogue that lies behind a task. As a modelling guideline, these *starting* deferred server actions (without any incoming transition) can be named according to that task to accentuate integration from a semantic point of view. They unambiguously lead to a client page and its connected immediate server action(s),

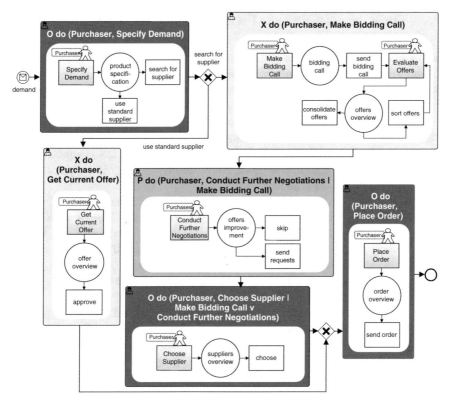

Fig. 6.4 Order placement process: H-BPM diagram (step 4)

representing the initial dialogue. For complex dialogues, further processing is based on branching semantics of the typed workflow chart (see Sect. 4.4). After the *final* immediate server action (without any outgoing transition) has been submitted, which corresponds to the end of the user task, subsequent process execution is performed in accordance with the defined control flow in the process model. Note that if there exist multiple, final immediate server actions, then homonymous guards must be defined for the subsequent exclusive gateway in the process model. Finally, it needs to be mentioned that the actor information assigned to deferred server actions actually becomes redundant due to the deontic classification of user tasks. However, it can be retained to preserve look and feel of workflow charts and to support intelligibility.

To sum up, the resulting H-BPM diagram comprises all relevant aspects for business process modelling and execution (i.e. control flow, actor, interaction, and data) based on a formally defined integration method. In this way, process modellers and analysts can benefit from this intuitive, integrated view and concentrate on their modelling tasks free from distraction by following the defined steps of the H-BPM method.

6.4   The enhanced Process Platform (eP^2) Architecture

In this section, we describe the architecture of eP^2, consisting of several components and addressing horizontal and vertical model integration. The core of the reference architecture for a BPM system is the so-called *Workflow Transition Interpreter*.

This component interprets H-BPM process models whose basis is described in [16] and which were extended by different aspects (cf. Chaps. 2–5). Thus, the aim of the eP^2 architecture is, on the one hand, to show that the proposed process description language with all its extensions in the form of integrated models is applicable for executable process definitions and, on the other hand, to provide a platform for business process execution and user support.

The eP^2 architecture includes, besides a workflow engine, components for actor management, user interaction, data management, as well as different interfaces to define the communication between the components. The models themselves are created using a model development tool which is not actually a part of eP^2 but depicted in the component diagram to document the relation.

The component diagram in Fig. 6.5 shows the high-level structure of eP^2, whereas Fig. 7.1 depicts the runtime instances.

Afterwards, we describe the functionality of each component and give a detailed description of the provided interfaces and their defined operations. We describe the interface operations in a generic style along the lines of typical descriptions of the signatures of such operations in programming languages. This section provides an overview of the architecture; a detailed specification is given in Chap. 7.

6.4.1   Process Model Repository

The *Process Model Repository* component provides functionality for persistent storage like access to and version management of models. In particular, it is the central access point in eP^2 for all models used within the architecture (*Process Model*, *Actor Model*, *Data Model*, and *Dialogue Model* (see also Fig. 6.5)).

CRUDModel Interface. The *Process Model Repository* component provides the interface *CRUDModel*, which offers the classical create, read, update, and delete operations (*crud*) as well as functionality for version management.

The operation *addModel* adds the given model to the repository connected with the provided metadata. The metadata contain information about initial version, keywords, and a description of the model.

```
void addModel(Model model, modelMetaData metaData)
```

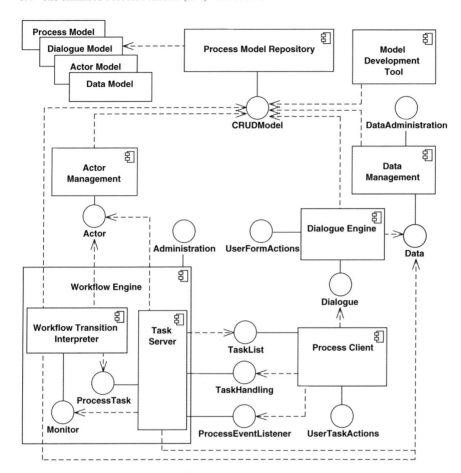

Fig. 6.5 Architectural overview of eP^2

The operation *deleteModel* deletes the model identified by the parameter *model-Name* in the given version from the repository. If all versions of the model should be deleted, the version string has to be defined as "all". If either the name or the version does not exist, an exception will be thrown.

```
void deleteModel(String modelName, String version) throws
    notFoundException
```

The operation *getModel* returns the model that refers to the parameter *modelName* in the given version. If the model cannot be found, an exception is thrown. If the version is *null* or empty, the latest version of the model will be returned.

```
Model getModel(String modelName, String version) throws
    notFoundException
```

The operation *updateModel* updates the already existing model with the new model data. If the model cannot be found, an exception is thrown. The operation returns the new version number of the updated model.

```
String updateModel(Model model) throws notFoundException
```

The operation *searchModel* searches for models in the repository. It returns a set of models that match the search string. The search string may also contain a list of logically connected keywords or wildcards.

```
Set searchModel(String searchString)
```

6.4.2 Workflow Engine

The *Workflow Engine* component encapsulates the *Workflow Transition Interpreter* component (as the core of eP^2) and the required infrastructure for the interpreter like the component *Task Server*.

Administration Interface. The functionality of the *Administration* interface should comprise operations for controlling workflow instances as well as monitoring running processes and tasks (not yet defined in detail).

6.4.3 Task Server

The *Task Server* component is part of the *Workflow Engine* and is, in particular, responsible for distributing tasks. So-called "UserTasks" and "ManualTasks" (see [21, p. 163]) are distributed to the component *Process Client*, whereas "Script-Tasks" and "ServiceTasks" (see [21, p. 159ff]) are processed by a task implementation tool (not modelled as an own component in Fig. 6.5 but implicitly part of the *Task Server* component).

ProcessTask Interface. The *Task Server* provides the interface *ProcessTask* to communicate with the *Workflow Transition Interpreter*.
The operation *processTask* is called by the *Workflow Transition Interpreter* when a newly created user or manual task instance gets active in order to instruct the *Task Server* to assign the instance to the corresponding users. If the parameter *adHocParentInstance* specifies that the instance is part of an ad-hoc sub-process, the *Task Server* has to take care that if the ordering attribute is sequential, only one user can process a single task instance at the same time. The parameter *transactionSubInstance* identifies the instance of a transaction sub-process. All task instances of a transaction sub-process are identified by the same *transactionSubInstance*. When the first task instance of the transaction is ready for processing, the *Task Server*

has to open and manage a transaction (see interface *Data* in Sect. 6.4.8). The parameter *deonticClassificationsForUsers* (tpye *Set*) includes a deontic classification for users (type *deonticClassificationsForUsers*) per certain user.

```
void processTask(Instance taskInstance, InputSet
    currentISet, Instance adHocParentInstance, Instance
    transactionSubInstance, Set
    deonticClassificationsForUsers)
```

The operation *invokeScript* is called upon the availability of a script task instance to pass it to a task implementation tool. The parameter *transactionSubInstance* (if specified) refers to an instance of a transaction sub-process to that the given script belongs to.

```
void invokeScript(Instance taskInstance, InputSet
    currentISet, String script, Instance
    transactionSubInstance)
```

The operation *invokeService* is called upon the availability of a service task instance to pass it to a task implementation tool. The parameter *transactionSubInstance* (if specified) refers to an instance of a transaction sub-process to that the given service operation belongs to.

```
void invokeService(Instance taskInstance, InputSet
    currentISet, String operation, Instance
    transactionSubInstance)
```

The operation *cancelTask* is called by the *Workflow Transition Interpreter* for every task instance that has to be cancelled (for example, when the *completionCondition* and *cancelRemainingInstances* attributes of an ad-hoc sub-process are true, then all active instances of the ad-hoc sub-process have to be cancelled). Subsequently, the *Task Server* has to call *removeTask* (see interface *TaskList* in Sect. 6.4.5) for the given task instance.

```
void cancelTask(Instance taskInstance)
```

The operation *completeTransaction* is called upon the completion of a transaction sub-process instance to request the *Task Server* to commit the open transaction assigned to the given *subProcessInstance*.

```
void completeTransaction(Instance subProcessInstance)
```

The operation *resetDeonticClassifications* provides a set containing *deonticClassificationsForUsers* for every user. Calling this operation can be necessary for alternative tasks when e.g. a user decided to perform a task, then another task can become forbidden.

```
void resetDeonticClassifications(Instance taskInstance, Set
    deonticClassificationsForUsers)
```

TaskHandling Interface. The interface *TaskHandling* provides operations to control the state of tasks and to deliver lists of task and process instances to users (via the *Process Client* component) or to a task processing tool. Furthermore, this interfaces is used for passing user actions (e.g. when a task was completed, skipped, or rejected) to the *Workflow Transition Interpreter* component via the *Task Server* component (cf. Fig. 6.6).

It is recommended that the operation *getAllTasks* is called by the *Process Client* whenever a user logs in to the system. Upon calling this operation, the user is automatically registered as active. The return value contains all task instances (of the type *ExtendedTaskInstance*), which the user is allowed to process (for the user's worklist cf. Chap. 4).

```
Set getAllTasks(User user, ClientInstance clientInstance)
```

The operation *tryStartTask* has to be called by the *Process Client* before a task instance can be processed. When the return value is true, processing can be started. In addition, when a user selects the task for performing, the *Task Server* has to change the state of the given task instance and to request all registered *Process Clients* to remove this task (see interface *TaskList* in Sect. 6.4.5).

```
Boolean tryStartTask(ExtendedTaskInstance taskInstance,
    User user)
```

The operation *cancelUserAndManualTask* requests the *Task Server* to reset the state of the given task instance and to offer it again to all *Process Clients*. (The *Task Server* has to take care that data changes are rolled back.)

```
void cancelUserAndManualTask(ExtendedTaskInstance
    taskInstance)
```

The operation *getAllProcessesToBeAllowedToStart* is called by the *Process Client* to get a set of all processes which the given user is allowed to start.

```
Set getAllProcessesToBeAllowedToStart(User user)
```

The operation *logOff* has to be called when a user logs off from the system. The parameter *user* identifies the logged-in user and the parameter *clientInstance* identifies the corresponding instance of the *Process Client* component.

```
void logOff(User user, ClientInstance clientInstance)
```

The operation *taskCompleted* informs the *Task Server* about the completion of a task instance. Subsequently, the *Task Server* has to call the operation *taskCompleted* from the *Monitor* interface (see Sect. 6.4.4) for that task instance to inform the *Workflow Transition Interpreter*, which has to set the proper lifecycle state (cf. Fig. 7.2).

```
void taskCompleted(ExtendedTaskInstance taskInstance)
```

The operation *taskSkipped* has to be called when a user decides not to process a task (i.e. when the deontic classification allows skipping the task) to inform the *Task Server* component, which in turn has to call the operation *taskSkipped* of the *Monitor* interface to inform the *Workflow Transition Interpreter*. The parameter *taskInstance* identifies the task instance to be skipped.

```
void taskSkipped(ExtendedTaskInstance taskInstance)
```

The operation *taskRejected* has to be called when a user decides not to process a task (i.e. when the deontic classification allows rejecting the task) to inform the *Task Server* component, which subsequently calls the operation *taskRejected* of the *Monitor* interface to inform the *Workflow Transition Interpreter*. The parameter *taskInstance* identifies the task instance to be skipped.

```
void taskRejected(ExtendedTaskInstance taskInstance)
```

ProcessEventListener Interface.   This interface provides an operation for catching events from other components, i.e. an activated start event from the *Process Client* to start a process instance or an error event occurred at task processing. The supported events are start events and error events. Both events are handled by creating an appropriate trigger object (type *eventTriggerTypes*), setting whose properties, and adding this trigger object to the appropriate event pool (see Sect. 5.5). The operation *handleProcessEvent* creates a trigger object (type *eventTriggerTypes*), sets whose properties from properties of the given process event and adds the trigger to the appropriate event pool.

```
void handleProcessEvent(ProcessEvent pEvent)
```

6.4.4 Workflow Transition Interpreter

The *Workflow Transition Interpreter* encapsulates the ASM ground model for H-BPM process diagrams and is responsible for managing running process instances by monitoring their state. It also runs through business processes and passes activated tasks (i.e. tasks whose lifecycle state is "Active" [21, p. 428]) to the *Task Server* using the interface *ProcessTask*. In this way the *Workflow Transition Interpreter* component interprets (business) process models. A detailed ASM ground model for the *Workflow Transition Interpreter* component is presented in [16] respectively in [15].

Monitor Interface.   The *Monitor* interface provides operations to inform the *Workflow Transition Interpreter* about the states of task instances or external information. The following interface operations correspond to monitored and shared functions in the respective ASM ground models (see [16]).
The operation *abortedByEnvironment* informs the *Workflow Transition Interpreter* that all instances of any process should be aborted.

```
Boolean abortedByEnvironment()
```

The operation *cancelTransactionTask* has to be called to inform the *Workflow Transition Interpreter* if the given task instance is part of a transaction sub-process (this is known by the *Task Server*, because the parameter *transactionSubProcInstance* was sent when the task was started) for each task that has to be cancelled.

```
Boolean cancelTransactionTask(Instance taskInstance)
```

The operation *taskCompleted* informs the *Workflow Transition Interpreter* that the given task instance has been completed by the appropriate user (represents the return value).

```
user taskCompleted(Instance taskInstance)
```

The operation *taskSkipped* informs the *Workflow Transition Interpreter*, when a user decided to skip the given task instance (i.e. when the deontic classification allows skipping the task).

```
Boolean taskSkipped(Instance taskInstance)
```

The operation *taskRejected* informs the *Workflow Transition Interpreter*, when a user decided to reject the given task instance (i.e. when the deontic classification allows rejecting the task).

```
Boolean taskRejected(Instance taskInstance)
```

The operation *taskSelected* informs the *Workflow Transition Interpreter*, when a user decided to process the given task instance (needed for recalculating the deontic classifications).

```
user taskSelected(Instance taskInstance)
```

6.4.5   Process Client

The *Process Client* component is responsible for providing user tasks as well as manual tasks to users. For user tasks, it uses the *Dialogue Engine* component (see Sect. 6.4.7), which provides dialogues (via the interface *Dialogue*) and displays and updates the corresponding data. Manual tasks are performed without the aid of any application (see [21, p. 163]), therefore, no connection to the *Data Management* component is required. As illustrated in Fig. 6.5, the *Process Client* component provides (i) the interface *TaskList* for communicating with the *Task Server* component regarding the distribution of activated tasks and (ii) the interface *UserTaskActions* for handling user actions regarding task management.

TaskList Interface.   The *TaskList* interface is provided by the *Process Client* to be informed by the *Task Server* whenever a task has to be removed from or added to a user's collection of open tasks or when the deontic classification of a task has changed.

The operation *removeTask* informs the *Process Client* that the given task instance was selected by another user for processing. Therefore, the *Process Client* has to update the collection of open tasks either by removing the given task instance from the collection or by recalling the operation *getAllTasks* of the *TaskHandling* interface.

```
void removeTask(ExtendedTaskInstance taskInstance)
```

The operation *addTask* informs the *Process Client* that the given task instance has become active, therefore, the *Process Client* has to update the collection of open tasks either by adding the given task instance to the collection or by recalling the operation *getAllTasks* of the *TaskHandling* interface. The second parameter contains information concerning deontic classifications and may be used for illustrating the task in the worklist.

```
void addTask(ExtendedTaskInstance taskInstance,
    DeonticClassificationsForUsers userClassification)
```

The operation *resetDeonticClassificationOfTask* is called for a logged-in user, when, after having skipped or completed a task, the deontic classification has changed to inform the *Process Client* component.

```
void resetDeonticClassificationOfTask
    (ExtendedTaskInstance taskInstance,
    DeonticClassificationsForUsers userClassification)
```

UserTaskActions Interface.   The *UserTaskActions* interface provided by the component *Process Client* handles different user actions (e.g. selection of a task from the collection of open tasks or completion of a manual task). Such actions must be passed to the *Task Server* component by using the *TaskHandling* interface, which again passes most of them to the *Workflow Transition Interpreter* component via the interface *Monitor* (see Fig. 6.6 for an example). For this reason, some operations (e.g. *taskSkipped* or *taskRejected*) are defined in the interfaces *TaskHandling* and *Monitor*.

The operation *selectedByUserForProcessing* handles the user action for selecting a task that should be processed. It checks whether the task is a user task and, if so, instructs the proper *Dialogue Engine* component to provide the related dialogue. Furthermore, when the *Dialogue Engine* component has finished the dialogue processing, the *Task Server* is informed (via the *TaskHandling* interface, who in turn informs the *Workflow Transition Interpreter* via the interface *Monitor* (cf. Fig. 7.3).

```
void selectedByUserForProcessing(ExtendedTaskInstance
    taskInstance)
```

The operation *manualTaskCompleted* handles the user action for marking the given task instance—which is always a manual task—as completed. As manual tasks are processed without the aid of IT systems (cf. [21]), a separate user action is necessary to inform the component *Task Server*, which in turn informs the *Workflow Transition Interpreter* via the interface *Monitor*. (Note that a user task is automatically completed when the corresponding dialogue has successfully been processed.)

```
void manualTaskCompleted(ExtendedTaskInstance taskInstance)
```

The operation *logOff* handles the user action for logging off from the system. The given parameter refers to the *Process Client* instance of the user (each user has an own instance cf. Fig. 7.1).

```
void logOff(ClientInstance clientInstance)
```

The operation *taskSkipped* handles the user action for skipping the task instance identified by the parameter (only possible if the deontic classification allows to skip the task). Figure 6.6 demonstrates how the *Workflow Transition Interpreter* component is informed about skipping a task.

```
void taskSkipped(ExtendedTaskInstance taskInstance)
```

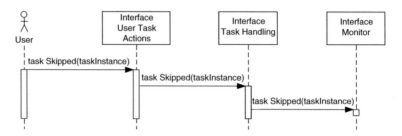

Fig. 6.6 Interactions when a user skips a task

The operation *taskRejected* handles the user action for rejecting the task instance identified by the parameter (only possible if the deontic classification allows to reject the task). The interactions are similar (only the name of the called operation differs) to those shown in Fig. 6.6.

```
void taskRejected(ExtendedTaskInstance taskInstance)
```

The operation *taskCanceled* handles the user action for cancelling the task instance identified by the parameter.

```
void taskCanceled(ExtendedTaskInstance taskInstance)
```

The operation *startProcess* handles the user action for starting the given process. In this case the component *Task Server* has to be informed by using the *ProcessEventListener*, which deals with events. Subsequently the *Task Server* delivers the trigger to the event pool of the environment (see Sect. 5.5). These interactions are illustrated in Fig. 7.4.

```
void startProcess(Process process)
```

6.4.6   Actor Management

The *Actor Management* component is responsible for managing roles and the assignment of users to these roles. Since the *Actor Model* (see Chap. 3) also might contain hierarchies, the *Actor Management* component also has to provide requests for an escalation path along the defined hierarchy.

Actor Interface.   The *Actor* interface provides required operations to access information of the *Actor Model*.

The operation *getUsersByRole* returns a set of all users assigned to the given role in the defined process.

```
Set getUsersByRole(Process process, Role role)
```

The operation *getUserRoles* returns a set of all roles of the user identified by the given user in the defined process.

```
Set getUserRoles(Process process, User user)
```

The operation *getEscalationRole* returns the superior role (in the role hierarchy) to the role of the given user in the defined process.

```
Role getEscalationRole(Process process, User user)
```

The operation *getEscalationUsers* returns a set of all users who have assigned a superior role to the role of the given user in the defined process.

```
Set getEscalationUsers(Process process, User user)
```

The operation *getAllProcessesUserMayStart* returns a set of all processes, which the given user is allowed to start.

```
Set getAllProcessesUserMayStart(User user)
```

6.4.7   Dialogue Engine

The *Dialogue Engine* component is able to interpret certain parts of the *dialogue model*, which are assigned to a single user (according to the assignment information of the corresponding task), and to provide user interfaces based on this model (see Chap. 4). This means that it manages and provides the dialogue of a given task, which may refer to a one-step dialogue or a complex dialogue. Furthermore, the *Dialogue Engine* component is responsible for reading and displaying required data to the user as well as for storing user inputs of a dialogue, for which it uses the interface operations provided by the *Data Management* component. As illustrated in Fig. 6.5, the *Dialogue Engine* component provides (i) the interface *Dialogue* for communicating with the *Process Client* component regarding the preparation of user interfaces and (ii) the interface *UserFormActions* for handling user actions regarding form processing. In this architecture, each *Process Client* component has its own *Dialogue Engine* object.

Dialogue Interface.   The *Dialogue* interface is defined to provide user interfaces requested from the *Process Client* for user tasks.

The operation *processDialogue* shows the dialogue for the given task instance. The parameter *user* denotes the responsible user and may be required for database operations. The parameter *transactionId* is only specified if the given task instance belongs to a transaction sub-processes; for all other instances it is undefined. If the parameter *transactionId* is undefined, a *commit* of the *Data* interface has to be performed after having processed the dialogue.

```
Boolean processDialogue(Instance taskInstance, User user,
    TransactionId transactionId)
```

UserFormActions Interface.   The *UserFormActions* interface provided by the component *Dialogue Engine* handles user actions regarding form processing (i.e. the submission of data inserted in a form).

The operation *submit* handles the user action for submitting the given *data* via the selected form *action*.

```
Boolean submit(DataView data, ImmediateServerAction action)
```

6.4.8   Data Management

The *Data Management* component provides access to the data model as well as to the data available in the initial *Data Model*.

Data Interface.   The *Data* interface provides operations to access and manage persistent domain data.

The operation *read* reads the data selected by the given query. The return value is of the type *DataView*.

```
DataView read(String query)
```

The operation *update* updates the given data view. The return value indicates whether the update was successful.

```
Boolean update(DataView dataView)
```

The operation *create* creates a new data view identified by the proper parameter and returns the newly created data view (including identification number).

```
DataView create(DataView dataView)
```

The operation *delete* deletes the given data view.

```
void delete(DataView dataView)
```

The operation *commit* commits the given transaction. The return value indicates whether the commit was successful.

```
Boolean commit(TransactionId transactionId)
```

The operation *rollback* rolls back the given transaction. The return value indicates whether the rollback was successful.

```
Boolean rollback(TransactionId transactionId)
```

The operation *openTransaction* creates a transaction and returns the identification number of this transaction.

```
TransactionId openTransaction()
```

DataAdministration Interface.   This interface is not yet defined but should handle data administration.

6.5   Summary

In this chapter, we presented a novel, homogeneous integration framework which is capable of formally integrating indispensable aspects of business process automation. The four-step-integration approach of the proposed H-BPM method precisely guides process analysts and modellers via defined steps, providing a complete walk-through for modelling business processes in a trustworthy way. All integration measures are designed in due consideration of all horizontal refinements for business process diagrams investigated in this book, i.e. deontic logic [18, 20] in Chap. 2, actor modelling [19] in Chap. 3, user interaction modelling [1, 2, 10] in Chap. 4, and a communication concept in Chap. 5. In this way, the H-BPM method enables seamless modelling of multifaceted aspects of business processes on all levels of abstraction by means of formal refinement.

The process model builds on the classical BPMN-style model (step 1) and incorporates event pools and additional event trigger properties to enable an enhanced communication concept. As the next step, those types of activities which are to be performed by humans—in BPMN called user tasks and manual tasks—are refined. These tasks can be associated with user roles and rules for detailing the relation between task and roles or individual users (step 2). At runtime, when such a task is activated, a *deontic classification* can be computed which tells each user their permissions and obligations with respect to this task. Outside the process model, users can then, depending on their permissions, perform, reject, or skip a task, which is then fed back to the process model to enable it to continue.

Regarding the integration of user interaction modelling in H-BPM (step 3), the three-staged interaction paradigm of workflow charts, i.e. (i) selecting a task from the worklist, (ii) rendering form data, and (iii) submitting the data, can be reduced to a two-staged interaction of submit/response-style systems for dialogues. This means that, applying the integration approach for refining user tasks by dialogues, the handling of workflow and dialogue states is divided among different components of the the eP^2 architecture (step 4). Referring to the basic states and operations of processing a workflow chart, the tasks of the worklist client (i.e. providing the worklist to the assigned user and supporting the selection of a worklist item) are undertaken by the *Task Server* and the *Process Client*, whereas the responsibilities of the dialogue client (i.e. rendering and submitting forms) is a matter of the *Dialogue Engine*.

The *Task Server* also makes use of its connection to the *Actor Management* component to handle assignment information for user tasks. It further controls a *Process Client* component instance to present the worklist for a single user and to support task selection, which corresponds to the notion of a deferred server action in the context of the typed workflow chart. The *Dialogue Engine* locally works on a dialogue without requiring any actor information (as the single-user constraint needs to be ensured already when the dialogue is identified). It focuses on rendering reports and forms on client pages and on supporting submission of user data of selected immediate server actions, which are included within the forms on client pages. Finally, data operations are handled within the *Data Management* component.

References

1. Atkinson, C., Draheim, D., Geist, V.: Typed business process specification. In: Proceedings of the 14th IEEE International Enterprise Distributed Object Computing Conference. pp. 69–78. EDOC '10, IEEE Computer Society (2010)
2. Auer, D., Geist, V., Draheim, D.: Extending BPMN with submit/response-style user interaction modeling. In: Proceedings of CEC '09. pp. 368–374. IEEE Computer Society (2009)
3. Awad, A., Grosskopf, A., Meyer, A., Weske, M.: Enabling resource assignment constraints in BPMN, [working paper BPT Technical Report 04-2009], Business Process Technology, Hasso Plattner Institute, Potsdam (2009)
4. Awad, A., Decker, G., Lohmann, N.: Diagnosing and repairing data anomalies in process models. In: Business Process Management Workshops. pp. 5–16. Springer (2010)
5. Bachman, C.W.: Summary of current work ansi/x3/sparc/study group: database systems. SIG-MOD Rec. **6**(3), 16–39 (1974)
6. Börger, E.: Approaches to modeling business processes: a critical analysis of BPMN, workflow patterns and YAWL. Softw. Syst. Model **11**(3), 305–318 (2012)
7. Börger, E., Sörensen, O.: BPMN core modeling concepts: inheritance-based execution semantics. In: Embley, D.W., Thalheim, B. (eds.) Handbook of Conceptual Modeling: Theory, Practice and Research Challenges, pp. 287–335. Springer, Heidelberg (2011)
8. Clements, P., Bachmann, F., Bass, L., Garlan, D., Ivers, J., Little, R., Nord, R., Stafford, J.: Documenting Software Architectures: Views and Beyond. Addison-Wesley, Boston (2003)
9. Draheim, D., Geist, V., Natschläger, C.: Integrated framework for seamless modeling of business and technical aspects in process-oriented enterprise applications. Int. J. Softw. Eng. Knowl. Eng. **22**(05), 645–674 (2012)
10. Geist, V.: Integrated executable business process and dialogue specification. Dissertation, Johannes Kepler University, Linz, Austria (2011)
11. Gortmaker, J., Janssen, M., Wagenaar, R.W.: Towards requirements for a reference model for process orchestration in e-government. In: Böhlen, M.H., Gamper, J., Polasek, W., Wimmer, M. (eds.) TCGOV. Lecture Notes in Computer Science, vol. 3416, pp. 169–180. Springer (2005)
12. Hofmeister, C., Nord, R., Soni, D.: Applied Software Architecture. Addison-Wesley Object Technology Series. Addison-Wesley, Boston (2000)
13. Kloppmann, M., Koenig, D., Leymann, F., Pfau, G., Rickayzen, A., Riegen, C., Schmidt, P., Trickovic, I.: WS-BPEL Extension for People - BPEL4People. IBM, SAP (2005)
14. Kossak, F., Geist, V.: An enhanced communication concept for business processes. In: Kolb, J., Leopold, H., Mendling, J. (eds.) Enterprise Modelling and Information Systems Architectures – Proceedings of EMISA 2015. Lecture Notes in Informatics, vol. 248, pp. 77–91. Gesellschaft für Informatik (2015)

15. Kossak, F., Illibauer, C., Geist, V., Kubovy, J., Natschläger, C., Ziebermayr, T., Kopetzky, T., Freudenthaler, B., Schewe, K.D.: A rigorous semantics for BPMN 2.0 process diagrams: the ground model in detail. http://www.scch.at/en/HagenbergBPM (2014). Accessed 12 Oct 2015
16. Kossak, F., Illibauer, C., Geist, V., Kubovy, J., Natschläger, C., Ziebermayr, T., Kopetzky, T., Freudenthaler, B., Schewe, K.D.: A Rigorous Semantics for BPMN 2.0 Process Diagrams. Springer, Berlin (2015)
17. Minoli, D.: Enterprise Architecture A to Z: Frameworks, Business Process Modeling, SOA, and Infrastructure Technology. Auerbach Publications, Boca Raton (2008)
18. Natschläger, C.: Deontic BPMN. In: Hameurlain, A., Liddle, S., Schewe, K., Zhou, X. (eds.) Database and Expert Systems Applications. Lecture Notes in Computer Science, vol. 6861, pp. 264–278. Springer (2011)
19. Natschläger, C., Geist, V.: A layered approach for actor modelling in business processes. Bus. Process. Manag. J. **19**, 917–932 (2013)
20. Natschläger-Carpella, C.: Extending BPMN with Deontic Logic. Logos, Berlin (2012)
21. Object Management Group: Business Process Model and Notation (BPMN) 2.0. http://www.omg.org/spec/BPMN/2.0 (2011). Accessed 6 Oct 2015
22. Object Management Group: OMG Unified Modeling Language (OMG UML), version 2.5. http://www.omg.org/spec/UML/2.5 (2015). Accessed 6 Oct 2015
23. Pinheiro da Silva, P., Paton, N.: UMLi: The unified modeling language for interactive applications. In: Proceedings of the UML '00, York. Lecture Notes in Computer Science 1939. pp. 117–132. Springer (2000)
24. Recker, J., Indulska, M., Rosemann, M., Green, P.: How good is BPMN really? Insights from theory and practice. In: Ljungberg, J., Andersson, M. (eds.) 14th European Conference on Information Systems, pp. 1582–1593. Goeteborg, Sweden (2006)
25. REWERSE Working Group I1: R2ML—the REWERSE I1 Rule Markup Language. http://oxygen.informatik.tu-cottbus.de/rewerse-i1/?q=R2ML (2015). Accessed 10 Nov 2015
26. Rozanski, N., Woods, E.: Software Systems Architecture: Working with Stakeholders Using Viewpoints and Perspectives. Addison-Wesley, Boston (2011)
27. Scheer, A.W.: ARIS - Business Process Modeling. Springer, Berlin (2000)
28. Scheer, A., Thomas, O., Adam, O.: Process modeling using event-driven process chains. In: Dumas, M., van der Aalst, W., ter Hofstede, A. (eds.) Process-Aware Information Systems: Bridging People and Software Through Process Technology, pp. 119–146. Wiley, New Jersey (2005)
29. Schewe, B., Schewe, K.D.: A user-centered method for the development of data-intensive dialogue systems: an object-oriented approach. In: Proceedings of the IFIP International Working Conference on Information System Concepts: Towards A Consolidation of Views. Chapman & Hall (1995)
30. Schewe, K.D.: Horizontal and vertical business process model integration. In: Decker, H., Lenka, L., Link, S., Basl, J., Tjoa, A. (eds.) Database and Expert Systems Applications. Lecture Notes in Computer Science, vol. 8055, pp. 1–3. Springer, Berlin (2013)
31. Schewe, K.D., Schewe, B.: Integrating database and dialogue design. Knowl. Inf. Syst. **2**, 1–32 (2000)
32. Seffah, A., Vanderdonckt, J., Desmarais, M.: Human-Centered Software Engineering. Springer, Berlin (2009)
33. Spielmann, M.: Verification of relational transducers for electronic commerce. J. Comput. Syst. Sci. **66**(1), 40–65 (2003)
34. ter Hofstede, A.M., van der Aalst, W.M.P., Adams, M., Russell, N. (eds.): Modern Business Process Automation: YAWL and its Support Environment. Springer, Heidelberg (2010)
35. Wohed, P., van der Aalst, W., Dumas, M., ter Hofstede, A., Russell, N.: On the suitability of BPMN for business process modelling. In: Dustdar, S., Fiadeiro, J., Sheth, A. (eds.) Business Process Management. Lecture Notes in Computer Science, vol. 4102, pp. 161–176. Springer (2006)

36. Wolter, C., Schaad, A.: Modeling of task-based authorization constraints in BPMN. In: Alonso, G., Dadam, P., Rosemann, M. (eds.) Business Process Management: 5th International Conference, BPM 2007, Brisbane, Australia, pp. 64–79. Springer, Berlin (2007)
37. Zachman, J.: A framework for information systems architecture. IBM Syst. J. **26**(3), 267–292 (1987)

Chapter 7
Formal Specification of the eP^2 Architecture

In this chapter, we present the common signature and we specify the common behaviour of all components of the enhanced Process Platform (eP^2) architecture, which are illustrated in Fig. 6.5 and described in Sect. 6.4. Additionally, we rigorously specify each component and its interactions—by refining the common behaviour—each in an own section.

Thereby, each component is specified as an own Abstract State Machine (ASM) ground model [5, 7], including the signature, which extends the common signature and is specific to this component by listing all static, controlled, shared, and out functions (if existing). Furthermore, the signature of each ground model includes exported and imported functions and rules, whereby exported functions are usually out or shared functions (though they may include controlled functions as well), and exported rules basically conform to interface operations supplied by this component. Imported functions correspond to monitored functions and imported rules to called interface operations provided by other components. For improving understandability, each rule and function is augmented with explanatory comments.

The interactions between those components correspond to synchronously or asynchronously called interface operations, which are already described in Sect. 6.4. Therefore, each component which provides interfaces specifies a rule or a derived function for each operation of those interfaces, in which it reacts to the call of the respective operation. Such a reaction may also comprise further calls to other interface operations of other components. For allowing other components to call provided interface operations, these operations are exported by the provider component and imported by the caller component, as mentioned above.

In order to handle asynchronous calls of interface operations of another component—whose parameter list may differ—in a unified way, we have specified (i) the universe *parameters* which contains all parameters in a list, where the sequence of these parameters corresponds to those defined for the related operation; and (ii) the rule *CallOperationAsync* to standardise asynchronous calls (for both, see Sect. 7.3.1).

The formal specification based on the ASM method defines the behaviour of the system in a formal, unambiguous way. This approach utilises different levels of

© Springer International Publishing Switzerland 2016
F. Kossak et al., *Hagenberg Business Process Modelling Method*,
DOI 10.1007/978-3-319-30496-0_7

abstraction to define the system behaviour similar to abstraction levels used in the implementation. Although the specification does not define how to implement the system and the implementation might be structured in a completely different way, it nevertheless makes sense to follow the structure of the specification.

This chapter is structured as follows. Section 7.1 provides a motivation for specifying the architecture by means of ASMs. Subsequently, we provide related work in Sect. 7.2. The signature of all specifications, including universes, notations used, common basic function as well as common rules and derived functions, is presented in Sect. 7.3, whereas Sect. 7.4 defines the common behaviour of all components. Afterwards, Sect. 7.5 comprises an own ASM ground model for each component of the eP^2 architecture. Finally, we conclude this chapter with a summary in Sect. 7.6.

7.1   Motivation

A serious issue concerning system architectures often is how to guarantee that the executable behaviour of a particular model is exactly the same as intended by the system architect. In addition, misbehaviour should be exposed as early as possible, potentially already in the design phase. A lot of facts influence the architectural design phase, e.g. requirements, domain knowledge, and experience, in which different architectural models are created, most of them using a graphical notation (Unified Modeling Language (UML), Business Process Model and Notation (BPMN), etc.). Graphical notations seem intuitive enough to be well understood almost at first sight. Unfortunately, they typically lack the precise mathematical basis that is required to render them really unambiguous. On the other hand, attempts on formalisation can become quite complex very soon. Though the ASM method has a solid mathematical foundation, ASMs can be correctly understood as pseudo-code or virtual machines working over abstract data structures, not requiring practitioners to have special training to use this method.

For this reason, we apply the notion of ASMs to formalise the eP^2 components, their interfaces and behaviour, and to specify the collaboration of the components in a rigorous way. Moreover, by using a formal notation, we avoid ambiguities in the system from the very start. Subsequently, we fulfil the main goals of a software architecture description comprising, among others, (i) efficiently support the system development, (ii) present different aspects of the architecture, and (iii) prescribe components at arbitrary levels of abstraction [1].

7.2   Related Work

Already in 1995, Inverardi and Wolf [9] presented an approach to formally specify software architectures, whereby the software system was viewed as chemicals, whose reactions were controlled by explicitly stated rules. This metaphor was devised by

Banâtre and Le Métayer in 1990 in the domain of theoretical computer science [3]. Berry and Boudol [4] reformulated this metaphor as CHemical Abstract Machine (CHAM), which was used to describe the semantics of various models. CHAM provides a framework for specifications, which allows to construct and use modular specifications at different abstraction levels. Inverardi et al. extended CHAM to be used for specifying architectures.

Allen [2] shows in a dissertation that an Architectural Description Language (ADL), which is based on a formal abstract model of system behaviour, can be used as practical means to describe and analyse software architectures and architectural styles. In this thesis, the architectural description language WRIGHT is used, which is characterised by using explicit, independent connector types as interaction patterns, by describing the abstract behaviour of components by a CSP-like notation, by using predicates to characterise styles, and a collection of static checks to state the completeness and the consistency of the architectural specification.

In 2004, He et al. [8] presented a formal software architecture description model called SAM. SAM is a framework based on Petri nets and temporal logic, whereby Petri nets are used for the visualisation of the structure and for modelling the behaviour, whereas temporal logic is used to specify the required properties of software architectures.

In 2004, Oquendo [13] provides the Π-ADL, which was designed to address specifications of dynamic and mobile architectures. This formal, well-founded theoretical language is based on higher order typed Π-calculus. Compared to other ADLs, which are describing architectures from a structural viewpoint, the Π-ADL describes the architecture from the structural and behavioural viewpoint.

A further formal approach, in this case to service component architecture, within the SENSORIA project is presented by Fiadeiro et al. [6]. The concepts and techniques, which support the composition model, the definition of external interfaces as well as a way to assemble complex applications from single components are reported. Furthermore, this method includes modelling primitives to orchestrate the participating components.

The Yet Another Workflow Language (YAWL) system [14] is a service-oriented architecture, consisting of an extensible set of YAWL services—each offering one or multiple interfaces. Besides several service-oriented architecture styles, the YAWL system adopts the Representational State Transfer (REST) style. YAWL has a proper formal foundation, which makes its specifications unambiguous and automated verification becomes possible. YAWL offers two approaches to verification, whereby one is based on Reset nets (Petri net with reset arc), the other is based on transition invariants.

As the described approaches state, much research has been done since the early nineties of the past century to formalise architectures. A lot of these mentioned approaches use ADLs to formally specify a certain architecture, e.g., by Allen, He et al., and Oquendo. However, in contrast to the other methods, the approach of Oquendo also includes a behavioural view like the ASM method which we use. Inverardi et al. presented an extension of CHAM, which allows modular specifications and different abstraction levels as the ASM method used by us for the formal specification of the architecture. The approach provided by Fiadeiro et al. differs in the usage of a composition model and the orchestration of the components, but like our specification, it defines external interfaces. A younger but different approach offers the YAWL system, which focuses on service-oriented architectures and uses an extension of Petri nets, the so-called Reset nets, as a formal foundation.

7.3   Common Signature

Although each component of the eP^2 architecture (see Fig. 6.5) is an own ASM ground model, in this section we describe all universes.

Furthermore, to avoid copies, we define common used controlled, monitored, and shared functions, which are used in the specification of different components of the eP^2 architecture in this section.

Additionally, for asynchronous calls of interface operations, we specified the rule *CallOperationAsync* (see Sect. 7.3.4), which is defined here to allow whose usage in all components of the eP^2 architecture without the necessity to copy the specification of this rule in each component, which asynchronously calls interface operations.

7.3.1   Universes

We use capital letters for primitive types and lowercase for all other universes (as in [11]).
Universes imported from the ground model
This section contains universes, which are already defined in the ground model (see [11]).

The universe *instances* includes instances of tasks ("UserTask", "ManualTask", "ServiceTask", and "ScriptTask") as well as instances of transaction sub-processes (a subset of the universe *flowNodes* defined in [11]).

universe instances

The universe *catchEventTypes* includes event types for catching events (defined in [11]).

universe catchEventTypes := {"StartEvent",
    " IntermediateCatchEvent ",
    " BoundaryEvent " }

The universe *throwEventTypes* includes event types for throwing events (defined in [11]).

universe throwEventTypes := {"EndEvent",
    " IntermediateThrowEvent " }

The universe *eventTypes* includes event types that throw or catch events (defined in [11]).

universe eventTypes := catchEventTypes ∪ throwEventTypes

The universe *processes* covers all process diagrams (in contrast to process instances running on those processes), including top-level processes, as well as activities, including (but not limited to) sub-processes. This universe basically covers elements which can be instantiated and which have a lifecycle defined for their instances (with the exception of elements with simple lifecycles such as complex gateways). Processes overlap with flow nodes through activities.

universe processes

The universe *triggers* represents events in a closer sense, that is, something which happens at a particular time. *Triggers* are triggering catching event nodes and are created by throwing event nodes or by the environment.

universe triggers

The universe *inputSets* defines the input of a task and corresponds to the universe *inputSets* (defined in [11])

universe inputSets

The universe *correlationInfo* represents all information needed for correlation, especially between process instances and event triggers. Thereby it becomes possible to associate a message with a particular process instance.

universe correlationInfo

The universe *eventTriggerTypes* includes all possible event trigger types which are explicitly considered in this specification.

Additional Universes
This section contains universes, which are used in the specification of all eP^2 components and are not defined in the ground model (see [11]).

The universe *interfaces* defines all interfaces of all components.

universe interfaces := {"Monitor", "ProcessTask", " Administration ",
    " TaskHandling ", " ProcessEventListener ", " TaskList ", " Dialogue ",
    "Data", " DataAdministration ", " Actors ", "CRUDModel",
    " UserTaskActions ", " UserFormActions "}

The universe *taskNodes* is a subset of the universe *flowNodes*, which is defined in [11] and includes only flow nodes of tasks .

universe taskNodes

The universe *extendedTaskInstances* represents a task instance (type *instances*) extended by a transaction id that is only set for tasks of a transaction sub-process; otherwise, it is undefined. The transaction id has to be known by the *Dialogue Engine* component (see Sect. 7.5.8).

universe extendedTaskInstances

The universe *processEvents* represents a data structure for handling events, comprising, e.g., the process, which is only set for start events, the event type (type *eventTypes*), the trigger type (type *eventTriggerTypes*), and the task instance (type *instances*).

universe processEvents

The universe *users* refers to entities which can select and perform user tasks and manual tasks.

universe users

The universe *componentInstances* includes instances of all eP^2 components.

universe componentInstances

The universe *clientInstances* includes instances of the component *Process Client*; therefore, it is a subset of the universe *componentInstances*.

universe clientInstances

The universe *transactionId* includes all ids of transactions got from a data management system.

universe transactionId

The universe *operations* defines a data structure containing an operation name, a caller (type *componentInstances*) and the actual parameters (type *parameters*) of a called interface operation.

universe operations

The universe *parameters* defines a list containing all values of the actual parameters (in the sequence as defined for the related operation). Note that this list contains different types. We use this universe for asynchronous calls of interface operations whereby we can handle different parameters of those operations in an unitary way.

universe parameters

The universe *clientPages* represents information for the user in terms of reports on a computer screen. It corresponds to the homonymous universe defined in Sect. 4.4.4.

universe clientPages

The universe *immediateServerActions* represents forms for user input. It corresponds to the homonymous universe defined in Sect. 4.4.4.

universe immediateServerActions

The universe *deferredServerActions* represents links to client pages in the user's worklist. It corresponds to the homonymous universe defined in Sect. 4.4.4.

universe deferredServerActions

The universe *dialogueNodes* corresponds to the universe *nodes* defined in Sect. 4.4.4. It aggregates the elements of the universes *clientPages*, *immediateServerActions* and *deferredServerActions*.

universe dialogueNodes := clientPages ∪ immediateServerActions ∪
    deferredServerActions

The universe *dataViews* represents a data view obtained from the *Data Management* component.

universe dataViews

The universe *models* represents all models (*Process Model, Dialogue Model, Actor Model*, and *Data Model*).

universe models

The universe *modelMetaData* represents the meta data of a model (containing information about initial version, keywords, and a description of the model).

universe modelMetaData

The universe *roles* represents all roles.

universe roles

The universe *asyncCallingData* defines data (the name of a called interface function together with the parameters) and is used to handle such asynchronous interface operation calls. This type comprises the name of the called operation and the parameter list (type *parameters*), both can be obtained by a certain monitored function.

universe asyncCallingData

The universe *deonticClassifications* defines all possible deontic classifications of a task instance and is, therefore, determined at runtime.

universe deonticClassifications := {"Obligatory", "Permitted",
    "   AlternativeInclusive   ", "   AlternativeExclusive   ", " Forbidden "}

The universe *deonticClassificationsForUsers* is parameterised with a user, a deontic classification (type *deonticClassifications*) and a set of alternatives which is only defined for "AlternativeInclusive" and "AlternativeExclusive" otherwise it is undefined.

universe deonticClassificationsForUsers

7.3.2   Notations

In this section, we list constructs which are not defined in [11] but are necessary to specify the eP^2 architecture.

We introduce the primitive type "Graph" to support a data structure referring to a directed graph of elements.

The following construct stands for synchronously calling the operation *operationName* of the interface *InterfaceName* and is used when only one instance of the interface provider component exists (i.e., *Workflow Transition Interpreter, Task Server, Actor Management, Data Management,* and *Process Model Repository* (cf. Fig. 7.1).

```
InterfaceName.operationName(param1, param2,...paramN)
```

The following construct stands for calling the operation *operationName* of the interface *InterfaceName* of the instance *componentInstance* which is used when more than one interface provider instance exists, to differentiate those provider instances (i.e., *Process Client*).

```
InterfaceName(componentInstance).operationName(param1,
    param2,...paramN)
```

We use the special function *self* to identify the current instance of any component.

7.3.3   Common Basic Functions

7.3.3.1   Common Controlled Functions

Controlled functions are functions that are updatable only by the rules of the ASM [5].

The controlled function *providedInterfaces* includes the name of all interfaces that the certain component provides. It has to be initialised for each component in the rule *Initialise*.

controlled providedInterfaces $\rightarrow$ Set

The controlled function *asyncOperations* includes the name of all operations defined in the given interface, which may be asynchronously called by other components, to that the certain component has to react. This function has to be initialised for each component in the rule *Initialise*.

controlled asyncOperations : interfaces $\rightarrow$ Set

The controlled function *initialised* indicates whether the given component instance has called the rule *Initialise* for initializing its functions, interfaces and operations. Each component has to set the value to *true* in the rule *Initialise*.

controlled initialised : Integer $\rightarrow$ Boolean

The controlled function *ownCalledFunctions* for the given component represents a set of asynchronous calls to interface operations of other components, which are to be processed when the return value is present (see *ComponentBehaviour* and *HandleOwnCalls*).

controlled ownCalledFunctions : componentInstances → Set

7.3.3.2 Common Monitored Functions

In this section, we list monitored functions, which are used by more than one component, especially functions to get a certain value out of a parameter list (type *parameters*) and out of operations (type *operations*), which are set by the caller of the operation and used by the component, which provides the certain operation. Monitored functions are functions that are only updatable by the environment (cf. [5]).

The monitored function *operationName* for the given called operation (type *operations*) supplies the name of the called operation.

monitored operationName : operations → String

The monitored function *params* for the given called operation (type *operations*) supplies the actual parameters (type *parameters*, which comprises a list of different types whose sequence is defined in the specification of the certain operation).

monitored params : operations → parameters

The monitored function *user* for the given parameter list (type *parameters*) supplies the user.

monitored user : parameters → users

The monitored function *clientInstance* for the given parameter list (type *parameters*) supplies the client instance.

monitored clientInstance : parameters → clientInstances

The monitored function *taskInstance* for the given parameter list (type *parameters*) supplies the task instance (type *instances*).

monitored taskInstance : parameters → instances

The monitored function *transactionId* for the given parameter list (type *parameters*) supplies the transactionId (type *transactionId*).

monitored transactionId : parameters → transactionId

7.3.3.3 Common Out Functions

In this section, we provide out functions which are used by several components to avoid multiple specifying them. These are mainly functions that set different properties of operations (type *operations*). Out functions are dynamic functions which are monitored by the environment and updated (but not read) by a ASM *M* (cf. [5]).

The out function *operationName* for the given operation (type *operations*) sets the name of the operation.

```
out operationName : operations → String
```

The out function *caller* for the given operation (type *operations*) sets the caller component (type *componentInstances*) of the operation.

```
out caller : operations → caller
```

The out function *params* for the given operation (type *operations*) sets the parameter list (type *parameters*) of the operation.

```
out params : operations → parameters
```

7.3.3.4 Common Shared Functions

Shared functions are updatable by the rules of the ASM as well as by the environment (cf. [5]). The following functions are specified as shared functions, because they are set from outside (from the caller of an interface operation) but must be reset by the provider of the interface, when it has reacted to the call, therefore, these functions cannot be defined as monitored functions.

The shared function *asyncCalledOperations* stores all operations of all provided interfaces, which where asynchronously called by another component. Each entry of the set complies with a data structure that contains the name, the caller, the parameters (type *operation*) of the operation, and the receiver. The parameter of the type *componentInstances* is needed to differentiate between different component instances to that the call belongs. We use a set and not a list, because all operations are processed in parallel anyway.

```
shared asyncCalledOperations : componentInstances → Set
```

7.3.3.5 Common Exported Functions

In this section we specify common functions, which are exported to be read by other components.

The function *processModelRepository* represents the only instance of the *Process Model Repository* component.

```
EXPORT processModelRepository → componentInstances
```

The function *taskServer* represents the only instance of the *Task Server* component.

```
EXPORT taskServer → componentInstances
```

The function *actorManagement* represents the only instance of the *Actor Management* component.

```
EXPORT actorManagement → componentInstances
```

The function *dataManagement* represents the only instance of the *Data Management* component.

```
EXPORT dataManagement → componentInstances
```

7.3.4 Common Rules and Derived Functions

This section contains rules and derived functions, which are used in the specification of several components.

The rule *CallOperationAsync* asynchronously calls the operation identified by the parameter *operationName* of the component instance identified by the parameter *receiverComponent*. The parameter *params* contains all actual parameters (type *parameters*), whose sequence is defined in the specification of the certain operation to be called, thereby we can handle different parameters of interface operations in a unitary way. The parameter *caller* identifies the component, which calls the operation. The call is processed by inserting a new *operation* object in the shared function *asyncCalledOperations* of the given *receiverComponent*. The *receiverComponent* then has to react to those calls (see Sect. 7.4).

```
rule CallOperationAsync : String × parameters ×
     componentInstances × componentInstances
rule CallOperationAsync(operationName, params, caller,
     receiverComponent)
   let op = new(operation) in
   seqblock
     operationName(op) := operationName
     caller(op) := caller
     params(oc) := params
     insert op in asyncCalledOperations(receiverComponent)
   seqblock
```

The rule *eP2* (the main rule) creates instances (type *componentInstances*) of all components of the eP^2 architecture, which exists only once (so-called *singletons*) namely the *Workflow Transition Interpreter*, *Process Model Repository*, *Actor Management*, *Task Server*, and *Data Management* and initialise them with whose program (see Fig. 7.1). For the *Process Client* component we assume that on login of a user an own new *Process Client* instance including whose own new *Dialogue Engine* instance is created (cf. Fig. 7.1) and initialised from outside.

```
main rule eP2
main rule eP2 =
  processModelRepository := new (componentInstances)
    add processModelRepository to activeComponents
    program(processModelRepository) :=
       @ProcessModelRepositoryBehaviour

    taskServer := new (componentInstances)
    add taskServer to activeComponents
```

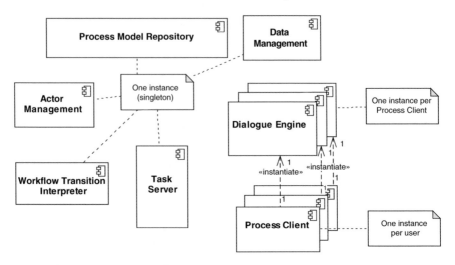

Fig. 7.1 Runtime instances of eP^2 components

```
program(taskServer) := @TaskServerBehaviour

actorManagement := new (componentInstances)
add actorManagement to activeComponents
program(actorManagement) := @ActorManagementBehaviour

dataManagement := new (componentInstances)
add dataManagement to activeComponents
program(dataManagement) := @DataManagementBehaviour

workflowTransitionInterpreter := new (componentInstance)
add workflowTransitionInterpreter to activeComponents
program(workflowTransitionInterpreter) :=
    @WorkflowTransitionInterpreter
```

7.4 Common Behaviour of All Components

The *Workflow Transition Interpreter* plays a central role in controlling the interaction of all components of the eP^2 architecture (see Fig. 6.5). As described in Sect. 6.4.4, this component runs through business processes and communicates with other components to handle certain types of nodes. The communication is based on the interface operations provided by the other components, which, if required, in turn call interface operations of further components. A particularly interesting component is the *Process Client*, because it is, on the one hand, controlled by the *Workflow Transition Interpreter* due to the process definitions and, on the other hand, by actual users who select tasks to be processed from their task collections (which are then presented by means of the *Dialogue Engine*).

The rule *ComponentBehaviour* defines the common behaviour of all components in an abstract way (except for the *Workflow Transition Interpreter*, whose ground model can be seen in [11] and whose enlargements in respect of the Hagenberg Business Process Modelling (H-BPM) are presented in the Sects. 7.5.1–7.5.3). Each of these components first has to ensure itself to be initialised and if so, it has to react to all asynchronously called operations of each provided interface, which was called by other components. The rules *Initialise, ReactToCall, CreateIncludingComponent*, and *HandleOwnCalls* are kept abstract for being refined in the specification of the proper component to fit for the particular purpose. The rule *RemoveCall* is responsible for keeping the collection of called operations of each component instance up-to-date. In parallel, the availability of the return value of each asynchronously called interface operation of other components are checked and handled by calling the rule *HandleOwnCalls*, which also has to be specified by each component.

```
rule ComponentBehaviour
rule ComponentBehaviour =
parblock
  if initialised(self) != true then // undef or false
    parblock
    Initialise()
    includingComponent = CreateIncludingComponent
    endparblock
    forall calledOperation ∈ asyncCalledOperations(self) do
    parblock
        ReactToCall(calledOperation)
        RemoveCall(calledOperation) // remove from the
            asyncCalledOperations
    endparblock
    // handle return values of own calls of interface function of
        other components
    forall callingData ∈ ownCalledFunctions do
        HandleOwnCalls(callingData)
endparblock
```

The abstract rule *CreateIncludingComponent* may create an inner component if necessary (e.g. the component *Process Client* uses an own instance of the component *Dialogue Engine*). In most cases, this rule will be kept empty.

```
abstract rule CreateIncludingComponent → Integer
```

The abstract rule *Initialise* has to be refined by each component to ensure that all functions required by the component are initialised. Furthermore, each component has to define the functions *providedInterfaces* and *asyncOperations* for each provided interface.

```
abstract rule Initialise
```

The abstract rule *ReactToCall* has to be refined by each component and has to include a case for each operation of the provided interfaces, which may be called asynchronously. The parameter indicates the called operation and includes a data structure containing the operation name, the caller, the parameters, and the receiving instance.

```
abstract rule ReactToCall : operations
```

The rule *RemoveCall* removes the given operation from the collection of asynchronously called operations of each component instance.

```
rule RemoveCall : operations
rule RemoveCall(calledOperation) =
  remove calledOperation from asyncCalledOperations(self)
```

The abstract rule *HandleOwnCalls* handles the return value of previously asynchronously called interface operations of other components. Each component knows which function it calls asynchronously and how to react, therefore, this rule must be implemented by each component to react to all operation calls.

```
abstract rule HandleOwnCalls : asyncCallingData
```

The rule *CreateAndAddAsyncCallingData* creates a new *asyncCallingData* object, fills it with the given parameters and adds it to *ownCalledFunctions*. Since this rule may be used by all components it is specified here.

```
rule CreateAndAddAsyncCallingData : componentInstances × String
    × parameters → asyncCallingData
rule CreateAndAddAsyncCallingData(component, calledOperationName,
    paramsOfCall)
  //create new asyncCallingData and add it to the
    ownCalledFunctions(component)
  let asyncCallingData = new (asyncCallingData)) in
  seqblock
      name(asyncCallingData) := calledOperationName
      parameters(asyncCallingData) := paramsOfCall
      add asyncCallingData to ownCalledFunctions(self)
  endseqblock
```

7.5   Detailed ASM Ground Models

7.5.1   Workflow Transition Interpreter

The *Workflow Transition Interpreter* was already introduced in [11]. It has to be modified in order to incorporate deontic classification and user modelling (see the next section) as well as the communication concept; but before, we have to integrate it in the eP^2 architecture. This requires a few steps which we describe very briefly but do not detail here.

- First, the *Workflow Transition Interpreter* will have to be based on the rule *ComponentBehaviour* (see Sect. 7.4).

- Second, we have to add a header with EXPORT and IMPORT clauses to summarise the interfaces on the side of the *Workflow Transition Interpreter*. (In the following section, we simply add the EXPORT keyword to the declaration of respective functions, and we add the respective other component's name to imported symbols.)

The important modifications concern deontic classification and user modelling, which will be specified in the next section, and the communication concept, which will be specified thereafter.

7.5.2 Integrating Deontic Classification and Actors

7.5.2.1 Introduction and Overview

In this section, we describe how to integrate the deontic classification of tasks and related aspects of actor modelling in the *Workflow Transition Interpreter* and how the respective interaction between the *Workflow Transition Interpreter* and other parts of a BPM system conforming to the eP^2 architecture (see also Sect. 6.4) should be handled.

To this end, we refine the semantics of the *Workflow Transition Interpreter* as given in [11] and summarised in [10]. As the specification of the *Workflow Transition Interpreter* has to be amended, the result will not always be a fully *conservative* refinement, although we try to limit actual changes to a minimum.

At the core of the changes lies the deontic classification of certain activities, in particular *user tasks* and *manual tasks*. In contrast to a "classical" task, a deontically classified task is marked as "obligatory", "optional", "alternative", and/or "forbidden". In most cases, the classification will depend on the runtime situation, that is, it will be obligatory etc. under a certain condition. A typical example is that a task is, in general, optional ("permitted"), but obligatory if a certain other task has already been performed. The classification will also depend on the actors—which we will call "users" in this context—and their roles.

The classification only applies to two kinds of tasks—user tasks and manual tasks. Both kinds of tasks need users to perform them. As in the BPMN standard, we understand *user tasks* as tasks where the BPM system leads and supports the users (as by workflow charts as described in Chap. 4) while there is no further support for a *manual task*. (In the case of a manual task, the user is simply expected to press a "Task completed" button eventually.)

When a user task or manual task becomes active, the respective user (or a group of users) is informed about this "to-do" by adding a representation of this task to their worklist (for worklists, see Chap. 4). There it must be visualised whether this task is obligatory, optional, or an alternative to certain other tasks for this user (or this group of users, and for the given process instance; forbidden tasks are not shown). In the case of alternatives, the users must additionally be informed whether those alternatives are *exclusive* (i.e., exactly one of them must be chosen) or *inclusive* (i.e., an arbitrary number of them may be chosen, but at least one).

Then the *Workflow Transition Interpreter* waits for feedback from the user. Possible reactions are "task selected", "task rejected", and "task skipped". "Task selected" is a choice for alternatives. "Task rejected" is a choice for *inclusive* alternatives in particular, for in this case, an arbitrary number of alternatives can be chosen by and by, and we need a way to say which alternatives will *not* be taken. "Task skipped" is a choice for *optional* tasks; in contrast to rejected tasks, the workflow simply continues after the task even if no actual work has been performed (in contrast to a rejected task, after which the workflow does *not* continue).

In the case of "task selected", if the task had been an exclusive alternative to other activities, those other tasks become "forbidden". Else, nothing happens: the task in question remains in its active state (until it is completed, maybe skipped, or interrupted). We keep waiting for feedback from the user that the task has been "completed". (If the selected task is an inclusive alternative and was the first among all alternatives to be selected, then the other alternatives will *de facto* become *optional*, i.e., no other alternative *has* to be selected. Still, it is useful for the user to know that those are alternatives belonging together and to the task just selected, therefore we do not re-classify them in this case.)

In the case of "task rejected", neither is the task performed nor is the workflow continued after the task. "Task rejected" is only possible for alternatives, in particular for inclusive alternatives, and if only one alternative is left after the rejection and no alternative was selected so far, then this last alternative becomes "obligatory" because one alternative *has* to be selected.

In the case of "task skipped", the intended behaviour is to just continue the workflow (pass on tokens) without doing anything else. (Note that "task skipped" is only a possibility for *optional* tasks and in general not e.g. for alternative tasks.)

In the case of "task completed", the task is simply finished and the workflow can continue. If we assume that for every user task or manual task, we get informed about "task selected" before the task is completed, no other action is required. (Otherwise, as in the case of "task selected", if that task had been an exclusive alternative to other tasks, those other tasks become "forbidden" and thus have to re-classified accordingly. For the sake of simplicity, we will not do this below, but implementers might want to add this for enhanced safety.)

For the *Workflow Transition Interpreter*, this means the following:

In order to inform the users about the respective deontic classifications of an active task, the precondition for each deontic classifier must be evaluated at runtime, with the user, the process instance, and possibly also the history of the given process instance (who performed which task so far) as important parameters. The task server is informed about all active user tasks and manual tasks. At the same time, for each user task or manual task, information about the deontic classification—evaluated separately for each user—must be made available to the task server. Possible classifications are "Obligatory", "Permitted", "AlternativeInclusive", "AlternativeExclusive", and "Forbidden". ("Forbidden" is particularly important for a re-classification of an initially alternative task; see below.)

(Note that manual tasks are to be treated like user tasks in all respects which are relevant in this place. Service tasks and script tasks are to be treated in a similar way in many respects, but they are not displayed to any user and cannot be selected, rejected, or skipped.)

After the lifecycle of a task has been set to "Active" and the users have been notified that the task is to be processed, we wait for feedback through one of the three monitored variables, *taskSelected*, *taskRejected*, or *taskSkipped*—whichever is first set to true (provided we do not receive any interruption signal).

If *taskSelected* is set to true, and if the task is an exclusive alternative task, then we have to re-classify all the other alternatives as "Forbidden" and abort them—that is, we have to terminate the respective task instances *without passing tokens on*. We achieve this by treating each forbidden alternative as if it had been *rejected* (see below). The selected task remains in lifecycle state "Active" until *taskCompleted* is additionally set to true (see below) or the task is interrupted.

If *taskRejected* is set to true (or the task was re-classified as "Forbidden"), then we set the lifecycle state of the task to "Rejected"—a state which we newly introduce (see Fig. 7.2). From this state, the task instance is closed without any token being produced (though tokens were consumed when the instance was created; see the rule *ControlOperation* in the context of the *ActivityTransition* in [11, Sect. 4.5]. If all other alternatives but one were rejected so far (or there were only two alternatives in total), then the only remaining alternative is reclassified to "Obligatory".

If *taskSkipped* is set to true, then we set the lifecycle state of the task to "Skipped"—also a newly introduced state (see Fig. 7.2). From this state, the task instance is closed *and tokens will be produced* at the outgoing sequence flows.

If *taskCompleted* is set to true (*after* the task was selected), we set the lifecycle state from "Active" to "Completing" (which is the usual behaviour for activities; see Fig. 7.2).

For every completed task, we have to remember *who* performed the task in an *instanceHistory*, because the deontic classification of following tasks may depend on this information.

7.5.2.2 Detailed Changes

A task is associated with a set of roles. This means that only users assigned to these roles can be permitted or obliged to perform the task in question.

```
static roles : flowNodes → Set
```

We query the assignment of users to roles by the rule *GetUsersByRole*, which we import from the *Actor* interface of the *Actor Management* component of eP^2 (see Sect. 7.5.7). We precede the rule name by the interface name from where we import the rule (separated by a dot).

```
rule Actor.GetUsersByRole : processes × roles → Set
```

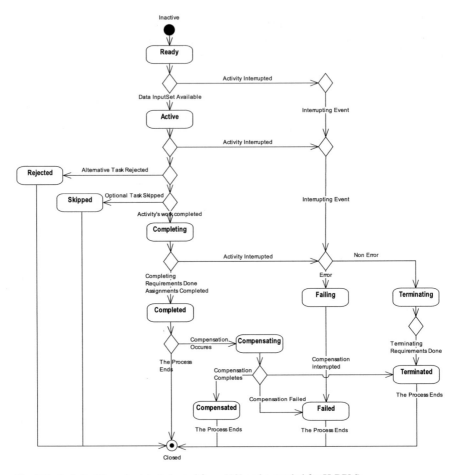

Fig. 7.2 Activity lifecycle state (adopted from [12] and extended for H-BPM)

With every user task, a *deonticExpression* is associated by means of which a deontic classification can be computed at runtime. Possible arguments (variables) are a
process (for accessing other tasks), an instance history (storing which completed
task was performed by which user for a given process instance), roles, and users.
A *deonticExpression* can be evaluated at runtime by means of the derived function
evaluateDeonticExpression (see further below).

```
static deonticExpression : flowNodes → expressions
```

Furthermore, we have a set of *actor rules* (see "Rule View" in Sect. 3.4.1) which can
span over several tasks (as well as several roles and users). It might be possible to
allocate each rule to one or a few tasks, but we want to retain the possibility to check
the rule system for consistency and to infer derived rules. Consequently, we keep a

set of such rules (expressions) for each process. Still, this rule set will have to be considered whenever we deontically classify a particular user task.

static actorRules : processes × Set

We additionally need to build up a history of each task instance where we remember, for each completed task, by whom it was performed. We need this in order to evaluate rules of the form "the user who performed task *A* also has to perform task *B*". The controlled function *instanceHistory* remembers the performing user for each process instance and for each user task and manual task within the respective process. This function is initialised with **undef** for each location (as usual). Note that the given instance is an instance *of the parent process* of the task in question (and not a task instance), while the given flow node is the task in question.

controlled instanceHistory : instances × flowNodes → users

For communication with the *Task Server* component (see Sect. 6.4), we need to provide the *Monitor* interface (see Sect. 6.4.4) and to use the *Task Server*'s *ProcessTask* interface. We inform the *Task Server* about newly activated user tasks and manual tasks by calling the operation "processTask" via the rule *CallOperationAsync*, which is specified in eP^2 as a common rule (see Sect. 7.3.4). The first parameter is the operation name (as a string), followed by a set of parameters, the own component instance, and the instance of the component to be called, in this case the *Task Server*. For the *Task Server* component instance, we can import the function *taskServer* from eP^2, which is controlled by eP^2 but monitored from the *Workflow Transition Interpreter*'s point of view.

rule eP2.CallOperationAsync : String × parameters ×
        componentInstances × componentInstances

monitored eP2.taskServer : componentInstances

From the *Monitor* interface, we require the notification whether a particular task instance has been selected, rejected, skipped, or completed. When a task has been selected or completed, we need to know which user selected or performed it. We store this in the *instanceHistory* because this may influence the deontic classification of following tasks for certain users, e.g. when we have a rule that the next task has to be performed by the same user, or by a strictly different user.

monitored Monitor.taskSelected : instances → users

monitored Monitor.taskRejected : instances → Boolean

monitored Monitor.taskSkipped : instances → Boolean

monitored Monitor.taskCompleted : instances → users

Now for required changes in existing parts of the specification (see [11]). In the rule *GetActive* of the *TaskTransition*, we have to inform the *Task Server* component that a new user task or manual task is waiting to be performed. We do this in the rule *ProcessUserTask* (see further below), which is called by *StartOperation* for the

relevant task types. Before, we have to collect and compute information required by
the *Task Server* about the deontic classification of the task. The deontic classification
is computed for each potential user separately, as different users may have different
permissions or obligations, play different roles, or have a different history with respect
to the task in question. A data structure containing such a classification for each user
is computed by the rule *SetClassificationsForUsers*.

In order to make this possible, we have to modify *GetActive* of the *ActivityTransition* by adding a call of *SetClassificationsForUsers* (with everything else unchanged).

```
rule GetActive(instance, flowNode) =
  if activationConditionActivity(flowNode) then
  seqblock
    parblock
      currentInputSet(instance) :=
          selectFirstAvailableInputSet(flowNode, instance)
      SetClassificationsForUsers(flowNode, instance)
      lifecycleState(instance, flowNode) := "Active"
    endparblock
    PrepareOperation(instance, flowNode)
    StartOperation(instance, flowNode)
  endseqblock
```

The sub-rule *SetClassificationsForUsers* is specified as **skip** by default (i.e., do nothing). Only in the context of *TaskTransition*, do we fill a respective structure of exported
functions which indicate, for the task instance and for each user, the respective deontic classification which is determined at runtime. We first describe this data structure
(made up of functions) before we define *SetClassificationsForUsers*.

The main output function, *deonticClassificationsForUsers*, is parameterised by
a task instance and gives a set of members of the respective custom universe, also
called *deonticClassificationsForUsers*. Members of the universe *deonticClassificationsForUsers* are associated with three functions which they parameterise: a *user*,
a *classification* (from another custom universe, *deonticClassifications*), and a set
of *alternatives* which may be **undef**; the latter is only defined if *classification* is
either "AlternativeInclusive", or "AlternativeExclusive". (If a task is classified as an
alternative, then the user as well as the system needs to know which are the other
alternatives.)

```
EXPORT controlled deonticClassificationsForUsers : instances →
    Set
  // Set of deonticClassificationsForUsers; for task instances

EXPORT controlled user : deonticClassificationsForUsers → users

EXPORT controlled classification : deonticClassificationsForUsers
      → deonticClassifications

EXPORT controlled alternatives : deonticClassificationsForUsers
      → Set
  // Set of task instances
  // only defined if classification ∈ { "AlternativeInclusive",
    "AlternativeExclusive" }
```

The rule *SetClassificationsForUsers* determines the deontic classification of the task in question, for the given task instance and for each user separately. With the result, the data structure given by the output function *deonticClassificationsForUsers* is filled.

```
rule SetClassificationsForUsers : flowNodes × instances
rule SetClassificationsForUsers(flowNode, instance) =
  let possibleUsers = possibleUsersForTask(flowNode) in
  seqblock
    deonticClassificationsForUsers(instance) := {}
    forall user ∈ possibleUsers do
    seqblock
      local deonticClassificationForUser :=
          new(deonticClassificationsForUsers)
      parblock
        user(deonticClassificationForUser) := user
        classification(deonticClassificationForUser) :=
            classifyTask(flowNode, instance, user)
      endparblock
      if classification(deonticClassificationForUser) ∈ {
          "AlternativeInclusive", " AlternativeExclusive " } then
        alternatives(deonticClassificationForUser) :=
            getAlternativesForTaskInstance(flowNode, instance)
      else
        alternatives(deonticClassificationForUser) := undef
      add deonticClassificationForUser to
          deonticClassificationsForUsers(instance)
    endseqblock
  endseqblock
```

The derived function *possibleUsersForTask* determines all users which have been assigned at least one of the roles with which the given task is associated. Thereby we use the rule *GetUsersByRole* provided by the Actor interface of the *Actor Management* component as specified in eP^2 (see Sect. 6.4).

```
derived possibleUsersForTask : flowNodes → Set
derived possibleUsersForTask(flowNode) =
  return users in
  seqblock
    users := {}
    forall role ∈ roles(flowNode) do
      add Actor.GetUsersByRole(getTopLevelProcess(flowNode),
          role) to users
  endseqblock
```

The derived function *classifyTask* assigns a deontic classification to a task at runtime with respect to a given task instance and a particular user. It makes use of the *deonticExpression* of the given *flowNode*, the set of *actorRules* associated with the respective top-level process (cf. "Rule View" in Sect. 3.4.1), and the *instanceHistory* of the respective instance of the parent process. The latter is a function which associates a user with a process instance and a user task, where the user performed the respective task within the given instance; therefore, we give the parent instance of the task instance as a parameter to *evaluateDeonticSystem*.

```
derived classifyTask : flowNodes × instances × users →
    deonticClassifications
derived classifyTask(flowNode, instance, user) =
    evaluateDeonticSystem(deonticExpression(flowNode),
        actorRules(getTopLevelProcess(flowNode)),
        instance,
        parentInstance(instance),
        user)
```

The abstract-derived function *evaluateDeonticSystem* computes a deontic classification from a deontic expression (as associated with a task) and a set of actor-centric rules with respect to a particular task instance and a particular user. The parent instance of the task instance (fourth argument) is required to access the history of this parent instance, i.e., who performed which task so far, which may be required to evaluate certain rules.

```
abstract-derived evaluateDeonticSystem : expressions × Set ×
    instances × instances × users → deonticClassifications
```

The derived function *getAlternativesForTaskInstance* obtains all instances of tasks which are alternatives to the given task with the same parent instance. We first look for alternative tasks according to the static process diagram and then determine the respective task instance for each task. Note that *activeInstances* of an activity also include instances in lifecycle state "Ready" (see [11, Appendix Sect. A.2.6.1]).

```
derived getAlternativesForTaskInstance : flowNodes × instances →
    Set
derived getAlternativesForTaskInstance(flowNode, instance) =
  return alternativeTaskInstances = {} in
    let alternativeTasks = getAlternativeTasks(flowNode) in
      foralll task ∈ alternativeTasks do
        choose instance in activeInstances(task) with
            parentInstance(task) = parentInstance(flowNode) do
          add task to alternativeTaskInstances
```

The abstract-derived function *getAlternativeTasks* obtains all tasks which are alternatives to the given task according to the static process diagram. In the standard case, when the given task immediately follows a splitting exclusive or inclusive gateway and we do not have loops, we may just look which other tasks immediately follow the same splitting gateway. In other cases, however, this may be more complicated.

```
abstract-derived getAlternativeTasks : flowNodes → Set
```

In the rule *StartOperation* (which is defined in the context of *ActivityTransition*—see the rule *GetActive* above resp. [11, Sect. 5.4.2]), for a user task or manual task, the subrule *ProcessUserTask* is called which was left abstract in the original specification. We can specify this rule now in order to notify the *Task Server* component that the task in question is scheduled for processing now. The *Task Server* will in turn relay this information so that ultimately all the users which are permitted or even obliged to perform that task are notified.

We have to call the operation *processTask* of the *ProcessTask* interface via the rule *CallOperationAsync* which is specified in the common functionality section of

eP^2 (Sect. 7.3.4). *processTask* takes the following parameters: a task instance, an input set, a Boolean parameter indicating whether the task is member of an ad hoc sub-process, an instance of a potential parent transaction sub-process (will typically be **undef**), and a structure containing the deontic classification for each potential user.

```
rule ProcessUserTask(instance, inputSet, isAdHoc,
    isTransactionInstance) =
  let parameterList = new(eP2.parameters),
      adHocParentInstance = getAdHocParentInstance(instance,
          isAdHoc),
      transactionSubProcessInstance =
          getTransactionSubProcessInstance(instance,
          isTransactionInstance) in
  seqblock
    add instance to parameterList
    add currentInputSet(instance) to parameterList
    add adHocParentInstance to parameterList
    add transactionSubProcessInstance to parameterList
    add deonticClassificationsForUsers(instance) to parameterList
    eP2.CallOperationAsync("processTask", parameterList, self,
        eP2.taskServer)
  endseqblock
```

The abstract-derived function *getAdHocParentInstance* returns the instance of an ad hoc sub-process which is a transitive parent instance of the given task instance, provided the Boolean parameter (*isAdHoc*) is true. In other words, if the task to which the given instance belongs is embedded in an ad hoc sub-process (possibly indirectly, e.g. the task belongs to a normal sub-process which is in turn part of an ad hoc sub-process), then this function returns the instance of this ad hoc sub-process which is the parent (or grandparent, etc.) instance of the given task instance. If the Boolean parameter (*isAdHoc*) is false, the function returns **undef**.

```
abstract-derived getAdHocParentInstance : instances × Boolean →
    instances
```

If *isTransactionInstance* is **true**, then the abstract-derived function *getTransaction-SubProcessInstance* returns the relevant instance of the transaction sub-process to which the task in question belongs; otherwise, this derived function returns **undef**. As with *getAdHocParentInstance* (above), the transaction sub-process need *not* be a *direct* parent of the task in question.

```
abstract-derived getTransactionSubProcessInstance : instances ×
    Boolean → instances
```

Now we have provided the *Task Server* component with all the information the users need to select the task in question and perform it or, as far as this is admissible, "reject" or "skip" it. Depending on the users' decisions, we will see either *taskSelected*, *taskRejected*, or *taskSkipped* set to true or to a user for the given task instance. The function *taskCompleted* is a follow-up to *taskSelected*.

The respective eP^2 interface provides four functions which are monitored for the *Workflow Transition Interpreter*.

```
monitored Monitor.taskSelected : instances → users

monitored Monitor.taskRejected : instances → Boolean

monitored Monitor.taskSkipped : instances → Boolean

monitored Monitor.taskCompleted : instances → users
```

In the original specification (see [11, Sect. 4.5.2]), we only waited for *taskCompleted* (which was of type Boolean there). Now we have to check for three other monitored functions.

For comparison, we show the original specification of *InstanceOperation* in the context of *ActivityTransition*. There we wait for *exitCondition(instance)* to become **true**, in which case we "exit" the activity in a regular way:

```
rule InstanceOperation(instance, flowNode) =
  ...
  if lifecycleState(instance, flowNode) ∈
      activeWaitingLifecycleStates then
  parblock
    CleanUpBeforeExit(instance, flowNode)
    if exitCondition(instance) then
    parblock
      ExitActivity(instance, flowNode)
      lifecycleState(instance, flowNode) :=
          getNewLifecycleState(instance, flowNode)
    endparblock
  endparblock
```

For a task, the derived function *exitCondition* shall simply check whether *taskCompleted(instance)* $\neq$ **undef** (originally: *taskCompleted(instance)* = **true**). The derived function *getNewLifecycleState* will return "Completing" in this case.

Now we have to make three additional checks.

- If *taskSelected* $\neq$ **undef**, we re-classify the alternatives of the given task instance as "Forbidden" and set their lifecycle states to "Rejected". No tokens are produced.
- If *taskRejected* is **true**, we set the lifecycle state of the task to "Rejected". No tokens are produced. Additionally, we re-classify the alternatives of the given task (which might lead to a single remaining alternative being re-classified as "Obligatory").
- If *taskSkipped* is **true**, we set the lifecycle state of the task to "Skipped". In this case, tokens *are* produced.

We thus extend the *InstanceOperation* of *ActivityTransition* in the following way:

```
rule InstanceOperation(instance, flowNode) =
  ...
  if lifecycleState(instance, flowNode) ∈
      activeWaitingLifecycleStates then
  parblock
    CleanUpBeforeExit(instance, flowNode)
```

```
if exitCondition(instance) then
parblock
  ExitActivity(instance, flowNode)
  lifecycleState(instance, flowNode) :=
       getNewLifecycleState(instance, flowNode)
endparblock
if Monitor.taskSelected(instance) then
  ReclassifyAlternatives(instance, flowNode)
if Monitor.taskRejected(instance) then
  RejectTask(instance, flowNode, true)
if Monitor.taskSkipped(instance) then
  ExitActivity(instance, flowNode)
endparblock
```

The rule *ReclassifyAlternatives* resets the deontic classifications for all instances of alternative tasks corresponding to the given task instance and for all users. The principal result (which is not explicit in the specification) is that, when a task classified as "AlternativeExclusive" was selected, all alternatives will be re-classified as "Forbidden", and when a task classified as "AlternativeExclusive" or "AlternativeInclusive" was rejected and there is only one alternative remaining, then this alternative will become "Obligatory". If an active task instance is reclassified as "Forbidden", then its lifecycle state has to be set to "Rejected". (Note that in the latter case, we must prevent the re-classification of alternatives to the automatically rejected task as this is already being done, and we would thus get an infinite cycle; we achieve this by setting a third parameter of *RejectTask* to **false**.)

```
rule ReclassifyAlternatives : instances × flowNodes
rule ReclassifyAlternatives(instance, flowNode) =
  let alternatives = getAlternativesForTaskInstance(flowNode,
       instance) in
    forall altTaskInstance in alternatives do
    seqblock
      forall user ∈ possibleUsersForTask(flowNode) do
        choose deonticClassification ∈
           deonticClassificationsForUsers(altTaskInstance) with
           user(deonticClassification) = user do
        seqblock
          classification(deonticClassification) :=
             classifyTask(flowNode, altTaskInstance, user)
          if classification(deonticClassification) = "Forbidden" then
            RejectTask(altTaskInstance, flowNode, false)
        endseqblock

      let parameterList = new(eP2.parameters) in
      seqblock
        add altTaskInstance to parameterList
        add deonticClassificationsForUsers(altTaskInstance) to
           parameterList
        eP2.CallOperationAsync("  ResetDeonticClassifications  ",
           parameterList, self, eP2.taskServer)
      endseqblock
    endseqblock
```

The rule *RejectTask* closes the task instance without producing tokens. The Boolean (third) parameter indicates whether alternatives shall be re-classified or not.

```
rule RejectTask : instances × flowNodes × Boolean
rule RejectTask(instance, flowNode, reclassifyAlternatives) =
  if exitPossible(flowNode, instance) then
  parblock
    CleanUp(instance, flowNode)
    lifecycleState(instance, flowNode) := "Rejected"
  endparblock
```

Furthermore, in the case of *taskCompleted(instance)* $\neq$ **undef**, we have to remember in *instanceHistory* which user completed the task. We can add this via the rule *ExitActivity*, which is called by the *InstanceOperation* (see above). More specifically, we can add this to the rule *CleanUp*, which is called by *ExitActivity* and which was left abstract in the original model in [11]. We now specify *CleanUp* for the *TaskTransition*:

```
rule CleanUp(instance, flowNode) =
parblock
  WriteParentInstanceHistory(instance, flowNode)
  CustomCleanUp(instance, flowNode)
endparblock
```

The rule *WriteParentInstanceHistory* takes note which user performed the given task (*flowNode*) in the context of the parent instance of the given task instance.

```
rule WriteParentInstanceHistory : instances × flowNodes
rule WriteParentInstanceHistory(instance, flowNode) =
  instanceHistory(parentInstance(instance), flowNode) :=
      taskCompleted(instance)
```

The abstract rule *CustomCleanUp* can be used for implementation-specific cleanup actions.

```
abstract rule CustomCleanUp : instances × flowNodes
```

7.5.3   Integrating the Enhanced Communication Concept

The semantic model of the *Workflow Transition Interpreter* has to be further modified in order to integrate the enhanced communication concept introduced in Chap. 5. We have already specified the most important respective refinements in Chap. 5, which we will now summarise and supplement.

When a trigger is thrown, we have to set the appropriate properties according to its *triggerType*. In Sect. 5.5, we have already refined the rule *ThrowEvent*. We will now further refine this rule in the light of the results of Sect. 5.7 by specifying the subrule *SetTypeDependentTriggerProperties*, which was left abstract so far.

```
rule ThrowEvent(triggerType, recipientNode, senderInstance,
      senderNode) =
  let newTrigger = new(triggers) in
  seqblock
    triggerType(newTrigger) := triggerType
    recipientNode(newTrigger) := recipientNode
    senderNode(newTrigger) := senderNode
    correlationInfo(newTrigger) :=
        correlationInfo(senderInstance)
    SetTypeDependentTriggerProperties(newTrigger, triggerType,
        recipientNode, senderNode)
    AddTrigger(newTrigger, outbox(parentNode(senderNode)))
  endseqblock
```

The rule *SetTypeDependentTriggerProperties* sets the newly defined trigger properties according to the *triggerType*, as far as these properties can be deduced from the trigger type, as analysed in the previous section, and the available information. We thereby include property values we classified as "typical". We make use of subrules to improve readability. We include "Link" triggers for completeness. Note that "Conditional" and "Timer" triggers cannot be thrown by event nodes. Also note that *senderNode* and *correlationInfo* have already been set in *ThrowEvent*. The default value of a function at a particular location is **undef** and will not be explicitly set, except if an undesired value may already have been set.

```
rule SetTypeDependentTriggerProperties : triggers ×
      eventTriggerTypes × flowNodes × flowNodes
rule SetTypeDependentTriggerProperties(trigger, triggerType,
      recipientNode, senderNode) =
  case triggerType of
    "Message" → SetMessageProperties(trigger, recipientNode,
        senderNode)
    "Signal " → SetSignalProperties(trigger)
    "Error " → SetSignalProperties(trigger)
    "Escalation " → SetSignalProperties(trigger)
    "Cancel " → SetAbortTriggerProperties(trigger, senderNode)
    "Compensation " → SetAbortTriggerProperties(trigger,
        senderNode)
    "Terminate " → SetAbortTriggerProperties(trigger, senderNode)
    "Link" → SetLinkTriggerProperties(trigger, recipientNode,
        senderNode)
```

In the case of a message, we can try to figure out the recipient node (if not already given) by means of a message flow (if one exists). We assume a unique message flow (if any) of which the source is the throwing event node. (We do not consider send tasks as defined by BPMN; see [11, Sect. 4.5.1] for a respective discussion.)

```
rule SetMessageProperties : triggers × flowNodes × flowNodes
rule SetMessageProperties(trigger, recipientNode, senderNode) =
parblock
  seqblock
    if recipientNode = undef then
      choose messageFlow in connectingObjects with
          connectingObjectType(messageFlow) = "MessageFlow" and
```

```
          sourceRef(messageFlow) = senderNode do
      if messageFlow ≠ undef then
          recipientNode(trigger) := targetRef(messageFlow)
    if recipientNode(trigger) ≠ undef then
      recipientProcesses(trigger) := {
          parentNode(recipientNode(trigger)) }
  endseqblock
  mayBePropagated(trigger) := false
  deleteUponCatch(trigger) := true
endparblock
```

The rule *SetSignalProperties* also works for "Error" and "Escalation" triggers (see Sect. 5.7).

```
rule SetSignalProperties : triggers
rule SetSignalProperties(trigger) =
parblock
  recipientNode(trigger) := undef
  mayBePropagated(trigger) := true
  recipientPool(trigger) := defaultPublicEventPool
  deleteUponCatch(trigger) := false
endparblock
```

The rule *SetAbortTriggerProperties* is designed for "Cancel", "Compensation", and "Terminate" triggers (cf. Sect. 5.7). If an abortion-related trigger is thrown within a process (and not by the environment), then we can expect that the recipients are activities of the same process.

```
rule SetAbortTriggerProperties : triggers × flowNodes
rule SetAbortTriggerProperties(trigger, senderNode) =
parblock
  recipientProcesses(trigger) := { parentNode(senderNode) }
  mayBePropagated(trigger) := true
  deleteUponCatch(trigger) := false
  lifetime(trigger) := 0
endparblock
```

"Link" triggers are supposed to be caught by the same process as that of the throwing node and on the same process level; this entails that the trigger shall *not* be propagated. We also suppose that a "Link" trigger should be caught *immediately*.

```
rule SetLinkTriggerProperties : triggers × flowNodes
rule SetLinkTriggerProperties(trigger, senderNode) =
parblock
  recipientProcesses(trigger) := { parentNode(senderNode) }
  mayBePropagated(trigger) := false
  deleteUponCatch(trigger) := true
  lifetime(trigger) := 0
endparblock
```

In Sect. 5.5, we have changed the type of the function *availableTriggers* from **shared** to **derived**, with the following specification:

```
derived availableTriggers : flowNodes → eventPools
derived availableTriggers(eventNode) =
  inbox(parentNode(eventNode))
```

We further need to change every expression of the form

```
trigger ∈ availableTriggers(flowNode)
```

to

```
containsTrigger(availableTriggers(flowNode), trigger)
```

We have also refined the rule *RemoveTrigger* in Sect. 5.5; however, we needed to add an *instance* as an additional parameter. This means that an appropriate argument also has to be added wherever *RemoveTrigger* is called. The rule is used in *EventOperation* and *EventOperationDefault*, where we can add *tokenInstance* as second argument.

```
rule RemoveTrigger(trigger, instance) =
  if deleteUponCatch(trigger) then
    RemoveTrigger(trigger, poolOfTrigger(trigger))
  else
    hasBeenCaughtByInstance(trigger, instance) := true

derived poolOfTrigger : triggers → eventPools
derived poolOfTrigger(trigger) =
  return pool in
    choose pool in eventPools with containsTrigger(pool, trigger)
```

This concludes the necessary refinement of the algorithmic part of the original ground model of the *Workflow Transition Interpreter*.

7.5.4 Ground Model of the Process Model Repository

This ground model specifies the functions and behaviour specific to the component *Process Model Repository* (cf. Sect. 6.4.1) .

7.5.4.1 Controlled Functions

The controlled function *modelId* stores the id of the given model.

```
controlled modelId : models → Integer
```

The controlled function *actualVersion* stores the actual version of the given id of a model.

```
controlled actualVersion : Integer → String
```

The controlled function *allVersions* includes all versions of the model identified by the given id.

```
controlled allVersions : Integer → Set
```

The controlled function *model* stores the given model at the location identified by the parameter *modelId* (Integer parameter) and *version* (String parameter) for an distinct explicit differentiation of different versions.

```
controlled model : Integer × String → models
```

The controlled function *metaData* stores the meta data of the given model identified
by the parameter *modelId* and the version identified by the parameter *version*.

```
controlled metaData : Integer × String → modelMetaData
```

7.5.4.2 Imported and Exported Functions and Rules

In this subsection, we specify rules and functions which are imported or exported
by the *Process Model Repository* component, to execute/provide synchronous calls
of/to interface operations, respectively to access certain data structures.

```
//interface CRUDModel
EXPORT AddModel : model × modelMetaData
EXPORT DeleteModel : String × String
EXPORT GetModel : String × String → models
EXPORT UpdateModel : model → String
EXPORT searchModel : String → Set
```

7.5.4.3 ProcessModelRepositoryBehaviour

The rule *ProcessModelRepositoryBehaviour* specifies the behaviour of the *Process
Model Repository* component by refining the rule *ComponentBehaviour*. This rule
does not include a specification how this component manages persistence of models.
In our high level abstraction, we do not explicitly specify exceptions occurring (e.g.
when an interface operation that is defined to throw an exception) in this case we set
the return value to undef.

```
rule ProcessModelRepositoryBehaviour = ComponentBehaviour where
```

The rule *Initialise* initialises the interfaces provided by the component *Process Model
Repository* (see also Sect. 6.4.1) namely *CRUDModel*. Additionally, this rule initialises some functions.

```
rule Initialise =
parblock
  providedInterfaces:= {"CRUDModel"}
    // all operations are called synchronously
  asyncOperations("CRUDModel") := {}
  asyncCalledOperations(self) := {}
    ownCalledFunctions(self) := {}
  initialised(self) := true
endparblock
```

The rule *CreateIncludingComponent* does nothing, because no own component is
needed.

```
rule CreateIncludingComponent = skip
```

The rule *ReactToCall* is called for each asynchronously called operation in any interface of the *Process Model Repository* component (see also Sect. 6.4.1). This rule does nothing, because no operation is called asynchronously.

```
rule ReactToCall(calledOperation) = skip
```

The rule *HandleOwnCalls* does nothing, because the *Process Model Repository* component does not call any interface operation asynchronously. This rule is called from the base *ComponentBehaviour* (see also Sect. 7.4).

```
rule HandleOwnCalls(asyncCallingData) = skip
```

7.5.4.4 Managing Called Functions of the *CRUDModel* Interface

The rule *AddModel* adds the given model including the meta data to the repository. It is assumed that the given model is not yet added to the repository (for a model that is already added to the repository the rule *updateModel* has to be used). This rule sets the functions *actualVersion, allVersions*, and *model* (no return value is required for this rule).

```
rule AddModel : model × modelMetaData
rule AddModel(model, metaData) =
parblock
  //store the parameters
  let id = getNextModelId in
    modelId(model) := id
    actualVersion(id) := "0.0"
    add actualVersion(id) to allVersions(id)
        //store the value in the controlled function
    model(id, actualVersion(id)) := model
        metaData(id, actualVersion(id)) := metaData
endparblock
```

The abstract-derived function *getNextModelId* returns the next possible id for a model.

```
abstract-derived getNextModelId : → String
```

The rule *DeleteModel* deletes the given model in the given version from the repository. When the version is "all", all versions of the model identified by the given *modelId* are deleted. If either the *modelId* or the *version* is undefined, an exception is thrown (no return value is required for this rule).

```
rule DeleteModel : String × String
rule DeleteModel(modelId, version) =
parblock
  //remove all versions
  if version = "all" then
  parblock
    forall v ∈ allVersions(modelId) do
      model(modelId, v) := undef)
```

```
    allVersions(modelId) := {}
  endparblock
  //remove given version
  else
  parblock
    remove version from allVersions(modelId)
    model(modelId, version) := undef
  endparblock
endparblock
```

The rule *GetModel* returns the given model in the given version from the repository. Because in some cases, this rule throws an exception, it is defined as rule.

```
rule GetModel : String × String → models
rule GetModel(modelId, version) =
  return res in
    let m = model(modelId, version) in
      res := m
```

The rule *UpdateModel* stores the given model in the function *model* and gets a new version by calling the derived function *getNextVersionForModel* and returns this version. Additionally, it sets the new version in the function *actualVersion* and adds the new version to *allVersions*.

```
rule UpdateModel : model → String
rule UpdateModel(model) =
  return res in
    let version = getNextVersionForModel(model) in
      model(modelId(model), version) := model
      actualVersion(modelId(model) := version
      add version to allVersions
      res := version
```

The abstract-derived function *getNextVersionForModel* returns the next possible version for the given model.

```
abstract-derived getNextVersionForModel : models → String
```

The derived function *searchModel*, which matches homonymous interface operation, searches for a model that corresponds to the given search string.

```
derived searchModel : String → Set
derived searchModel(searchString) =
  return res in
    local temp in
        seqblock
      forall m ∈ models with matchesSearchString(searchString,
          m) do
        temp(m) := modelId(m))

      res := {x|x ∈ temp and temp(x) != undef}
        endseqblock
```

The abstract-derived function *matchesSearchString* for a given search string and a given model checks whether the given model matches the given search string.

abstract-derived matchesSearchString : String × models → Boolean

7.5.5 Ground Model of the Task Server

This ground model specifies the functions and behaviour specific to the component *Task Server* (cf. Sect. 6.4.3).

7.5.5.1 Static Functions

The static function *ordering* defines the kind of ordering ("sequential" or "parallel") for the given ad hoc sub-process (defined in [11]).

static ordering : flowNodes → String

7.5.5.2 Controlled Functions

The controlled function *runningClients* contains a set of *clientInstances* objects that are inserted when the operation *tryStartTask* was called and removed when the operation *logOff* was called both operations are defined in the interface *TaskHandling*.

controlled runningClients → Set

The controlled function *openTransactions* contains the id of the transaction (of the type *transactionId*), which we got when a transaction was opened by calling the operation *openTransaction* of the interface *Data*. A transaction has to be opened when the first task of a transaction sub-process was submitted by the operation *processTask* in the interface *ProcessTask* (see Sect. 6.4.3). The parameter identifies the transaction sub-process instance. When a transaction is already open for a task of a certain transaction sub-process [11], this *transactionId* is used for all other task of the same transaction sub-process instance.

controlled openTransactions : instances → transactionId

The controlled function *actTransSubInstances* contains all instances of transaction sub-processes for that a transaction is open (see [11]).

controlled actTransSubInstances → Set

The controlled function *activeTasks* contains all task instances that are delivered for being processed (of the type *extendedTaskInstances*). When the processing of a task instance has finished, this task instance has to be removed from this *activeTasks* function.

controlled activeTasks → Set

The controlled function *arguments* stores the values of the parameters, given when the task instance was delivered by the interface *ProcessTask*, not only for tasks of the type "UserTask" and "ManualTask" but also for "ServiceTask" and "ScriptTask".

controlled arguments : instances → parameters

The controlled function *responsibleUser* for the given task instance stores the user who performs the task instance.

controlled responsibleUser : instances → users

The controlled function *allUserClassifications* for the given extended task instance, stores the set containing all deontic classifications for all users (a set of *deonticClassificationsForUsers*).

controlled allUserClassifications : extendedTaskInstances → Set

The controlled function *adHocParent* for the given extended task instance stores the corresponding parent instance of the task, when the parent is an ad hoc sub-process.

controlled adHocParent : extendedTaskInstance → instances

The controlled function *adHocProcessing* stores a boolean value indicating whether the task is being processed, which is necessary for tasks of ad hoc sub-processes with an sequential ordering attribute (cf. [12, p. 181]).

controlled adHocProcessing : extendedTaskInstance → Boolean

7.5.5.3   Monitored Functions

The monitored function *transactionSubProcInstance* for the given parameter list (type *parameters*) supplies the instance of a transaction sub-process when it exists.

monitored transactionSubProcInstance : parameters → instances

The monitored function *adHocParentInstance* for the given parameter list (type *parameters*) supplies the instance of the parent process when the parent is an ad hoc sub-process.

monitored adHocParentInstance : parameters → instances

The monitored function *deonticUserClassifications* for the given parameter list (type *parameters*) supplies a set with deontic classifications for users (type *deonticClassificationsForUsers*) for all related users.

monitored deonticUserClassifications : parameters → Set

The monitored function *getTopLevelProcess* for the given flow node supplies the process to that the given flow node belongs.

monitored getTopLevelProcess : flowNodes → processes

The monitored function *getFlowNode* for the given instance supplies the flow node.

monitored getFlowNode : instances → flowNodes

The monitored function *process* for the given process event (type *processEvents*) supplies the process (type *processes*).

monitored process : processEvents → processes

The monitored function *eventType* for the given process event (type *processEvents*) supplies the event type (type *eventTypes*).

monitored eventType : processEvents → eventTypes

The monitored function *triggerType* for the given process event (type *processEvents*) supplies the trigger type (type *eventTriggerTypes*).

monitored triggerType : processEvents → eventTriggerTypes

The monitored function *taskInstance* for the given process event (type *processEvents*) supplies the task instance (type *instances*).

monitored taskInstance : processEvents → instances

The monitored function *getTriggerTypeFromEventDef* for the given event definition (type *eventDefinitions*) supplies the trigger type (type *eventTriggerTypes*).

monitored getTriggerTypeFromEventDef : eventDefinitions →
    eventTriggerTypes

The monitored function *classification* for the given deontic classification for users (type *deonticClassificationsForUsers* returns the deontic classification (type *deonticClassifications*.

monitored classification : deonticClassificationsForUsers →
    deonticClassifications

7.5.5.4 Out Functions

Following out functions are specified to set values of certain types, which then can be used by other components.

The out function *user* for the given client instance (type *clientInstances*) supplies the user.

out user : clientInstances → users

The out function *taskInstance* for the extended task instance (type *extendedTaskInstances*) sets the task instance (type instances).

out taskInstance : extendedTaskInstances → instances

The out function *transactionId* for the extended task instance (type *extendedTaskInstances*) sets the transactionId (type transactionId).

out transactionId : extendedTaskInstances → transactionId

7.5.5.5   Shared Functions

A lot of the following shared functions represent return values of operations defined in the *Monitor* interface, because the *Workflow Transition Interpreter* listens to these shared functions (has not implemented the *Monitor* interface). No shared functions are specified for the return values of the *ProcessTask* interface as no operation of this interface requires a return value.

The shared function *taskSkipped* represents the return value of the operation *taskSkipped* of the interface *Monitor*.

shared taskSkipped : instances → Boolean

The shared function *taskRejected* represents the return value of the operation *taskRejected* of the interface *Monitor*.

shared taskRejected : instances → Boolean

The shared function *taskCompleted* represents the return value of the operation *taskCompleted* of the interface *Monitor*.

shared taskCompleted : instances → Users

The shared function *taskSelected* for the task instance (type *instances*) informs the *Workflow Transition Interpreter* component (via the *Monitor* interface), which user has selected the task for being processed, whereupon the *Workflow Transition Interpreter* component has to recalculate the deontic classifications.

shared taskSelected : instances → users

The shared function *cancelTransactionTask* for the task instance (type *instances*) informs the *Workflow Transition Interpreter* component (via the *Monitor* interface), when processing a task of a transaction sub-process causes an error.

shared cancelTransactionTask : instances → Boolean

The shared function *abortedByEnvironment* represents the return value of the operation *abortedByEnvironment* of the interface *Monitor*.

shared abortedByEnvironment → Boolean

The shared function *correlationInfo* for a given trigger (type *triggers*) sets the correlation info (see Sect. 5.4).

shared correlationInfo : triggers → correlationInf

The shared function *recipientProcesses* for a given trigger (type *triggers*) sets the recipient process (see Sect. 5.4).

shared recipientProcesses : triggers → process

The shared function *mayBePropagated* for a given trigger (type *triggers*) sets a boolean value, indicating whether the trigger may be propagated (see Sect. 5.4).

shared mayBePropagated : trigger → Boolean

The shared function *senderNode* for a given trigger (type *triggers*) sets the trigger type (see Sect. 5.4).

shared senderNode : triggers → taskNodes

The shared function *triggerType* for a given trigger (type *triggers*) sets the trigger type (see Sect. 5.4).

shared triggerType : triggers → eventTriggerTypes

7.5.5.6 Imported and Exported Functions and Rules

In this subsection, we specify rules and functions which are imported or exported by the *Task Server* component, to execute/provide synchronous calls of/to interface operations, respectively to access certain data structures.

```
IMPORT (Data Management) OpenTransaction : → transactionId
IMPORT (Data Management) Commit : transactionId
IMPORT (Actor Management) GetAllProcessesUserMayStart : users ×
    user → Set
IMPORT (Process Client) RemoveTask : extendedTaskInstances
IMPORT (Process Client) AddTask : extendedTaskInstances ×
    deonticClassificationsForUsers
IMPORT (Workflow Transition Interpreter) classification :
    deonticClassificationsForUsers → deonticClassifications
IMPORT (Workflow Transition Interpreter) getFlowNode : instances
    → flowNodes
IMPORT (Workflow Transition Interpreter) ordering : flowNodes →
    String
IMPORT (Workflow Transition Interpreter) getTopLevelProcess :
    flowNodes → processes
IMPORT (Workflow Transition Interpreter)
    getTriggerTypeFromEventDef : eventDefinitions →
    eventTriggerTypes
IMPORT (Process Client) process : processEvents → processes
IMPORT (Process CLient) eventType : processEvents → eventTypes
IMPORT (Process CLient) triggerType : processEvents →
    eventTriggerTypes
IMPORT (Process Client) taskInstance : processEvents → instances

//interface TaskHandling
EXPORT GetAllTasks : users × clientInstances → Set
EXPORT TryStartTask : extendedTaskInstances × users → Boolean
EXPORT TaskCompleted : extendedTaskInstances
EXPORT CancelUserAndManualTask : extendedTaskInstances
EXPORT GetAllProcessesToBeAllowedToStart : users → Set
EXPORT LogOff : users × clientInstances
EXPORT GetAllProcessesToBeAllowedToStart : users → Set
EXPORT TaskSkipped : extendedTaskInstances
EXPORT TaskRejected : extendedTaskInstances
//interface ProcessEventListener
EXPORT HandleProcessEvent : processEvents
```

```
//interface ProcessTask is asynchronously called → no export
//functions
EXPORT taskInstance : extendedTaskInstances → instances
EXPORT transactionId : extendedTaskInstances → transactionId
EXPORT user : clientInstances → users
EXPORT triggerType : triggers → eventTriggerTypes
EXPORT correlationInfo : triggers → correlationInf
EXPORT recipientProcesses : triggers → process
EXPORT mayBePropagated : trigger → Boolean
EXPORT senderNode : triggers → taskNodes
EXPORT taskSkipped : instances → Boolean
EXPORT taskRejected : instances → Boolean
EXPORT taskCompleted : instances → Users
EXPORT taskSelected : instances → users
EXPORT cancelTransactionTask : instances → Boolean
EXPORT abortedByEnvironment → Boolean
```

7.5.5.7   TaskServerBehaviour

The rule *TaskServerBehavior* specifies the behaviour of the component *Task Server* by refining the rule *ComponentBehaviour*.

```
rule TaskServerBehavior = ComponentBehaviour where
```

The rule *Initialise* initialises all interfaces provided by the component *Task Server* (see also Sect. 6.4.3). These interfaces are *ProcessTask, TaskHandling* and *ProcessEventListener*.

```
rule Initialise =
parblock
  providedInterfaces:= {"ProcessTask", " TaskHandling ",
      "  ProcessEventListener  "}
  asyncOperations("ProcessTask") := {" processTask ", " invokeScript ",
      " invokeService ", " cancelTask ", " completeTransaction ",
      "  resetDeonticClassifications  "}
  asyncOperations("TaskHandling") := {}
  asyncOperations(ProcessEventListener) := {}
  runningClients := {}
    activeTasks := {}
  asyncCalledOperations(self) := {}
    ownCalledFunctions(self) := {}
    initialised(self):= true
endparblock
```

The rule *CreateIncludingComponent* does nothing, because no own component is needed.

```
rule CreateIncludingComponent = skip
```

The rule *ReactToCall* is called for each asynchronously called operation in any interface of the *Task Server* component (see also Sect. 6.4.3). This rule contains a case rule that depending on the parameter *calledOperationName*, calls a corresponding rule that is responsible for processing the operation call.

```
rule ReactToCall(calledOperation) =
parblock
  let params = params(calledOperation) in
  let calledOperationName = operationName(calledOperation) in
    case calledOperationName of
    //interface ProcessTask
      " processTask " → PropagateUserTask(params)
      " invokeScript " → InvokeScript(params)
      " invokeService " → InvokeService(params)
      " completeTransaction " → CompleteTransaction(params)
      " cancelTask " → CancelTask(params)
      "    resetDeonticClassifications    " →
          ResetDeonticClassifications(params)
endparblock
```

The rule *HandleOwnCalls* does nothing, because the *TaskServer* component does not call any interface operation asynchronously except those of the *Monitor* interface where the location is set directly (without a call, since this interface is not yet implemented by the *Workflow Transition Interpreter* component). This rule is called from the base *ComponentBehaviour* (see also Sect. 7.4).

```
rule HandleOwnCalls(asyncCallingData) = skip
```

7.5.5.8 Managing Called Functions of the *ProcessTask* Interface

The rule *PropagateUserTask* reacts to a call of the operation *processTask* (*Process Task* interface). It propagates a task instance (type *extendedTaskInstances*) to all users that may process this task. The actual values of the parameters of the called function are given in the parameter params and are used by this rule. This rule first stores the actual parameters of the called function. Additionally, it checks whether the parameter *transactionSubProcInstance* is defined, and if so the derived function *getTransactionId* is called, to obtain the *transactionId* when it already exists or to open a new transaction. Moreover, this rule adds the *transactionId* to *actTransSubInstances* and sets the function *openTransactions* at the appropriate transaction sub-process instance. Furthermore, a new *extendedTaskInstances* object is created and the *taskInstance*, the *transactionId*, and the *deonticClassificationsForUsers* are set. Afterwards, when the task belongs to an ad hoc sub-process, the derived function *mayPropagateAdHoc* is called to check the *ordering* attribute and when it returns *true*, the rule *PropagateTaskToCertainUsers* is called to send the extended task to the appropriate users.

```
rule PropagateUserTask : parameters
rule PropagateUserTask(parametersOfCall) =
seqblock
  let taskInst = taskInstance(parametersOfCall) in
    let adHocSubInstance = adHocParentInstance(parametersOfCall) in
```

```
    local transId := undef in
    local mayPropagate := true
  parblock
    arguments(taskInst) := params(parametersOfCall)
    //check if the task belongs to a transaction sub-process
    if transactionSubProcInstance(parametersOfCall) != undef then
    seqblock
      transId := getTransactionId(parametersOfCall)
      add transId to actTransSubInstances
      openTransactions(transactionSubProcInstance(
          parametersOfCall)) := transId
    endseqblock
  endparblock
  let actParams = new(parameters) in
  let extendedTask = new(extendedTaskInstances) in
  seqblock
    taskInstance(extendedTask) := taksInst
    transactionId(extendedTask) := transId
      //we remember the deonticClassifications (Set) in the location
          allUserClassifications(extendedTask)
        allUserClassifications(extendedTask) :=
            deonticClassificationsForUsers(parametersOfCall)
    add extendedTask to actParams
        //we add the extendedTask to activeTasks
        add extendedTask to activeTasks

        //check whether a task of an ad hoc sub-procses may be
            propagated and store the ad hoc sub-process instance
        if(adHocSubInstance) != undef then
        seqblock
          mayPropagate := mayPropagateAdHoc
            adHocParent(extendedTask) := adHocSubInstance
    endseqblock
        //add the extendedTask to the worklist of certain users
        if mayPropagate then
          PropagateTaskToCertainUsers(deonticClassifications(
              extendedTask), actParams)
  endseqblock
endseqblock
```

The derived function *mayPropagateAdHoc* returns false, when the given ad hoc sub-process instance is not *undef* and the ordering attribute of the corresponding flow node is "sequential" and a user is processing another task of this ad hoc sub-process, otherwise it returns true (when a user already is working on a task of that ad hoc sub-process, or the ad hoc sub-process is undefined).

```
derived mayPropagateAdHoc : Instances →
derived mayPropagateAdHoc(adHocSubInstance) =
  return res in
        if adHocSubInstance = undef or
            ordering(getFlowNode(adHocSubInstance)) = "parallel" then
          res := true
        else
```

```
                //check whether task of same ad hoc sub-process is
                   already being processed
            if forsome extTask in activeTasks with
                adHocParent(extTask) = adHocSubInstance and
                adHocProcessing(extTask) != true then
                res := false
            else
                res := true
```

The rule *PropagateTaskToCertainUsers* checks all deontic classifications for users, (type *Set of deonticClassificationsForUsers*) given by the first parameter and adds the task to the worklist of the appropriate user, when the classification is not "Forbidden".

```
rule PropagateTaskToCertainUsers : Set × extendedTaskInstances
rule PropagateTaskToCertainUsers(deonticClassificationsForUsers,
    extendedTaskInst)
  forall deonticClassiForUser ∈ deonticClassificationsForUsers do
    if classification( deonticClassiForUser) != "Forbidden" then
        if forsome client ∈ runningClients holds user(client) =
            user(deonticClassiForUser) then
          //call addTask of the TaskList interface for the certain
              client
            TaskList(client).addTask(extendedTaskInst,
                deonticClassiForUser)
  endseqblock
```

The derived function *getTransactionId* searches in *actTransSubInstances* for an instance of a transaction sub-process that is equal to that inserted in the parameter and returns the appropriate *transactionId*, when it exists otherwise it opens a new transaction by calling the operation *OpenTransaction* of the interface *Data* and returns the return value of the operation call. Because the *transactionId* is returned and not stored and since opening a transaction is done by another component, this can be done in a derived function, which must not change the state of an ASM.

```
derived getTransactionId : parameters → transactionId
  return transId in
    //check if the task belongs to a transaction sub-process
    if transactionSubProcInstance(parametersOfCall) != undef then
      //check if the transactionId already exists
      if forsome instance ∈ actTransSubInstances holds instance =
          transactionSubProcInstance(parametersOfCall) and
        openTransactions(instance) != undef then
      choose instance ∈ actTransSubInstances with instance =
          transactionSubProcInstance(parametersOfCall) and
        openTransactions(instance) != undef do
        transId = openTransactions(instance)
    else
          //synchronously call openTransaction of the Data
              interface
        transId := Data.OpenTransaction()
```

The derived function *getExtendedTaskFromTaskInstance* returns the extended task instance from the *activeTasks* function that corresponds to the given instance.

```
derived getExtendedTaskFromTaskInstance : instances →
     extendedTaskInstances
derived getExtendedTaskFromTaskInstance(taskInstance) =
  return res in
     choose extTaskInst in activeTasks with taskInstance(extTask) =
          taskInstance do
          res := extTaskInst // only one may exist
```

The rule *InvokeScript* reacts to a call of the operation *invokeScript* (*ProcessTask* interface) and stores the parameters and obtains a transaction id by calling the rule *StoreParameters* and calls the rule *InvokeTheScript* that is kept abstract but is responsible for calling the script.

```
rule InvokeScript : parameters
rule InvokeScript(parametersOfCall) =
parblock
  StoreParameters(parametersOfCall)
  InvokeTheScript(script(parametersOfCall),
      currentISet(parametersOfCall))
endparblock
```

The rule *StoreParameters* first gets the task instance out of the given parameter. Afterwards it checks whether the given task belongs to a transaction sub-process, if so it calls the derived function *getTransactionId* to obtain the transaction id (either already defined or a new one). This rule inserts the obtained transaction id into the function *actTransSubInstances* and sets the function *openTransactions* at the given transaction sub-process instance to this transaction id.

```
rule StoreParameters : parameters
rule StoreParameters(parametersOfCall) =
parblock
  let taskInst = taskInstance(parametersOfCall) in
  local transId := undef in
    //check if the task belongs to a transaction sub-process
    if transactionSubProcInstance(parametersOfCall) != undef then
    seqblock
       transId := getTransactionId(parametersOfCall)
       add transId to actTransSubInstances
       openTransactions(transactionSubProcInstance(
          parametersOfCall)) := transId
    endseqblock
endparblock
```

The abstract rule *InvokeTheScript* invokes the script given by the first parameter with the input sets (type *inputSets*) provided in the second parameter.

```
abstract rule InvokeTheScript : String × inputSets
```

The rule *InvokeService* reacts to a call of the operation *invokeService* (*ProcessTask* interface), stores the parameters and obtains a transaction id by calling the rule *StoreParameters* and calls the rule *InvokeTheService* that is kept abstract but is responsible for calling the service.

```
rule InvokeService : parameters
rule InvokeService(parametersOfCall) =
parblock
  StoreParameters(parametersOfCall)
  InvokeTheService(service(parametersOfCall),
      currentISet(parametersOfCall))
endparblock
```

The abstract rule *InvokeTheService* invokes the service given by the first parameter with the input sets (type *inputSets*) provided in the second parameter.

```
abstract rule InvokeTheService : String × inputSets
```

The rule *CompleteTransaction* reacts to a call of the operation *completeTransaction* (*ProcessTask* interface) and ends a successful transaction sub-process. First it calls the operation *commit* of the interface *Data* of the *Data Management* component and removes the given transaction sub-process instance from the function *actTransSubInstances* and sets the function *openTransactions* at the given transaction sub-process instance to undefined.

```
rule CompleteTransaction : parameters
rule CompleteTransaction(parametersOfCall) =
parblock
  transSubId := transactionSubProcInstance(parametersOfCall)
  transId := getTransactionId(parametersOfCall)
  // call Commit of the Data interface synchronously
  let isSuccessfull = Data.Commit(transId)
  if(isSuccessfull) then
    parblock
       remove transId from actTransSubInstances
       openTransactions(transactionSubProcInstance) := undef
    endparblock
endparblock
```

The rule *CancelTask* (corresponds to the interface operation *cancelTask*) is called by the *Workflow Transition Interpreter* for every task instance that has to be cancelled. Therefore, the *Task Server* calls *removeTask* (see interface *TaskList* in Sect. 6.4.5) for all process clients to remove the task from their worklist.

```
rule CancelTask : parameters
rule CancelTask(parametersOfCall) =
  let taskInst = taskInstance(parametersOfCall) in
  parblock
    //update functions
    responsibleUser(taskInstance) := undef
    let extendedTaskInst =
       getExtendedTaskFromTaskInstance(taskInst)
    //remove the task from each client
    forall client ∈ runningClients do
      TaskList.RemoveTask(extendedTaskInst)
    endparblock
```

The rule *ResetDeonticClassifications* (conform to the interface operation *resetDeonticClassifications*) is called by the *Workflow Transition Interpreter* for every task instance for which the deontic classification for users has changed (this is only for alternative tasks when one task was e.g. selected for being processes in such a case another task can become forbidden). This rule stores the new got set of *deonticclassificationsForUsers* in the location *allUserClassifications* and calls the correspondent rule of the interface *TaskList* for every logged in user. For users not logged in, the deontic classification for a certain user will be evaluated in the rule *GetAllTasks* which is called when a new user logs on to the system.

```
rule ResetDeonticClassifications : parameters
rule ResetDeonticClassifications(parametersOfCall) =
  let taskInst = taskInstance(parametersOfCall) in
    let deonticClassificSet =
        deonticUserClassifications(parametersOfCall) in
      choose extendedTask in activeTasks with
          taskInst(extendedTask) = taskInst do
        parblock
          //reset the allUserClassifications (controlled function)
              for the task instance
            allUserClassifications(extendedTask) :=
                deonticClassificSet
          forall userClassific ∈ deonticClassificSet do
            if forsome client ∈ runningClients holds user(client) =
                user(userClassific)
              TaskList(client).resetDeonticClassificationOfTask(
                  extendedTask, userClassific)
        endparblock
```

7.5.5.9 Managing Called Functions of the *TaskHandling* Interface

The rule *GetAllTasks*, which corresponds to the interface operation *getAllTasks*, implies the login of a *Process Client* instance, therefore, the given *clientInstance* is added to *runningClients* (an additional adding does not matter in a set). Furthermore, all tasks, which are not chosen for being processed, are checked whether the deontic classification for the appropriate user is not "Forbidden" (the user is allowed to process it) and in the case the task is a task of an ad hoc sub-process whether processing is allowed by calling the derived function *mayPropagateAdHoc*. When both checks succeed, the task is added to a local variable, which is returned later. Note we do use a while and not a forall, because this would allow parallel access the collection of tasks.

```
rule GetAllTasks : users × clientInstances → Set
rule GetAllTasks(user, clientInst) =
  return res in
    parblock
        //store the parameters
        add clientInst to runningClients
        user(clientInstance) := user
        local allTasks := activeTasks, tasks := {} in
```

```
                  while allTasks != {} do // forall would access the
                      activeTasks parallel → inconsistent update
                    choose extTaskInstance ∈ allTasks do
                      if responsibleUser(taskInstance(extTaskInstance) =
                          undef then
                        if mayPropagateAdHoc(adHocParent(extTaskInst)) then
                            forall deonticClassiForUser ∈
                                allUserClassifications(extTaskInstance) with
                                    user(deonticClassiForUser) = user do
                              if classification(deonticClassiForUser) !=
                                  "Forbidden" then
                                parblock
                                    add extTaskInstance to tasks
                                    remove extTaskInstance from allTasks
                                endparblock
          // set the return value
          res := tasks
```

The rule *TryStartTask* (conform to the interface operation *tryStartTask*) first checks whether the given task instance is being processed by another user and if not, the given user is stored for the given task (function *responsibleUser*) and the out function *taskSelected* is set to the given user to inform the *Workflow Transition Interpreter* component and *true* is returned to inform the given user that he is allowed to process the task. For all other users the rule *RemoveTask* is called via the *TaskList* interface (for the certain client instance) to remove the task from their worklist.

```
rule TryStartTask : extendedTaskInstances × users → Boolean
rule TryStartTask(extendedTaskInst, user ) =
parblock
  return res in
      let taskInstance = taskInstance(extendedTaskInst)
          // nobody processes the task
          if responsibleUser(taskInstance) = undef then
          parblock
              responsibleUser(taskInstance) := user
              //inform the Workflow Transition Interpreter who has
                  selected the task
              taskSelected(taskInstance) := user
              //when the parent is an ad hoc sub-process set
                  adHocProcessing to true
              if adHocParent(extendedTaskInst) != undef
                adHocProcessing(extendedTaskInst) := true
              res := true
              //remove the task from all other users
              forall clientInst ∈ runningClients with user(clientInst)
                  != clientId do
                TaskList(clientInst).RemoveTask(taskInst)
          endparblock
          else
              res := false
endparblock
```

The rule *TaskCompleted* corresponds to the interface operation *taskCompleted*) and removes the given task instance from the collection of tasks (function *activeTasks*) and clears the value of function *arguments*. In the case when the given task instance is a task of an ad hoc sub-process, the location *adHocProcessing* is set to *undef*. Furthermore, it sets the shared function *taskCompleted* to the certain user for informing the *Workflow Transition Interpreter*. Up to now we do not call the operation *taskCompleted* defined in the *Monitor* interface, due to the fact that the *Workflow Transition Interpreter* component is specified to listen to these shared functions and has not implemented the *Monitor* interface.

```
rule TaskCompleted : extendedTaskInstances
rule TaskCompleted(extTaskInst) =
parblock
    let taskInstance = taskInstance(extTaskInst)
    let user = responsibleUser(extTaskInst)
  parblock
    //update functions
    arguments(taskInstance) := undef
    remove extTaskInst from activeTasks
        responsibleUser(extTaskInst) := undef
        if adHocParent(extendedTask) != undef then
          adHocProcessing(extTaskInst) := undef
    //inform Workflow Transition Interpreter who has performed
        the task
        taskCompleted(taskInstance) := user
  endparblock
endparblock
```

The rule *CancelUserAndManualTask* (conform to the interface operation *cancelUserAndManualTask*) first clears the function *responsibleUser* and if applicable also the function *adHocProcessing* for the given task instance and afterwards calls the rule *PropagateTaskToCertainUsers* which propagates the task (type *extendedTaskInstances*) to all users which a deontic classification not equal to "Forbidden".

```
rule CancelUserAndManualTask : extendedTaskInstances
rule CancelUserAndManualTask(extendedTaskInst) =
parblock
  //update functions
  responsibleUser(extTaskInst) := undef
    if adHocParent(extendedTask) != undef then
        adHocProcessing(extTaskInst) := undef
  //inform certain clients that a task instance is ready for
      being processed
  PropagateTaskToCertainUsers(
      deonticClassifications(extTaskInst), extendedTaskInst)
endparblock
```

The rule *GetAllProcessesToBeAllowedToStart*, which corresponds to the interface operation *getAllProcessesToBeAllowedToStart*, synchronously calls the rule *GetAllProcessesUserMayStart* of the *Actor* interface to get all processes the given user is allowed to start, which are returned afterwards.

```
rule GetAllProcessesToBeAllowedToStart : users → Set
rule GetAllProcessesToBeAllowedToStart(user) =
    return res in
      res := Actor.GetAllProcessesUserMayStart(user)
```

The rule *LogOff* (interface operation *logOff*) removes the given client instance from *runningClients* and clears related functions.

```
rule LogOff : users × clientInstances
rule LogOff(user, clientInst) =
parblock
  remove clientInst from runningClients
  user(clientInst) := undef
endparblock
```

The rule *TaskSkipped* is conform to the interface operation *taskSkipped* of the *TaskHandling* interface. It sets the location *taskSkipped* to inform the *Workflow Transition Interpreter* component (via the *Monitor* interface).

```
rule TaskSkipped : extendedTaskInstances
rule TaskSkipped(extendedTaskInst) =
parblock
  let taskInst = taskInstance(extendedTaskInst) in
    //inform WTI via Monitor interface (shared function)
    taskSkipped(taskInst) := true
endparblock
```

The rule *TaskRejected* corresponds to the interface operation *taskRejected* of the *TaskHandling* interface and sets the location *taskRejected* to inform the *Workflow Transition Interpreter* component (*Monitor* interface).

```
rule TaskRejected : extendedTaskInstances
rule TaskRejected(extendedTaskInst) =
parblock
  let taskInst = taskInstance(extendedTaskInst) in
    //inform WTI via Monitor interface (shared function)
    taskRejected(taskInst) := true
endparblock
```

7.5.5.10   Managing Called Functions of the *ProcessEventListener* Interface

The rule *HandleProcessEvent*, which relates to the interface operation *handleProcessEvent*, handles the given event by calling appropriate rules depending on the event type of the given process event (type *processEvents*). Supported Events are start events (when a user wants to start a new process) and error events—when something went wrong at processing a task (by the component *Process Client* or whose *Dialogue Engine* component).

```
rule HandleProcessEvent : processEvents
rule HandleProcessEvent(pEvent) =
  let eventType = eventType(pEvent) in
      if eventType = "StartEvent" then
          let proc = process(pEvent) in
             ThrowStartEvent(process)
        else
           ThrowOtherEvents(pEvent)
```

The rule *ThrowStartEvent* creates a new *correlationInfo* object and a new *trigger* object, sets the appropriate properties and adds the trigger to the respective event pool of the given process.

```
rule ThrowStartEvent : processes
rule ThrowStartEvent(process) =
  let correlationInf = new (correlationInfo) in
    let trigger = new (triggers) in
    seqblock
        correlationInfo(trigger) := correlationInf
        recipientProcesses(trigger) := {process}
        mayBePropagated(trigger) := false //implies the private
            event pool
      choose startEvent ∈ flowNodes(process) with
          parentNode(startEvent) = process and
          flowNodeType(startEvent) = "StartEvent" do
          choose eventDef ∈ eventDefinitions(startEvent) in
              triggerType(trigger) :=
                  getTrigerTypeFromEventDef(eventDef)
    AddTrigger(trigger, outbox(environment)) //background process
        collects from outbox and delivers to appropriate event
        pool
  endseqblock
```

The rule *ThrowOtherEvents* first checks whether the task instance whose processing leaded to the error event is part of a transaction sub-process and if so, the *Workflow Transition Interpreter* component is informed via the *Monitor* interface. Otherwise this rule creates a new *correlationInfo* object and a new *trigger* object, sets the appropriate properties and adds the *trigger* to the respective event pool of the given process.

```
rule ThrowOtherEvents : processEvents
rule ThrowOtherEvents(pEvent) =
    let correlationInf = new (correlationInfo) in
    let trigger = new (triggers) in
    let taskInst = taskInstance(pEvent) in
    let extendedTaskInst = getExtendedTaskFromTaskInstance(taskInst)
      //inform the Workflow Transition Interpreter when the
          corresponding task is a task of a transaction sub-process
      if(transactionId(extendedTaskInst) != undef then
         cancelTransactionTask(taskInstance) := true
        else
        seqblock
            correlationInfo(trigger) := correlationInf
```

```
recipientProcesses(trigger) :=
    {getTopLevelProcess(getFlowNode(taskInstance))}
senderNode(trigger) := getFlowNode(taskInstance)
mayBePropagated(trigger) := true
AddTrigger(trigger, outbox(environment)) //background
    process collects from outbox and delivers to
    appropriate event pool
endseqblock
```

7.5.6 Ground Model of the Process Client

This ground model specifies the functions and behaviour specific to the *Process Client* component (cf. Sect. 6.4.5) by refining the common behaviour of the eP^2 architecture components. This specification let issues concerning the illustration of single tasks in the worklist open, (e.g. the difference in deontic classification of different tasks, which are alternative or which may be skipped, etc.) although when adding a task to the worklist, user specific deontic classifications (type *deonticClassificationsForUsers*) are provided, which could be used for the illustration of the certain task. We assume that a new instance of a *Process Client* component is created when a user logs in to the system whereat also the function *user* for this new client instance is set.

7.5.6.1 Controlled Functions

The controlled function *taskList* contains all task instances (type *extendedTaskInstances*, which includes required information for transaction handling) that the logged in user is allowed to process (corresponds to a worklist cf. Chap. 4). The parameter refers to the component instance that is related to the logged in user as an own instance of the *Process Client* component is created for each user (cf. Fig. 7.1). The sequence of the task instances is not relevant, therefore we use a set.

controlled taskList : componentInstances → Set

The controlled function *startableProcesses* contains all processes (of type *processes*), which the logged in user is allowed to start. The parameter refers to the logged in user.

controlled startableProcesses : users → Set

The controlled function *userClassification* stores the deontic classification for users (type *deonticClassificationsForUsers*) for the given extended task instance (which can be used for illustration of the task in the collection of tasks).

controlled userClassification : extendedTaskInstances →
    deonticClassificationsForUsers

7.5.6.2   Monitored Functions

The monitored function *user* supplies the user for the given client instance (type *clientInstances*), which has to be set when the client instance was created.

monitored user : clientInstances → users

The monitored function *taskInstance* for the given extended task instance (type *extendedTaskInstances*) gets the task instance (type *instances*).

monitored taskInstance : extendedTaskInstances → instances

The monitored function *getFlowNode* for the given instance supplies the flow node.

monitored getFlowNode : instances → flowNodes

The monitored function *extendedTaskInstance* for the given parameter list (type *parameters*) supplies the extended task instance.

monitored extendedTaskInstance : parameters →
    extendedTaskInstances

The monitored function *transactionId* for the extended task instance (type *extendedTaskInstances*) supplies the transactionId (type transactionId).

monitored transactionId : extendedTaskInstances → transactionId

The monitored function *classification* for the given deontic classification for users (type *deonticClassificationsForUsers*) supplies the deontic classification (type *deonticClassifications*).

monitored classification : deonticClassificationsForUsers →
    deonticClassifications

The monitored function *flowNodeType* for the given flow node supplies the type of the flow node (type *flowNodeTypes*).

monitored flowNodeType : flowNodes → flowNodeTypes

7.5.6.3   Out Functions

Following out functions are specified to set values of certain types, which then can be used by other components.

The out function *process* for the given process event (type *processEvents*) sets the process (type *processes*).

out process : processEvents → processes

The out function *eventType* for the given process event (type *processEvents*) sets the event type (type *eventTypes*).

out eventType : processEvents → eventTypes

The out function *triggerType* for the given process event (type *processEvents*) sets the trigger type (type *eventTriggerTypes*).

out triggerType : processEvents → eventTriggerTypes

The out function *taskInstance* for the given process event (type *processEvents*) sets the task instance (type *instances*).

out taskInstance : processEvents → instances

The out function *transactionId* for the given parameter list (type *parameters*) sets the transactionId (type *transactionId*).

out transactionId : parameters → transactionId

The out function *user* for the given parameter list (type *parameters*) sets the user.

out user : parameters → users

The out function *taskInstance* for the given parameter list (type *parameters*) sets the task instance.

out taskInstance : parameters → instances

7.5.6.4   Shared Functions

The shared function *processDialogue* represents the return value of the operation *processDialogue* of the interface *Dialogue*. It is defined as shared because this component resets the value which was first set by the component *Dialogue Engine*.

shared processDialogue : instances × users × transactionId →
    Boolean

7.5.6.5   Imported and Exported Functions and Rules

In this section, we specify rules and functions which are imported or exported by the *Process Client* component, to execute/provide synchronous calls of/to interface operations, respectively to access certain data structures.

IMPORT (Task Server) GetAllTasks : users × clientInstances → Set
IMPORT (Task Server) TryStartTask : extendedTaskInstances ×
    users → Boolean
IMPORT (Task Server) GetAllProcessesToBeAllowedToStart : users →
    Set
IMPORT (Task Server) TaskCompleted : extendedTaskInstances
IMPORT (Task Server) LogOff : users × clientInstances
IMPORT (Task Server) TaskSkipped : extendedTaskInstances
IMPORT (Task Server) TaskRejected : extendedTaskInstances
IMPORT (Task Server) CancelUserAndManualTask :
    extendedTaskInstances
IMPORT (Task Server) HandleProcessEvent : processEvents

```
IMPORT (Task Server) taskInstance : extendedTaskInstances →
    instances
IMPORT (Task Server) transactionId : extendedTaskInstances →
    transactionId
IMPORT (Task Server) user : clientInstances → users
IMPORT (Workflow Transition Interpreter) getFlowNode : instances
    → flowNodes
IMPORT (Workflow Transition Interpreter) classification :
    deonticClassificationsForUsers → deonticClassifications
IMPORT (Workflow Transition Interpreter) flowNodeType : flowNodes
    → flowNodeTypes
IMPORT (Dialogue Engine) processDialogue : instances × users ×
    transactionId → Boolean

// interface TaskList
EXPORT RemoveTask : extendedTaskInstances
EXPORT AddTask : extendedTaskInstances ×
    deonticClassificationsForUsers
// interface UserTaskActions
EXPORT SelectedByUserForProcessing : extendedTaskInstances
EXPORT ManualTaskCompleted : extendedTaskInstances
EXPORT LogOff
EXPORT TaskSkipped : extendedTaskInstances
EXPORT TaskRejected : extendedTaskInstances
EXPORT TaskCanceled : extendedTaskInstances
EXPORT StartProcess : processes
//functions
EXPORT taskInstance : processEvents → instances
EXPORT eventType : processEvents → eventTypes
EXPORT process : processEvents → processes
EXPORT triggerType : processEvents → eventTriggerTypes
EXPORT user : parameters → users
EXPORT transactionId : parameters → transactionId
EXPORT taskInstance : parameters → instances
EXPORT operationName : operations → String
```

7.5.6.6   ProcessClientBehaviour

The rule *ProcessClientBehaviour* specifies the behaviour of the *Process Client* by refining the rule *ComponentBehaviour*.

```
rule ProcessClientBehaviour
rule ProcessClientBehaviour = ComponentBehaviour where
```

The rule *Initialise* initialises all interfaces provided by the *Process Client*; in this case, the *TaskList* and the *UserTaskActions* interface. First, some functions are initialised. The main part of this rule is to call the operation *getAllTasks* of the *TaskHandling* interface (provided by the *Task Server* component) to receive all tasks that the given user is allowed to process. Furthermore, all processes (type *processes*) which the user is allowed to start, are initialised by calling the operation *getAllProcessesTo-BeAllowedToStart* of the *TaskHandling* interface.

```
rule Initialise =
parblock
    providedInterfaces := {"TaskList", " UserTaskActions "}
    asyncOperations("TaskList") := {}
    asyncOperations(" UserTaskActions ") := {}
    asyncCalledOperations(self) := {}
    ownCalledFunctions(self) := {}
    userSelectedTask := undef
    // call getAllTasks of the TaskHandling interface
        synchronously
    taskList(self) := TaskHandling.GetAllTasks(user(self), self)
    startableProcesses(user(self)) :=
        TaskHandling.GetAllProcessesToBeAllowedToStart(user(self))
    initialised(self) := true
endparblock
```

The rule *CreateIncludingComponent* creates an new instance of the component *Dialogue Engine* and returns it.

```
rule CreateIncludingComponent =
    return res in
        //create an own Dialogue Engine instance
        ownDialogEngine := new (DialogueEngine)
        //start the new Dialogue Engine component
        program(ownDialogueEngine) := @DialogueEngineBehaviour
        res = ownDialogEngine
```

The rule *ReactToCall* does nothing, since all operations of the provided interfaces (*TaskList* and *UserTaskActions*) are called synchronously.

```
rule ReactToCall(calledOperation) = skip
```

The rule *HandleOwnCalls* is called for each operation in any interface of any component that was previously called asynchronously by the *Process Client* component to react to the return value. This rule is called from the base *ComponentBehaviour* (see also Sect. 7.4).

```
rule HandleOwnCalls(asyncCallingData) =
    case name(asysncCallingData) of
        " processDialogue " →
            HandleProcessDialogueResponse(asyncCallingData)
        //no other interface operations of other components are
            called
```

The rule *HandleProcessDialogueResponse* first checks whether the return value of the call to the operation *processDialogue* of the interface *Dialogue* is available and if so, the location *processDialogue* is reset, and the *asyncCallingData* is removed from *ownCalledFunctions*. Depending on the return value either the operation *TaskCompleted* from the *TaskHandling* interface is called synchronously to inform the component *Task Server* about completing the task instance or a new process event (type *processEvents*) is created and forwarded to the *Task Server* component by calling the rule *HandleProcessEvent* defined in the interface *ProcessEventListener*. Furthermore, the task is removed from the worklist (*taskList*) only when dialogue processing has succeeded.

```
rule HandleProcessDialogueResponse : asyncCallingData
rule HandleProcessDialogueResponse(asyncCallingData) =
  //check the availability
    let extendedTaskInst =
        extendedTaskInstance(parameters(asyncCallingData)) in
  let taskInst = taskInstance(extendedTaskInst) in
    let transactionId = transactionId(parameters(asyncCallingData)
        in
  let user = user(self) in
      if processDialogue(taskInst, user, transactionId) != undef
          then
        seqblock
          //remember the return value (Boolean)
          let retValShow = processDialogue(taskInstance, user,
              transactionId)) in
            //reset the location
            processDialogue(taskInstance, user, transactionId)) :=
                undef
            //remove the call from ownCalledFunctions
            remove asyncCallingData from ownCalledFunctions(self)
              if retValShow then
                seqblock
                //inform the Task Server component that the task is
                    completed
                TaskHandling.TaskCompleted(extendedTaskInstance)
                    //remove the task from the taskList
                  remove extendedTaskInst from taskList(self)
              endseqblock
              else // an Error occurred
                let pEvent = new (processEvent) in
                  seqblock
                    triggerType(pEvent) := "Error"
                    taskInstance(pEvent) := taskInst
                    ProcessEventListener.HandleProcessEvent(pEvent)
                  endsecblock
        endseqblock
```

7.5.6.7   Managing Called Operations of the *TaskList* Interface

The rule *RemoveTask* (corresponding to the interface operation *removeTask*) removes the task instance (type *extendedTaskInstances*) given by the actual call parameters from the user's task collection (worklist).

```
rule RemoveTask : extendedTaskInstances
rule RemoveTask(extendedTaskInst) =
  remove extendedTaskInst from taskList(self)
```

The rule *AddTask*, which corresponds to the interface operation *addTask*, adds the task instance (type *extendedTaskInstances*) given by the actual call parameters to the collection of tasks of the assigned user and sets the function *userClassification* for the given extended task instance to the given deontic classification for users represented by the second parameter.

```
rule AddTask : extendedTaskInstances ×
    deonticClassificationsForUsers
rule AddTask(extendedTaskInst, userClassification) =
parblock
  add extendedTaskInst to taskList(self)
  userClassification(extendedTaskInst) := userClassification
endparblock
```

The rule *ResetDeonticClassificationOfTask* is called for a logged in user, when after
skipping or completing a task the deontic classifications have changed. This rule
relates to the interface operation *resetDeonticClassificationOfTask*.

```
rule ResetDeonticClassificationOfTask : extendedTaskInstances ×
    deonticClassificationsForUsers
rule ResetDeonticClassificationOfTask(extendedTaskInst,
    userClassification) =
  //get the old task if it exists
    if forsome oldExtendedTask ∈ taskList(self) holds
        taskInstance(oldExtendedTask) =
        taskInstance(extendedTask) then
      choose oldExtendedTask ∈ taskList(self) with
          taskInstance(oldExtendedTask) =
          taskInstance(extendedTask) do
        parblock
          if classification(userClassification) = "Forbidden" then
              remove oldExtendedTask from taskList
            //reset the classification
            userClassification(oldExtendedTask) :=
                userClassification
        endparblock
    //task is not in taskList
    else if classification(userClassification) != "Forbidden"
            add extendedTaskInstance to taskList
```

7.5.6.8 Managing Called Operations of the *UserTaskActions* Interface

The *UserTaskActions* interface handles different user actions, which must be passed
to the *Task Server* component by using the *TaskHandling* interface who again passes
most of them to the *Worklfow Transition Interpreter* component via the interface
Monitor.

The rule *SelectedByUserForProcessing*, which corresponds to the interface operation *selectedByUserForProcessing*, calls the operation *TryStartTask* of the interface
TaskHandling. If the user is allowed to process the task, and the task is a "UserTask",
this rule calls the rule *ProcessTaskByAidOfDialogueEngine*, which in turn calls the
operation *processDialogue* of the *Dialogue* interface. Otherwise, for manual tasks
no dialogue is shown, because a manual task is performed without the aid of any
IT-system (see [12, p. 163]). Figure 7.3 depicts subsequent interactions when a user
selects a user task for being processed.

```
rule SelectedByUserForProcessing : extendedTaskInstances
rule SelectedByUserForProcessing(extendedTaskInst) =
    let user = user(self) in
    parblock
        let isAllowed =
            TaskHandling.TryStartTask(extendedTaskInst, user) in
            if(isAllowed) then
                if flowNodeType(getFlowNode(taskInstance(
                    extendedTaskInst))) = "UserTask" then
            ProcessTaskByAidOfDialogueEngine(extendedTaskInst)
    endparblock
```

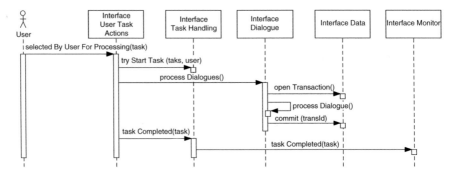

Fig. 7.3 Interactions when a user selects a user task for processing

The rule *ProcessTaskByAidOfDialogueEngine* asynchronously calls the operation *processDialogue* of the *Dialogue* interface to be assisted by the *Dialogue Engine* in processing the given task instance.

```
rule ProcessTaskByAidOfDialogueEngine : extendedTaskInstances
rule ProcessTaskByAidOfDialogueEngine(extendedTaskInst) =
  let taskInst = taskInstance(extendedTaskInst),
    let transId = transactionId(extendedTaskInst),
    let params = new(parameters) in
    seqblock
      add taskInst to params
        add transId to params
        add user(self) to params // for setting the location
            (return value)
        //create new asyncCallingData and add it to the
            ownCalledFunctions(component)
        CreateAndAddAsyncCallingData(self, "processDialogue", params)
        CallOperationAsync("processDialogue", params, self,
            includingComponent)
    endseqblock
```

The rule *ManualTaskCompleted*, which is conform to the interface operation *manualTaskCompleted*, synchronously calls the operation *TaskCompleted* to inform the component *Task Server* about completing the task instance (represented by the parameter) and removes it from the collection of tasks (worklist). This rule is intended only for manual tasks, because for user tasks this is done when the corresponding dialogues have been processed (in the rule *HandleProcessDialogueResponse*).

```
rule ManualTaskCompleted : extendedTaskInstances
rule ManualTaskCompleted(extendedTaskInstance) =
  parblock
        //inform the Task Server component that the task is completed
        TaskHandling.TaskCompleted(extendedTaskInstance)
        //remove the task from the taskList
        remove extendedTaskInst from taskList(self)
    endparblock
```

The rule *LogOff* (corresponding to the interface operation *logOff*) synchronously calls the operation *logOff* of the *TaskHandling* interface to inform the component *Task Server* that the user has logged off.

```
rule LogOff
rule LogOff =
    let user = user(self) in
        //inform the Task Server component
        TaskHandling.LogOff(user, self)
```

The rule *TaskSkipped*, which equates to the interface operation *taskSkipped*, synchronously calls the operation *TaskSkipped* defined in the *TaskHandling* interface to inform the component *Task Server*. The subsequent interactions are illustrated in Fig. 6.6.

```
rule TaskSkipped : extendedTaskInstances
rule TaskSkipped(extendedTaskInst) =
  //inform the Task Server component
    TaskHandling.TaskSkipped(extendedTaskInst)
```

The rule *TaskRejected* (conform to the interface operation *taskRecected*) synchronously calls the homonymous interface operation, defined in the *TaskHandling* interface to inform the component *Task Server*.

```
rule TaskRejected : extendedTaskInstances
rule TaskRejected(extendedTaskInst) =
  //inform the Task Server component
    TaskHandling.TaskRejected(extendedTaskInst)
```

The rule *TaskCanceled* (interface operation *taskCanceled*) synchronously calls the operation *CancelUserAndManualTask* defined in the *TaskHandling* interface to inform the component *Task Server*.

```
rule TaskCanceled : extendedTaskInstances
rule TaskCanceled(extendedTaskInst) =
    //inform the Task Server component
    TaskHandling.CancelUserAndManualTask(extendedTaskInst)
```

The rule *StartProcess*, which corresponds to the interface operation *startProcess*, creates a new *processEvent* object and sets its properties, afterwards it calls the rule *HandleProcessEvent* of the interface *ProcessEventListener* provided by the component *Task Server*. This and further interactions are illustrated in Fig. 7.4.

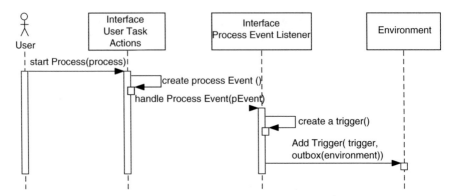

Fig. 7.4 Interactions when a user starts a process

```
rule StartProcess : processes
rule StartProcess(process) =
  let pEvent = new (processEvents) in
    seqblock
      process(pEvent) := process
        eventType(pEvent) := "StartEvent"
        ProcessEventListener.HandleProcessEvent(pEvent)
    endseqblock
```

7.5.7 Ground Model of the Actor Management

This ground model specifies the functions and behaviour specific to the component
Actor Management (cf. Sect. 6.4.6).

7.5.7.1 Controlled Functions

The controlled function *actorModel* stores the *Actor Model*.

controlled actorModel → models

7.5.7.2 Imported and Exported Functions and Rules

In this subsection we specify rules which are imported or exported by the *Actor
Management* component, to provide synchronous calls to interface operations.

IMPORT (Process Model Repository) searchModel : String → Set

```
EXPORT GetUsersByRole : processes × roles → Set
EXPORT GetUserRoles : processes × users → Set
EXPORT GetEscalationRole : processes × users → Role
EXPORT GetEscalationUsers : processes × users → Set
EXPORT GetAllProcessesUserMayStart : users × user → Set
```

7.5.7.3   ActorManagementBehaviour

The rule *ActorManagementBehaviour* specifies the behaviour of the *Actor Management* component by refining the rule *ComponentBehaviour*.

```
rule ActorManagementBehaviour = ComponentBehaviour where
```

The rule *Initialise* initialises the interfaces provided by the component *Actor Management* namely *Actors* (see also Sect. 6.4.6). First, this rule initialises some functions. Additionally, the actor model is requested by the *CRUDModel* interface provided by the component *Process Model Repository*.

```
rule Initialise =
parblock
  providedInterfaces := {"Actors"}
  asyncOperations("Actors") := {}
  asyncCalledOperations(self) := {}
  ownCalledFunctions(self) := {}
  // initialise the actorModel function
  seqblock
    let searchString = createQueryForGetActorModel in
    // call searchModel of the CRUDModel interface synchronously
    actorModel := CRUDModel.searchModel(searchString)
  endseqblock
  initialised(self) := true
endparblock
```

The rule *CreateIncludingComponent* does nothing, because no own component is needed.

```
rule CreateIncludingComponent = skip
```

The abstract-derived function *createQueryForGetActorModel* returns a query string for searching the actor model.

```
abstract-derived createQueryForGetActorModel → String
```

The rule *ReactToCall* does nothing, since all operations of the *Actor* interface are called synchronously.

```
rule ReactToCall(calledOperation) = skip
```

The rule *HandleOwnCalls* does nothing, because the *Actor Management* component does not call any interface operation asynchronously. This rule is called from the base *ComponentBehaviour* (see also Sect. 7.4).

```
rule HandleOwnCalls(asyncCallingData) = skip
```

7.5.7.4   Managing Called Functions of the *Actor* Interface

Although all operations defined in the *Actor* interface start with "get", which may
appear to refer to derived functions rather than rules, we specify them as rules,
because each calls a further abstract rule, which should not be restricted to not being
able to change the state of the Actor Management component. (For instance, the
Actor Management might have to retrieve information from other components and
store it locally.)

The rule *GetUsersByRole*, which meets the interface operation *getUsersByRole*,
calls the rule *GetAllUsersForProcess*, which returns all users for the given role in
the given process.

```
rule GetUsersByRole : processes × roles → Set
rule GetUsersByRole(process, role) =
return res in
seqblock
  // set the return value
  res := GetAllUsersForProcess(process, role)
endseqblock
```

The abstract rule *GetAllUsersForProcess* returns all users that are assigned to the
given role in the given process model.

```
abstract rule GetAllUsersForProcess : processes × roles → Set
```

The rule *GetUserRoles* (interface operation *getUserRoles*) calls the rule *GetAllRoles-
ForUserInProcess*, to get all roles of the user identified by the parameter *user* of the
given process model and returns it.

```
rule GetUserRoles : processes × users → Set
rule GetUserRoles(process, user) =
return res in
  // set the return value
  res := GetAllRolesForUserInProcess(process, user)
```

The abstract rule *GetAllRolesForUserInProcess* returns all roles of the user identified
by the parameter *user* in the given process model.

```
abstract rule GetAllRolesForUserInProcess : models × user → Set
```

The rule *GetEscalationRole* (relates to the interface operation *getEscalationRole*)
calls the rule *GetEscalationRoleForUserInProcess*, to get the escalation role of the
user identified by the parameter *user*.

```
rule GetEscalationRole : processes × users → Role
rule GetEscalationRole(process, user) =
return res in
  // set the return value
  res := GetEscalationRoleForUserInProcess(process, user)
```

The abstract rule *GetEscalationRoleForUserInProcess* returns the escalation role of
the given user in the given process model.

abstract rule GetEscalationRoleForUserInProcess : models × user
     → Role

The rule *GetEscalationUsers*, which corresponds to the interface operation *getEscalationUsers*, calls the rule *GetEscalationUsersForUserInProcess*, to get all escalation users of the user identified by the parameter *user*.

rule GetEscalationUsers : processes × users → Set
rule GetEscalationUsers(process, user) =
return res **in**
  // set the return value
  res := GetEscalationUsersForUserInProcess(process, user)

The abstract rule *GetEscalationUsersForUserInProcess* returns all escalation users of the user identified by the parameter *user* in the given process model.

abstract rule GetEscalationRoleForUserInProcess : models ×
users → Set

The abstract rule *GetAllProcessesUserMayStart* (interface operation *getAllProcessesUserMayStart*) returns all process models (type *processes*), which the given user is allowed to start.

abstract rule GetAllProcessesUserMayStart : users × user → Set

7.5.8   *Ground Model of the Dialogue Engine*

This ground model specifies the functions and behaviour specific to the component *Dialogue Engine* (cf. Sect. 6.4.7). With respect to the typed approach for user interaction modeling proposed in Chap. 4, this component takes over the tasks of the *dialogue client*, i.e., to display (reporting) information to the user and to submit user inputs to a server system.

For integrating user interaction modelling in eP^2, we decide in favour of explicitly marking dialogues in the workflow chart due to improved intelligibility (see Sect. 6.3). Therefore, providing the appropriate mapping (i.e., the static functions *dialogue* and *startingDeferredServerAction*), which defines which dialogues belong to which user tasks, is the responsibility of the process designer. The mapping can vary regarding the granularity between tasks and dialogues. This corresponds to determining a convenient and situation-specific granularity of workflow states compared to dialogue states on the basis of explicit dialogue identification. According to the recommendations given in Sect. 6.3, we assume that a user task is refined at least by a *one-step dialogue*, consisting of a (starting) deferred server action, a single, subsequent client page, and its connected (final) server actions. This would mean that every dialogue state belongs to a workflow state, resulting in a high number of elementary tasks, and that workflow control always returns to the worklist after having submitted a form. Alternatively, a user task can be refined by a *complex dialogue*, including multiple client pages and server actions wired together (in terms of multiple one-step dialogues).

Client pages and immediate server actions are displayed to the user in terms of reports and forms (involving required data operations), whereas (starting) deferred server actions represent links—indicating the name of the corresponding user task—in the worklist (see Sect. 4.4.1). Note that actor information associated with deferred server actions is no longer relevant in this case, because it must be ensured that a user task only contains parts of a dialogue model that are designed to be processed by a single user without any parallel paths (see Sect. 4.4.3).

7.5.8.1 Static Functions

The static function *dialogue* provides the corresponding dialogue (either a one-step or a complex dialogue) for each user task, defining the alternating sequence(s) of deferred server action(s), client page(s), and immediate server action(s). This implies to have access to the *CRUDModel* interface of the component *Process Model Repository* to get the dialogue (defined in the *Dialogue Model*) of each user task in the *Process Model* (cf. Fig. 7.1).

```
static dialogue : taskNodes → Graph
```

The static function *startingDeferredServerAction* yields the deferred server action representing the starting point of the given dialogue.

```
static startingDeferredServerAction : Graph →
    deferredServerActions
```

7.5.8.2 Monitored Functions

The monitored function *getFlowNode* provides the related (static) flow node for a given task instance.

```
monitored getFlowNode : instances → flowNodes
```

The monitored function *selectedNode* provides the user-selected immediate server action (refer to the description of the homonymous function in Sect. 4.4.4 for details).

```
monitored selectedNode : componentInstances →
    immediateServerActions
```

The monitored function *dataInput* provides the data view for submission provided by user (refer to the description of the homonymous function in Sect. 4.4.4 for details).

```
monitored dataInput : componentInstances → dataViews
```

7.5.8.3 Shared Functions

The shared function *processDialogue* represents the return value of the operation *processDialogue* of the interface *Dialogue*. The given *instance* identifies the user task node that is assigned to the given *user* and maybe part of a *transaction* sub-process.

```
shared processDialogue : instances × users × transactionId →
   Boolean
```

7.5.8.4   Imported and Exported Functions and Rules

In this section, we specify rules and functions which are imported or exported by the *Dialogue Engine* component, to execute/provide synchronous calls of/to interface operations, respectively to access certain data structures.

```
IMPORT (Data Management) OpenTransaction : → transactionId
IMPORT (Data Management) Commit : transactionId → Boolean
IMPORT (Data Management) Rollback : transactionId → Boolean
IMPORT (Process Model Repository) searchModel : String → Set
IMPORT (Workflow Transition Interpreter) getFlowNode : instances
   → flowNodes
IMPORT (ProcessClient) operationName : operations → String
IMPORT (ProcessClient) user : parameters → users
IMPORT (Process Client) transactionId : parameters →
   transactionId
IMPORT (Process Client) taskInstance : parameters → instances
IMPORT (Process Model Repository) dialogue : taskNodes → Graph
IMPORT (Process Model Repository) startingDeferredServerAction :
   Graph → deferredServerActions
```

```
//interface UserFormActions
EXPORT Submit : dataViews × immediateServerActions → Boolean
//interface Dialogue is called asynchronously → no export
//functions
EXPORT processDialogue : instances × users × transactionId →
   Boolean
```

7.5.8.5   DialogueEngineBehaviour

The rule *DialogueEngineBehaviour* specifies the behaviour of the *Dialogue Engine* component by refining the rule *ComponentBehaviour*.

```
rule DialogueEngineBehaviour = ComponentBehaviour where
```

The rule *Initialise* initialises the interfaces provided by the component *Dialogue Engine* (see also Sect. 6.4.7), i.e., *Dialogue* and *UserFormActions*. Additionally, all required instance-specific functions are initialised.

```
rule Initialise =
parblock
  providedInterfaces := {"Dialogue", " UserFormActions "}
  asyncOperations("Dialogue") := {" processDialogue "}
```

```
asyncOperations("UserFormActions") := {}
asyncCalledOperations(self) := {}
ownCalledFunctions(self) := {}
initialised(self) := true
endparblock
```

The rule *CreateIncludingComponent* will be skipped, because no including components are needed.

```
rule CreateIncludingComponent = skip
```

The rule *ReactToCall* is called for each operation in any interface of the *Dialogue
Engine* component (see also Sect. 6.4.7). This rule contains a case rule that, depending
on the parameter *calledOperationName*, calls the respective rule for processing the
operation call.

```
rule ReactToCall(calledOperation) =
  let params = params(calledOperation) in
  let calledOperationName = operationName(calledOperation) in
    case calledOperationName of
      " processDialogue " → ProcessDialogue(params)
```

The rule *HandleOwnCalls* can be skipped again, because the *Dialogue Engine* component does not call any interface operation asynchronously.

```
rule HandleOwnCalls(asyncCallingData) = skip
```

7.5.8.6 Managing Called Functions of the *Dialogue* Interface

The rule *ProcessDialogue*, which corresponds to the interface operation *processDialogue*, handles all form-oriented activities that may exist behind a user task. These
activities are described as user interactions in the form of an alternating sequence
of deferred server action(s), client page(s), and immediate server action(s). Regarding data operations, the rule first opens a transaction if the transferred *transactionId*
is undefined, which means that the task in question is no part of a transaction sub-
process. After all necessary data changes have been completed, the previously opened
transaction is committed (or rolled back) at the end of the rule, which relates to the
end of the task. If a *transactionId* is defined, those will be used for changing and
storing dialogue data. All data operations are guided by the defined sequences of
dialogue nodes by calling the rule *EditDialogue*.

```
rule ProcessDialogue : parameters
rule ProcessDialogue(parametersOfCall) =
  let taskInst = taskInstance(parametersOfCall) in
  let user = user(parametersOfCall) in
  local transId = transactionId(parametersOfCall) in
    let isTransSubProc = transId != undef in
    local success in
    seqblock
    if !isTransSubProc then
```

```
           // synchronous call
      transId := Data.OpenTransaction()
      success := EditDialogue(taskInst, transId)
        if !isTransSubProc then
          if success then
            Data.Commit(transId)
            else
              Data.Rollback(transId)
        // set return value location
        processDialogue(taskInst, user, transId) := success
   endseqblock
```

The rule *EditDialogue* shows the dialogue for the given task instance and handles the submission of user data using the derived function *enabledNodes* defined in Sect. 4.4.4. For presenting information to the user, the rule *ShowDialogue* defined in Sect. 4.4.4 can be applied with the parameters given below, which implies calling the operation *read* of the *Data Management* component. The submission of user input can be handled by calling the rule *SubmitData* also defined in Sect. 4.4.4, which either calls the operation *create*, *update*, or *delete* of the *Data Management* component (using the given *transactionId*). Note that no commit or rollback must be done in this place, because this is done in the rule *ProcessDialogue* or by the component *Task Server* in the case of a transaction sub-process. The return value indicates whether the dialogue has been successfully processed or not.

```
rule EditDialogue : instances × transactionId → Boolean
rule EditDialogue(taskInstance, transactionId) =
  return res = true in
    local deferredServerAction := startingDeferredServerAction(
        dialogue(getFlowNode(taskInstance))) in
    local endOfDialogue := false in
    local immediateServerAction, clientPage in
        while !endOfDialogue do
      seqblock
        clientPage := choose cp ∈
            enabledNodes(deferredServerAction,
            deferredServerActions, clientPages)
        res := res and ShowDialogue(clientPage,
            enabledNodes(clientPage, clientPages,
            immediateServerActions))
        immediateServerAction := selectedNode(self)
        res := res and SubmitData(immediateServerAction,
            transactionId)
        endOfDialogue :=
            isFinalDialogueNode(immediateServerAction)
        deferredServerAction := choose dsa ∈
            enabledNodes(immediateServerAction,
            immediateServerActions, deferredServerActions)
      endseqblock
```

The derived function *isFinalDialogueNode* checks if the given dialogue node (which by definition refers to an immediate server action) represents a final node of the encircling dialogue, and thus represents the end of the dialogue. This is the case if the node reached does not have any outgoing transitions. (Note that this proposition is sufficient, because the dialogue is not allowed to contain parallel paths.)

```
derived isFinalDialogueNode : dialogueNodes → Boolean
derived isFinalDialogueNode(immediateServerAction) =
  | enabledNodes(immediateServerAction, immediateServerActions,
      deferredServerActions) | = 0
```

7.5.8.7 Managing Called Functions of the *UserFormActions* Interface

The rule *Submit* (corresponding to the interface operation *submit*) submits the given user input, represented by *data views*, via the selected *immediate server action*). This means that exactly one one-step dialogue has been successfully processed, resulting in either showing the next one-step dialogue—in the case of a complex dialogue defined for a certain task—or showing the task collection (worklist) to the user.

```
abstract rule Submit : dataViews × immediateServerActions →
    Boolean
```

7.5.9 Ground Model of the Data Management

This ground model specifies the functions and behaviour specific to the component *Data Management* (cf. Sect. 6.4.8).

7.5.9.1 Imported and Exported Functions and Rules

In this section, we specify rules and functions which are imported or exported by the *Data Management* component, to execute/provide synchronous calls of/to interface operations, respectively to access certain data structures.

```
//interface Data
EXPORT OpenTransaction :  → transactionId
EXPORT Commit : transactionId
EXPORT Read : String → dataViews
EXPORT Update : dataViews → Boolean
EXPORT Create : dataViews → dataViews
EXPORT Delete : dataViews
EXPORT Rollback : transactionId → Boolean
```

7.5.9.2   DataManagementBehaviour

The rule *DataManagementBehaviour* specifies the behaviour of the *Data Management* component by refining the rule *ComponentBehaviour*.

```
rule DataManagementBehaviour = ComponentBehaviour where
```

The rule *Initialise* initialises the interfaces provided by the component *Data Management* (see also Sect. 6.4.8) namely *Data* and *DataAdministration* whereby the interface *DataAdministration* has not been defined yet. Additionally, this rule initialises some functions.

```
rule Initialise =
parblock
  providedInterfaces:= {"Data", " DataAdministration "}
  // all operations are synchron
  asyncOperations("Data") := {}
  asyncOperations(" DataAdministration ") := {}
  asyncCalledOperations(self) := {}
  ownCalledFunctions(self) := {}
  initialised(self) := true
endparblock
```

The rule *CreateIncludingComponent* does nothing, because no own component is needed.

```
rule CreateIncludingComponent = skip
```

The rule does nothing, because no interface operation is called synchronously.

```
rule ReactToCall(calledOperation) = skip
```

The rule *HandleOwnCalls* does nothing, because the *Data Management* component does not call any interface operation asynchronously. This rule is called from the base *ComponentBehaviour* (see also Sect. 7.4).

```
rule HandleOwnCalls(asyncCallingData) = skip
```

7.5.9.3   Managing Called Functions of the *Data* Interface

The rule *Read*, which is conform to the interface operation *read*, reads the data identified by the parameter *query* from the database by calling the rule *ReadFromDB*.

```
rule Read : String → dataViews
rule Read(query) =
    return res in
        // set the return value
        res := ReadFromDB(query)
endparblock
```

The abstract rule *ReadFromDB* reads the data identified by the parameter from the database. This rule processes the raw database access.

```
abstract rule ReadFromDB : String → dataViews
```

The rule *Update* (corresponding to the interface operation *update*) updates the data identified by the parameter in the database by calling the rule *UpdateInDB* that does the raw database access.

```
rule Update : dataViews → Boolean
rule Update(obj) =
  return res in
    return UpdateInDB(obj)
```

The abstract rule *UpdateInDB* updates the data identified by the parameter in the database. This rule processes the raw database access.

```
abstract rule UpdateInDB : dataViews → Boolean
```

The rule *Create* (interface operation *create*) creates a new data view (the values are identified by the parameter) in the database by calling the rule *CreateInDB*, which does the raw database access.

```
rule Create : dataViews → dataViews
rule Create(obj) =
  return res in
        // set the return value
        res := CreateInDB(obj)
```

The abstract rule *CreateInDB* updates the data identified by the parameter in the database (in the returned *dataViews* also ids are inserted). This rule processes the raw database access.

```
abstract rule CreateInDB : dataViews → dataViews
```

The rule *Delete* (relating to the interface operation *delete*) deletes the data view identified by the parameter in the database by calling the rule *DeleteFromDB*, which does the raw database access.

```
rule Delete : dataViews
rule Delete(obj) =
  DeleteFromDB(obj)
```

The abstract rule *DeleteFromDB* deletes the data view identified by the parameter from the database. This rule processes the raw database access.

```
abstract rule DeleteFromDB : dataViews
```

The rule *Commit* (interface operation *commit*) commits the transaction identified by the parameter in the database by calling the rule *CommitInDB*, which does the raw database access.

```
rule Commit : transactionId → Boolean
rule Commit(transactionId) =
return res in
  // set the return value
  res := CommitInDB(transId)
```

The abstract rule *CommitInDB* commits a transaction identified by the parameter in the database. This rule processes the raw database access.

```
abstract rule CommitInDB : transactionId → Boolean
```

The rule *Rollback* (relates to the interface operation *rollback*) rolls the transaction identified by the parameter back in the database by calling the rule *RollbackInDB*, which does the raw database access.

```
rule Rollback : transactionId → Boolean
rule Rollback(transId) =
return res in
  // set the return value
  res := RollbackInDB(transId)
```

The abstract rule *RollbackInDB* rolls a transaction identified by the parameter back in the database. This rule processes the raw database access.

```
abstract rule RollbackInDB : transactionId → Boolean
```

The rule *OpenTransaction* (conform to the interface operation *openTransaction*) opens a transaction in the database by calling the rule *OpenTransactionInDB*, which does the raw database access.

```
rule OpenTransaction → transactionId
rule OpenTransaction =
    return res in
        res := OpenTransactionInDB()
```

The abstract rule *OpenTransactionInDB* opens a transaction in the database. This rule processes the raw database access.

```
abstract rule OpenTransactionInDB → transactionId
```

7.5.9.4 Managing Called Functions of the *DataAdministration* Interface

The interface *DataAdministration* has not been specified yet, because it is also not defined now (see Sect. 6.4.8).

7.6 Summary

Modelling information systems is challenging and various models are usually used to model various aspects (particularly regarding business processes, actors, dialogues, data, and communication). Integrating those models allows to cover additional aspects and to model the whole system. We have already discussed details of the different concepts and a static view on integration in Chaps. 2–6.

In this chapter, we presented a formal specification of the dynamic view on the eP^2 system described in Sect. 6.4. The eP^2 system consists of several components which implement the required functionality to run and interpret the integrated models. That is, it encompasses a component to run business processes modelled using the H-BPM method, a component which interprets the dialogue model, a component for the management of actors, a component for data management interpreting the data model, and a component implementing the process client.

The specification in this chapter describes the eP^2 system in a formal way utilising ASMs to define the interfaces and interface behaviour of the components. We present a common signature, which is applicable to all components including universes, common functions, and common rules. Additionally, we provide a specification of the common behaviour of all components. Finally, we specify an own ASM ground model for every component, by refining the common behaviour, whereby each ground model comprises the signature which is specific to this component. Thereby, we need to extend the specification of the component *Workflow Transition Interpreter*, which was specified in [11], for being able to capture all horizontal refinements of H-BPM.

All in all, the specification of the eP^2 architecture is a further step towards the implementation of a framework that utilises integrated models for the implementation of information systems. The application of rigorous methods for the definition of the models and the description of the structure assures correctness and clarity and also helps to facilitate the implementation of the framework by, at least, partly generated code.

References

1. Albin, S.: The Art of Software Architecture: Design Methods and Techniques. Wiley Application Development Series. Wiley, Chichester (2003)
2. Allen, R.J.: A Formal Approach to Software Architecture. Ph.D. thesis, Pittsburgh, PA, USA (1997), aAI9813815
3. Banâtre, J.P., Le Métayer, D.: The gamma model and its discipline of programming. Sci. Comput. Program. **15**(1), 55–77 (1990)
4. Berry, G., Boudol, G.: The chemical abstract machine. In: Proceedings of the 17th ACM SIGPLAN-SIGACT Symposium on Principles of Programming Languages. pp. 81–94. POPL '90, ACM, New York, NY, USA (1990)
5. Börger, E., Stärk, R.: Abstract State Machines: A Method for High-Level System Design and Analysis. Springer, Berlin (2003)
6. Fiadeiro, J.L., Lopes, A., Bocchi, L.: A formal approach to service component architecture. In: Proceedings of the Third International Conference on Web Services and Formal Methods. pp. 193–213. WS-FM '06, Springer, Berlin (2006)
7. Gurevich, Y.: Sequential abstract state machines capture sequential algorithms. ACM Trans. Comput. Log. **1**(1), 77–111 (2000)
8. He, X., Yu, H., Shi, T., Ding, J., Deng, Y.: Formally analyzing software architectural specifications using sam. J. Syst. Softw. **71**(1–2), 11–29 (2004)
9. Inverardi, P., Wolf, A.: Formal specification and analysis of software architectures using the chemical abstract machine model. IEEE Trans. Softw. Eng. **21**(4), 373–386 (1995)
10. Kossak, F., Illibauer, C., Geist, V., Kubovy, J., Natschläger, C., Ziebermayr, T., Kopetzky, T., Freudenthaler, B., Schewe, K.D.: A rigorous semantics for BPMN 2.0 process diagrams: the ground model in detail. http://www.scch.at/en/HagenbergBPM (2014). Accessed 12 Oct 2015

11. Kossak, F., Illibauer, C., Geist, V., Kubovy, J., Natschläger, C., Ziebermayr, T., Kopetzky, T., Freudenthaler, B., Schewe, K.D.: A Rigorous Semantics for BPMN 2.0 Process Diagrams. Springer, Berlin (2015)

12. Object Management Group: Business Process Model and Notation (BPMN) 2.0. http://www. omg.org/spec/BPMN/2.0 (2011). Accessed 06 Oct 2015

13. Oquendo, F.: Pi-ADL: an architecture description language based on the higher-order typed pi-calculus for specifying dynamic and mobile software architectures. SIGSOFT Softw. Eng. Notes pp. 1–14 (2004)

14. ter Hofstede, A.M., van der Aalst, W.M.P., Adams, M., Russell, N. (eds.): Modern Business Process Automation: YAWL and its Support Environment. Springer, Heidelberg (2010)

Chapter 8
Summary and Outlook

In this chapter, we summarise our work on developing the Hagenberg Business Process Modelling (H-BPM) method, a novel and homogeneous integration framework for business processes modelling based on a rigorous semantics for BPMN 2.0 process diagrams [5], which also includes indispensable extensions in the form of horizontal refinements. The proposed extensions address actor modelling [7], closely tied to an intelligible way for denoting permissions and obligations with respect to deontic logic [6, 9], user interaction modelling [1, 2, 4], and an enhanced communication concept. In addition, we present the enhanced Process Platform (eP^2) architecture which is capable of integrating all aspects using Abstract State Machines (ASMs).

We further discuss future research work on continuing aspects, such as a view-based data approach, process adaptability, and exception handling mechanisms to handle unexpected situations in business processes.

In an investigation of related work, we evaluated some Business Process Management (BPM) methods and business modelling languages with regard to the above mentioned extensions provided by H-BPM (cf. Sect. 1.2), where we summarised the results in Table 1.1. As this table points out, none of the existing BPM methods supports all of the extensions to business process modelling which we address in the H-BPM method. Most of them treat issues of actors and data, but communication is modelled only by Subject-Oriented Business Process Management (S-BPM). Only S-BPM and ARIS (only partly) facilitate HCI as we provide it in our approach to user interaction modelling in business processes. Furthermore, modalities (permissions and obligations) are not supported by any approach. Model integration, a main focus of our H-BPM method, is just provided by S-BPM, ARIS, and partly by the Horus method. Some of the investigated business process modelling languages deal with actors and data, either in the basic language or in an extension, but none supports modalities. Furthermore, the only process modelling languages which facilitate user interaction modelling are Yet Another Workflow Language (YAWL) and Unified Modeling Language (UML)—the latter, when an additional profile is specified. BPMN, UML, and Systems Modelling Language (SysML) at least partly provide communication aspects, whereas Event-Driven Process Chains (EPCs) and YAWL

© Springer International Publishing Switzerland 2016
F. Kossak et al., *Hagenberg Business Process Modelling Method*,
DOI 10.1007/978-3-319-30496-0_8

provide them only in an extension. Just YAWL provides full model integration, UML and SysML at least partly, and WF-net in an extension to the language.

By using the four-step-integration approach of H-BPM, process analysts and modellers are guided via defined steps, providing a complete walk-through for modelling business processes in a trustworthy way. So, the H-BPM method enables seamless modelling of multifaceted aspects of business processes on all levels of abstraction by means of formal refinement.

A first step in actor modelling is to introduce a deontic classification of tasks which are supposed to be performed by human actors (users), and to associate user roles with these tasks to signify general permissions or obligations. Depending on a particular runtime situation, such a task can be obligatory, optional, alternative to other tasks, or forbidden for a particular user. The classification typically depends on the control structure of the process, but can also be affected by explicit rules and general permissions for particular user roles.

We suggest to optically highlight such permissions by colours and letters (like "P(a)" for "task A is optional"); however, alternative representations are provided in [8]. Optically classified tasks can then be displayed in the user interface in a *worklist*. Moreover, process diagrams can be simplified in their structure and can be made better understandable by optic highlighting of deontic classifications.

Further and independent elements of actor modelling are an *organisation chart*, which comprises roles, the role hierarchy, and individuals of the company, and a *global rule set*, which allows to specify task dependencies that cannot be made explicit in the process view. From these manually-defined rules, further rules can be logically derived and the whole rule system can be checked for consistency.

Workflow charts [1, 3, 4] define a dialogue-based approach to *user interaction modelling* by integrating workflow definition and application programming. They represent a convenient way to put more emphasis on HCI when describing business processes. A workflow chart is specified as a tripartite graph consisting of typed nodes for (i) rendering reports, (ii) providing forms for user input, and (iii) representing task items of the users' worklists (see Chap. 4). Supporting the worklist paradigm, assignment information, as well as parallelism, this approach provides a flexible process technology based on dialogues. A *dialogue*, in its simplest form, refers to a one-step dialogue, i.e. a single client page with its connected server actions, or it represents a complex dialogue, consisting of multiple client pages and server actions wired together.

The formal integration of dialogues into activity-oriented business process modelling languages, such as BPMN, represents an innovative approach for refining process models (in particular user tasks) by dialogues and data views (see Chaps. 6 and 7). It offers clear benefits to BPM due to improved modelling capabilities on a conceptual level by also including the dialogue model. Thus, this approach can help to overcome structural interruptions of BPM tools, i.e. the unnatural separation of visual business process diagrams and state transitions that are often implemented using third-generation programming languages. The platform-independent approach can also be applied in the context of Enterprise Application Integration

(EAI) to orchestrate stand-alone IT systems that have evolved in the course of "natural growth" by specifying new dialogues.

This not only establishes an added value for developing process-oriented enterprise applications but also allows process designers to flexibly specify which parts of a business process apply to workflow technology and which parts make up the system dialogues. Furthermore, it provides the opportunity to design the user's work with one system as efficiently as possible. The system dialogues become pervasive and, thus, all benefits of the BPM technology including support for advanced techniques, such as business process monitoring or simulation, are available [4]. Furthermore, the structure of dialogues becomes changeable, which leads to a natural partition of business logic into services of appropriate granularity.

We also propose an enhanced communication concept. The event concept of BPMN provides a few simple event types which will suffice in standard situations. However, more complex processes will require more differentiated communication types. We propose a system of event trigger properties and a few different types of event pools to generically cover a wide range of communication patterns.

In order to make full-blown use of the introduced communication concept, an additional user interface will have to be added and respective eP^2 inter-component interfaces will have to be defined. Users will need to be enabled to set extra event trigger properties, to select from triggers available in an inbox, and to opt in to or out of public event pools. Furthermore, access restrictions for event pools may be added and integrated with actor modelling.

Finally, the different aspects that we have addressed here, i.e. deontic classifications, actors, dialogues, and the communication concept, require formal integration in a process platform architecture, which we call the eP^2 architecture. This architecture consists of several components and is capable to run and interpret the integrated models (see Sect. 6.4).

The core of the architecture is the *Workflow Transition Interpreter* component, specified in [5] and extended to incorporate deontic classification and user modelling as well as an enhanced communication concept. The *Workflow Transition Interpreter* component runs through business processes and passes active task instances via the interface *ProcessTask* to the *Task Server* component, which in turn uses the interface *TaskList*, provided by the component *Process Client*, to deliver the tasks to appropriate users. Thereby, an own instance of a *Process Client* component exists for each user, which comprises an own instance of the component *Dialogue Engine*. Feedback about the status of tasks is passed from the *Process Client* to the *Task Server* component (via the interfaces *TaskHandling* and *ProcessEventListener*) and further passed from the *Task Server* to the *Workflow Transition Interpreter* component (by using the interface *Monitor*).

The *Process Client* manages user and manual tasks and reacts to user actions of the interface *UserTaskActions*, whereby it uses the interface *Dialogue* (for user tasks) provided by the component *Dialogue Engine*, which is responsible for providing the dialogue of a given user task (either a one-step dialogue or a complex dialogue) as well as for reading and displaying required data and for storing user inputs of dialogues.

The component *Actor Management* is responsible for the management of roles and the assignment of users to these roles and provides the interface *Actor* for communicating with other components.

The *Process Model Repository* component supplies the interface *CRUDModel* to provide access to the models within the architecture (i.e. *Process Model, Actor Model, Data Model*, and *Dialogue Model*) and version management of those models developed by a *Model Development Tool*, which is actually not a part of eP^2.

A further part of the eP^2 architecture is the component *Data Management* that provides access to the data model by providing the interface *Data*.

Furthermore, we provide a formal specification of the eP^2 architecture, its components, interfaces, behaviour, and the collaboration of the components by means of ASMs. Each eP^2 component is specified as an own ASM ground model and the interactions between those components correspond to synchronously or asynchronously called interface operations (see Chap. 7).

In the following, we give an outlook on further aspects that shall be integrated in the rigorous semantic model of H-BPM.

First of all, we extended the actor model presented in Chap. 3 with speech act theory to support communication, coordination, and cooperation between actors. We suggested some basic speech acts and proposed an extension of the process model. However, the realisation of speech acts in the eP^2 architecture is left for future work. The main challenge is that a task classified with a speech act must perform a special action and the required action must be supported by the *Workflow Transition Interpreter* and the *Task Server* component.

In addition, still demanding issues in BPM are the ability to react to exceptional events that constitute a deviation from the expected process behaviour and to support process changes at build- or runtime in order to respond to implicit or explicit process needs. Such process changes may range from small corrections of volatile process portions to larger adaptations like dynamic configurations of the process or complex recovery actions.

While the subject of adaptivity and exception handling has been addressed in various other contexts, the investigation of those aspects in formal business process models is novel. In particular, the best known industrial and academic standards, e.g. BPMN or YAWL, do not address adaptivity and exception handling in a fully integrated and sufficiently formal way. Missing are, for example, adaptations of business processes based on the qualifications, preferences, and goals of the executing actor as well as on collaboration of actors to dynamically define parts of the business process at runtime. Furthermore, no clear semantics exists to define exceptions and recovery strategies, e.g. cancellation, suspension, or compensation, and to rigorously specify under which conditions such strategies have to be applied.

We will address these issues by elaborating different levels of adaptivity in future work and suggest solutions that are general enough to be applicable in various key BPM standards.

References

1. Atkinson, C., Draheim, D., Geist, V.: Typed business process specification. In: Proceedings of the 14th IEEE International Enterprise Distributed Object Computing Conference, EDOC'10, pp. 69–78. IEEE Computer Society, Washington (2010)
2. Auer, D., Geist, V., Draheim, D.: Extending BPMN with submit/response-style user interaction modeling. In: Proceedings of CEC'09, pp. 368–374. IEEE Computer Society, Washington (2009)
3. Draheim, D.: Business Process Technology—A Unified View on Business Processes, Workflows and Enterprise Applications. Springer, Heidelberg (2010)
4. Geist, V.: Integrated executable business process and dialogue specification, Dissertation, Johannes Kepler University, Linz (2011)
5. Kossak, F., Illibauer, C., Geist, V., Kubovy, J., Natschläger, C., Ziebermayr, T., Kopetzky, T., Freudenthaler, B., Schewe, K.D.: A Rigorous Semantics for BPMN 2.0 Process Diagrams. Springer, Heidelberg (2015)
6. Natschläger, C.: Deontic BPMN. In: Hameurlain, A., Liddle, S., Schewe, K., Zhou, X. (eds.) Database and Expert Systems Applications, Lecture Notes in Computer Science, vol. 6861, pp. 264–278. Springer, Heidelberg (2011)
7. Natschläger, C., Geist, V.: A layered approach for actor modelling in business processes. Bus. Process Manag. J. **19**, 917–932 (2013)
8. Natschläger, C., Geist, V., Kossak, F., Freudenthaler, B.: Optional activities in process flows. In: Rinderle-Ma, S., Weske, M. (eds.) EMISA 2012—Der Mensch im Zentrum der Modellierung, pp. 67–80 (2012)
9. Natschläger-Carpella, C.: Extending BPMN with Deontic Logic. Logos Verlag Berlin (2012)

Index

© Springer International Publishing Switzerland 2016
F. Kossak et al., *Hagenberg Business Process Modelling Method*,
DOI 10.1007/978-3-319-30496-0